JED HARRIS
THE
CURSE OF
GENIUS

OTHER BOOKS BY
MARTIN GOTTFRIED

Broadway Musicals
Opening Nights
A Theater Divided

JED HARRIS

THE

CURSE OF

GENIUS

MARTIN GOTTFRIED

LITTLE, BROWN AND COMPANY
Boston   Toronto

Second Printing

Acknowledgments of permission to quote previously published material appear on page 274.

Library of Congress Cataloging in Publication Data

Gottfried, Martin.
  Jed Harris, the curse of genius.
  Includes index.
  1. Harris, Jed. 2. Theatrical producers and directors—United
States—Biography. I. Title.
PN2287.H249G67 1984   792'.0232'0924 [B]   83–16174
ISBN 0-316-32156-7

MV

Designed by Patricia Girvin Dunbar

Published simultaneously in Canada
by Little, Brown & Company (Canada) Limited

PRINTED IN THE UNITED STATES OF AMERICA

This book is dedicated to Martha Weinman Lear because she never lost patience, interest or enthusiasm during its creation. Would that it reached the standards of her own precise and graceful writing.

AUTHOR'S NOTE: There is a considerable amount of dialogue in this book. Every word is as recalled by participants or witnesses. Within the fair bounds of memory, the conversations bear, I believe, a good proximity to what was said.

Among those who provided this dialogue, or were in other ways essential to the book, are these gracious people:

George Abbott, Edward Chodorov, Irving Lazar, José Ferrer, Geraldine Morris, Lillian Gish, Charles Abramson, Jean Dalrymple, James Proctor, William Roerick, Archie Carter, Ina Claire, Frederic Wakeman, Peter Witt, Dorris Johnson, Dame Judith Anderson, Judy Feiffer, Ruth Goetz, Louise Platt, Shirley Berick, Alexander H. Cohen, Jean Barkow, Alvin Deutsch, Nathan Wartels, Ray Malsin, William Fitelson, Joseph and Bobbie Weinstein, Irving Cooper, Jay Darwin, Donald Davis, Martha Scott, Katherine Parker, Billy Caplan, Isabel Wilder, Arthur Miller, Beatrice Straight, Peter Cookson, Paul and Millicent Osborn, Howard and Evelyn Teichmann, Kay Brown, Sigmund Miller, Del Hughes, Michael Straight, Art Franklin, Pat Burroughs, Dick Cavett, Robin Breed, Betsy von Furstenberg, John Whedon, Lois Jacoby, Ralph Shapiro, Gertrude Shapiro, Gilda Davis, Alice Carey, Michael Abbott, Bernard Jacobs, Daniel Petrie, Peggy Jacobsen, and Jacques Traubee.

Of particular and necessary help were the members of Jed Harris's immediate family, Mildred, Sylvia, Florence, and Abigail Harris, and Nina Wilcox Mersen.

In the course of research the biographer develops a sense of larger family with his sources. Some members of that family died before being able to see the fruit of their cooperation: Marc Connelly, David Bunim, Paul Streger, Herbert Michaelmore, and the endearing Anita Green. I miss them and special men who were friends before they were sources, L. Arnold Weissberger and Harold Clurman.

I am particularly grateful for permission to reproduce the photographs from the Billy Rose Theatre Collection in the New York Public Library at Lincoln Center and the Astor, Lenox and Tilden Foundations. The Billy Rose Theatre Collection includes the Vandamm Studio photographs.

Michael Mattil of Little, Brown seemed sent by God with theatrical lore and demands for accuracy. As for my editor, Genevieve Young, during the two years of this book's writing she was tactless enough to be accurate with criticism, merciless enough to see that it was dealt with, and relentless enough in her belief in this book and its author to bring them both through, alive. Blessed be she.

CONTENTS

A GENIUS FOR
MAKING ENEMIES

THE LEGEND looked like an old man dressed up to not look seedy. His thin gray hair was parted in the middle and plastered down, without concession to current style. He wore a dark ascot inside his open shirt collar. The padding of his camel's hair sports jacket overlapped his shoulders, too wide. He fidgeted with his hearing aid and coughed, trying vainly to clear his throat between draws on a cigarette. He'd just been released from the hospital and sipped a glass of water through an L-shaped straw he'd stolen on the way out.

In the Hollywood television studio, Pat Burroughs, his forty-year-old girlfriend, stood and watched beside one of the cameramen. *The Dick Cavett Show* was usually taped in New York, but when Jed Harris heard that Cavett was in Los Angeles, he telephoned. He had a book to publicize. He was penniless and ill and desperate for it to succeed.

Cavett introduced him as "legendary, the golden boy of our theater's golden age," and Harris peered up from beneath lids that, once notoriously hooded, now just seemed eighty years' heavy. He said nothing.

Cavett, stagestruck since childhood, was excited by a chance to interview the Jed Harris he'd heard so much about; the Jed Harris he had thought was dead. He arranged for a studio and crew and now Pat Burroughs looked on apprehensively. Beside the preppy production assistants she appeared gauche in her white orlon sweater and gray gabardine slacks, but she was more concerned with Harris's hearing and alertness. The medication made him so groggy.

He had been the subject of her doctoral thesis. They'd been together for several years now. The relationship had never been placid, but this last stretch had been actively acrimonious.

They had stayed with her mother in Winston-Salem, the seventy-nine-year-old former golden boy not embarrassed to be dependent on his girl-friend's sixty-five-year-old mother. Though he complained about everything else, he never complained about this final and ludicrous deposit. A lifetime earlier he had declared international celebrity something he put little stock by. Apparently he had meant it.

Then, always fleeing somewhere, he told Pat they were going to Califor-nia. She scraped up two thousand dollars, bought a used Thunderbird, and while he dozed she drove from one TraveLodge Motel to the next. They wound up in a sorry one-bedroom Malibu garden apartment.

Now Cavett smiled smartly at the camera and recited Harris's credits as a theatrical producer and director. These were faded and spiritless references to forgotten glories. Cavett seemed to realize, as he spoke, that the play titles would mean little to most people and so he abbreviated the list in midstream. Yet he was awed, he said, by the presence of Harris and he kept using that word, "legend."

Videotape made it possible to come back from the grave. Months after Harris died the interviews were broadcast. After thirty years of oblivion, he had five nights on television, more time than Cavett had ever offered anyone. Old enemies watched with contempt for Harris's deviousness, his dishon-esty, his malevolence to the end. Old friends watched with admiration for his courage in carrying off "The Jed Harris Show" just one last time, and in plain sight of death. Now, as they all watched, he *was* dead.

◆

Jones Harris stood in the lobby of the Booth Theatre and greeted those who had come to the memorial for his father. His clothes, a costume, seemed from some old issue of *Vanity Fair* magazine. Pictured there as a young man, Jed had looked like a matinee idol: a pale, bony, ivory face; dark and piercing eyes; glossy black hair brushed flat like shelf paper. The body was less im-portant. It existed to support the head. It could just as soon have been made of puppet sticks, or drawn. Fifty years later, duplicating his father's look Jones seemed an eccentric dandy, but like all eccentrics, sure of himself. His father's death should have come as a relief from a lifetime of rejection, but he had no such luck.

"I never much cared for my son," Harris told Cavett on the posthumously broadcast show.

It had made people cringe for Jones, but perhaps that was what Harris wanted: everyone to hate him. Now his emotionally abused son was fifty years old and the host of a memorial service.

"I'm sure you know Ruth Gordon," Jones repeated as he introduced his mother to the arrivals. Of course they knew her. The actress had long been celebrated and was now beloved, an institution. She wore a black suit, a broad-brimmed hat and dark red suede pumps. A tiny, eighty-three-year-old woman in high heels. Thin hair, limp from a lifetime of dye, was the only betrayal of her age.

She beamed, as actors do in public places. She grinned and winked and shook hands all around. She had been born Ruth Gordon Jones. Jones Harris had been named for her. He was the child of show people. His mother's career had lasted more than fifty years. His father's was another story.

Jed Harris had been one of those fabulous young men for whom the Roaring Twenties were named. His rise had been heady even for those roller-coasting times: within just two years this unknown youngster had produced four smash hits; shows so polished and energetic they came to symbolize Broadway, just as he came to personify it. He was earning forty thousand dollars a week. He made the cover of *Time*. It was 1928, and he was twenty-eight. An original.

And then he embarked on a slow, painful decline that ended in his virtual disappearance. By the time he died the shock wasn't over the ending of a fabulous career. The shock was that he had been alive all these years.

The memorial service was held early in the warm evening of May 4, 1980, at the Booth Theatre on the corner of West 45th Street and Shubert Alley. It was in the lobby of this very theater that Jones had once stopped his father to say hello. They hadn't seen each other for two years. Jed had said, "What are you doing, following me?" He could be funny. You had to hand it to him.

The Booth's seating capacity was just over a thousand people. About three hundred came, and Jones met them with a neat balance of cordial solemnity. He looked young in the thirties clothes; the tight and skinny double-breasted dark blue suit that was snugly buttoned across his chest; the black wool tie almost invisible against his navy blue shirt; the gray fedora tilted over his heavy-bearded, swarthy face.

Jones had never seen much of his mother. He chatted with her now. Her husband, the writer and director Garson Kanin, looked on, short, bald, and wiry. Kanin had a long list of stage and movie credits, but despite celebrity he was an outsider here, and Jones seemed disinclined to improve that status.

The Booth Theatre's walls are paneled in walnut. It has more than the usual number of aisles, which breaks up the long rows of seats and lends the orchestra floor an engaging intimacy. The deep blue of the seats, the carpets and the curtain are in rich contrast to the wood walls; the theater has something of the atmosphere of a university club.

The mourners drifted in. They funneled through the double doors where the ticket taker usually stood, flowing down the aisle to break off in small clusters and take seats with an embarrassed awareness of a superabundance of choice. Few of them were recognizable. Norman Mailer was the most famous person there and he'd never even met Jed Harris. He had come out of friendship for Jones. Jed had made enemies of everybody who was anybody. This audience was in fact distinguished by those absent.

Helen Hayes wasn't there. George Abbott wasn't there. Nor were Judith Anderson or Wendy Hiller or Lillian Hellman. James Cagney and Arthur Miller hadn't come, nor had Katharine Hepburn, Laurence Olivier, or Orson Welles. They had all suffered miserable experiences with Harris, experiences still vivid. Some of them still refused to talk about him.

His first wife, Anita Green, was home in her bohemian Greenwich Village apartment. Louise Platt, his second wife, was in Cutchogue, Long Island with her scrapbooks. She had scissored Harris out of all the snapshots. Bebe Allan, his third and last wife, was dead. She'd sued him for divorce only months after they were married. She wouldn't have come to the memorial. His younger brother Saul didn't come. Not even Harris's own daughter Abigail came. "I don't believe there is a person walking the face of the earth," she later said, "who would have a good word to say for my father." And yet Abigail hugged herself recalling the big stuffed goose he'd brought when she'd been a little girl sick in bed. A soft white goose, she remembered, with a yellow bill.

Abigail's ten-year-old daughter Chedsey was there, clutching the hand of her great-aunt, Harris's sister Mildred. Chedsey was there to honor the grandfather who'd never bothered to meet her.

"Such things leave me cold," he said, "seeing your seed sprout up and multiply."

Chedsey was almost as tall as Ruth Gordon and hardly had to stretch to kiss her. Mildred introduced her to Uncle Jones, saying nothing to Pat Burroughs beside him.

At 6:45 Jones accepted L. Arnold Weissberger's suggestion that the services begin since whoever was coming had probably come. Weissberger was to introduce the speakers. He was the dean of New York's theatrical attorneys. He had represented Harris during the final years, when there had been nothing to represent.

Weissberger was a man of wit and courtliness. A born fan, he doted on celebrated clients and even published his candid photographs of them in a book called *Famous Faces*. Being star-struck and charming and diplomatic made him the perfect speaker for such occasions.

He strolled on stage in the familiar gray pin-stripe suit with his signature white carnation in the lapel. He wore this costume every day until he died nine months later. (His own memorial service was given at the Royale Theatre and the place was packed. Stars stood, everyone came.)

The other speakers trooped out from the wings like obedient students, to spread themselves across the stage on folding metal chairs. Whether it is appropriate or ironic, theatrical values are not suspended for the deaths of show people. These memorial services, like any shows, are judged by the fame of the speakers and the size of the audience. The show was flopping. Jed Harris was playing to half a house. The eulogizers had little box office appeal and not all of them even *liked* him.

The playwright Marc Connelly, for instance, had taken *The Green Pastures* to another producer after Harris had tried to muscle in on the author's credit. That had been fifty years ago, though, and the Pulitzer Prize Connelly had received for the play had eased his rancor. Now ninety and intermittently senile, the playwright had few friends still alive. He welcomed the invitation to speak, even on behalf of an old enemy. His speech rambled. It was that kind of day for Jed Harris.

The other speakers were drama critic Richard Watts, John Huston the film director, the actresses Martha Scott and Lillian Gish, Garson Kanin and Ruth. Watts was near death and shaky. Huston was out of place among theater people and, as if by mutual consent, sat apart. Weissberger was having trouble with his opening remarks because he had to avoid the most interesting thing about Harris: the reputation for evil-doing. The attorney tried to be light and conventional in his eulogizing. He praised Harris for being a genius as a director and producer, but virtues are boring. What had made Jed Harris *Jed Harris* had been more elusive and scary, but this was hardly the occasion.

"Brilliant," Weissberger said, "provocative Jed Harris," and so on. "Altogether absorbing."

The other speakers smiled and applauded in their seats like mimes, except for Huston who didn't seem to understand stage courtesies. He sat there, windburnt, white haired, sueded and leathered, a Hollywood director. He had not been close to Harris. His father, the actor Walter Huston, had, but

Walter was dead. Of all these people, John Huston had been the only one Jones wanted. Weissberger held out for Lillian Gish because he doted on her. He also urged that Ruth speak, to heal old wounds. Jones had stamped his foot at that, and at Gish too, and, most adamantly of all—nobody knew why—at Steve Allen, the television performer who had befriended Harris. Jones ultimately relented on everyone but Allen.

Weissberger introduced Miss Gish as if she were the saint of the silver screen. She pit-pattered to the microphone pursing pink lips through pale makeup. Sweet, sad, an ancient sparrow, she clasped her white gloves and chirped with equal emphasis about the *Uncle Vanya* she'd done with Harris in 1935 and a Chinese dinner she'd had with him forty years later.

Then she startled the audience.

"Jed!" she cried. "Wherever you are! There are a lot of people here that love you."

She caressed the microphone.

"Oooh, you had a genius for making enemies but I don't think you disliked anybody in the world as much as you disliked Jed."

She was quaint and melodramatic, yet she had been the first to venture into reality. But self-hatred, was that all it would come to? The malevolence only neurosis?

Martha Scott continued Gish's candor. "Jones," she began, "I am so happy that you thought of having me."

Just because Jones had organized the memorial didn't mean his name could be mentioned in public. It had never been mentioned in public before, not in connection with Jed and not in Ruth's presence. As if having dared enough, Miss Scott said no more on that subject. She reminisced about acting in *Our Town*, the play that had marked the peak and the end, really, of Harris's career.

"Strange, wonderful, demoniacal man of the theater," she said. "A man totally committed to the theater and blind to everything but the play."

It was chilly, suddenly, that warm May evening. Talk of *Our Town* conjured up ghosts, and there were so many ghosts in the Booth Theatre: the cast of characters in Jed's life, ghosts of people *he* had haunted. Margaret Sullavan, George S. Kaufman, Thornton Wilder, S. N. Behrman, Ben Hecht and Charlie MacArthur, Herman Shumlin, Moss Hart, Noël Coward. The unforgiving wraiths swirled through the theater.

Garson Kanin spoke, thanking Jones. It wouldn't get him anywhere. And Richard Watts, as senile as Connelly. Huston had little to say. He talked more about Jed's mistress Pat Burroughs than about Harris. Finally Weissberger introduced Ruth Gordon, and Jones must have tensed in his seat. Here it came, the reconciliation at last for the family that had never existed. For Jones was Ruth and Jed's son and they had never married.

In 1929, having or being an illegitimate child was more than scandalous. News of the event would have destroyed Ruth's career, or so Jed had feared, and considering the devastation such a birth visited, twenty-five years later, on the career of Ingrid Bergman, the fear was not unfounded. The babe was hatched in secret, the danger of scandal and the secret creating a unique family bond. In many ways, Jones had remained a secret ever since.

"Well," Ruth began in her familiar yap. "Gotta tell ya how at home I feel here," and everyone laughed because being sassy was her stock in trade and they liked it and knew she'd put on a show.

"Jed said," she grinned, "'The way to make it is to have brains, luck, money, and the greatest of all is courage.' He had it. Another thing he said was, 'To be sexy you've got to have menace.' He had it. Well, there are good days and there are bad days."

She chuckled and winked, like a mechanical doll, but like Louise Platt, Ruth Gordon seemed to be scissoring Harris right out of her life. She had written about Jed and Jones in a memoir, *My Side*, but otherwise refused to discuss them. When she spoke at the memorial service, she did not mention their life together. In fact, Ruth did not say, at the memorial service, just why she was speaking there. It was as if enough was enough.

Her coda. "He was the boy without a limit. He was the intellectual who could go to *Hellzapoppin'* and laugh so hard he had to leave the theater and no matter how many times he went to *Hellzapoppin'* he could never stay till the finish."

There had been so much excitement, secrecy, pain, hysteria. Now she stood, at eighty-three, stage center at the Booth, the survivor.

"George S. Kaufman said, 'Jed thinks he's Napoleon.'" Ruth grinned, not mentioning what else Kaufman had said during the forty years he refused to talk to Harris. "'He thinks he's Napoleon and I think he is too,' that's what George Kaufman said about Jed." Ruth paused and winked, so feisty she didn't have to put her hands on her hips to put her hands on her hips. "And *I* think he was too, but five'll getcha ten that Napoleon couldn't wear a hat as good as Jed Harris.

"He would take that hat and that brim and he would pull it down just right and was that ever sexy and didn't he ever have menace and Ben Hecht, he could have written two more books and one more play but he wasted his time staying home trying to get *his* hat to look like Jed Harris's."

They roared. She didn't mention Hecht's vicious novel about Jed, *A Jew in Love*. The final applause came in a compact outburst and the house lights went up. As at the end of any performance, the audience stretched and un-wound, gathering its stuff and starting out. The people made their way up the aisle, backs to the stage and the scenery on it. The Booth Theatre's cur-rent tenant was a play called *The Elephant Man*. Its setting was of a stark Victorian hospital. The play was about a freak of nature who was frightening at first sight, yet vulnerable and even beautiful beneath his horrifying exte-rior; a monster who was intelligent and unique; an artist.

NEWARK

ESTHER AND MEYER WOLF HOROWITZ were young and freshly married when they immigrated to New York City in 1898 from the village of Lemburg in the southeast corner of Austria. They came on a tidal flow of hopeful Jews, but within a year they turned around and went right back.

Esther had hated Meyer's working at a common job. She hated the steaming crowds on the sidewalks of the Lower East Side. She hated, most of all, the tenement apartment on East 10th Street and so, while a historic rush of Jews was surging one way, this young couple went the other.

In Lemburg, Esther gave birth to Jacob Hirsch Horowitz on February 25, 1900. When he became Jed Harris he would say that he'd been born in Newark. He later decided that having been born in Newark was one of the few things less impressive than having been born in Lemburg, so he settled on Vienna and many of his obituaries endorsed that.

However brief and unhappy had been their stay in America, it had been long enough to make provincial European life no longer acceptable to the Horowitzes and now they could not mistake the approaching storm of anti-Semitism. When a former neighbor wrote from Newark to suggest that Meyer start a grocery business there, Esther was receptive to the idea. That was working for yourself, she later told her children. So they emigrated a second time, this time with an infant son.

They found a one-bedroom apartment on Clayton Street in Newark, and with the help of a small loan from the *lundtsman* who had suggested the grocery business, Meyer opened a store. He sold produce and grains and dairy products to both the retail and wholesale trades.

The young couple remained in the Clayton Street apartment for three years until, the business prospering, they decided to have a second child. Mildred was born in 1904 when Jacob was four years old. He was already too big for the crib in his parents' bedroom.

Esther found five and a half rooms on Spruce Street. Meyer expanded the business. Everything seemed plentiful: wooden baskets on the shop's shelves, overflowing with oranges, grapefruits, prunes. Burlap sacks of wheat, rye, oats, and flour, packed to bursting on the heavy wood planks of the floor. Cheeses and butter in the cool tin tubs.

Meyer and his two clerks wore bibbed, ankle-length white aprons, tied twice around their waists. The men were all in white, it seemed, except for their high black shoes and bushy black beards and round, broad-brimmed black hats. The place looked like Lemburg.

During the day Meyer tended to his retail business. After supper he reopened the shop to keep the accounts and then he went out and made calls on the wholesale trade. He no longer walked the mile to and from the store to save the nickel trolley fare. He rode in one of the two horse-drawn wagons he'd bought for wholesale deliveries.

Number 156 Spruce Street was a sturdy brick building of four stories, with two apartments on each floor. The Horowitzes were on the second floor, front. To Esther's disgust, it was a working-class building in a working-class neighborhood. She told little Mildred they were the only middle-class people there, but at least, she said, the whitewashed facade set the building a cut above the others in the neighborhood.

Esther decorated the apartment, she filled it up. She began with a matched set of leather armchairs and a sofa from Bamberger's Department Store, adding the inevitable upright piano and Oriental rug that seemed to signify culture to so many immigrants. Jacob had already begun taking violin lessons. Mildred would play the piano.

Once the wallpapering of the dining room was finished, Esther bought a big round oak table, matching chairs, and another leather sofa, but the room remained resolutely ceremonial; meals were served in the kitchen. It was homier there, with a spotless linoleum covering the floor and a yellow oil-cloth on the enameled metal table. In winter the coal stove would heat the room to a cozy glow.

The icebox was always crammed with cheeses and fruit that Papa brought

10

home from the store. The only treat Esther forbade was spicy delicatessen meat. She thought it vulgar. But then, she considered all traditional Jewish food vulgar. Not for her the flanken, the boiled chicken, the *tsimmes*. Naturally she kept a kosher kitchen, but she had subtle taste in food and a passion for clam chowder and lobster. All shellfish is unkosher, as little Mildred had the temerity to remind her mother.

"Don't you say that to me," Esther tartly replied as she lighted the gas stove to set the water boiling. "Anything that's as delicious as lobster has to be kosher," and she didn't smile.

Esther Horowitz had found these larger quarters so that Jacob could have his own room, but Papa's twenty-year-old brother Morris moved in, so the boy's privacy was taken before he could enjoy it. Refusing to be frustrated, he moved into the dining room and slept on the sofa.

Like the store, the apartment too seemed to grow as if an organism. The living room sprouted lamps and lace curtains. Cut-glass crystal and little rocking chairs for the girls developed in the dining room. An oak bed emerged in Mama and Papa's room and it seemed enormous to the children. There were to be five of them: Sylvia, born in 1907; Florence (Florie) two years later, and ultimately a second son, Saul, in 1916. He would always be the second son.

Meanwhile, the Horowitzes lived beneath their means. They had arrived penniless. Perhaps that was why their psychology was to save until the future was secure, an indefinite wait.

The apartment now shrank, crammed with people and things. Morris finally moved out after getting engaged, but the girls had already taken over his room, each in turn having been pushed out of the crib. Now all three were in the second bedroom along with the sleep-in maid. With Jacob in the dining room and Saul in the crib, that made eight people in the five-room apartment, and Mama still insisted that they were living well. Their possessions proved it, she said: oak tables, leather sofas, hats with veils, her fur coat and matching muff.

It was not a religious home. Lighting the Friday night *shabbes* candles and keeping a kosher kitchen were cultural rather than religious rituals. Papa went to *shul* only on the high holidays. He was, however, a Hebrew scholar and read from the Talmud every day. As soon as Jacob was old enough he joined his father in this, and the boy was soon reading and speaking Hebrew fluently. Not religious but proud of his Jewishness, Meyer told Jacob that most of the immigrants wanted to be Americans rather than Jews. That is what "melting pot" means, he said. Everyone melted into *goyim*.

Esther and Meyer spoke Yiddish at home unless they didn't want the children to understand, and then they spoke Polish or Ukrainian. They read Yiddish-language newspapers. They went to the Yiddish theater. It was the only theater Jacob ever saw until he was twenty.

He sat snug between his parents, an only child for this evening at Newark's Yiddish theater. The actors on stage were footlit, their faces aglow. The papa in the play was resplendent in a purple satin robe and a black silk yarmulke. Fathers in the Yiddish theater were modeled after the Jewish God. This one had a frightening great bushy beard and he roared at the young man who wished to marry his daughter. He pointed a mighty arm to the door and ordered the disrespectful fellow out. The daughter fell to the sofa, weeping.

Seated between his parents, Jacob moaned, "*Oy veyze mir.*"

In tandem, his parents turned and glared at him for the rest of the play. When they got home he was given a beating. Years later, he rubbed his ear just recalling the incident.

The firstborn son of Jewish immigrants had an almost ritualistic upbringing. In a way he was expected to rescue his family from historic Jewish persecution by growing up to be a perfect man, the vaunted Jewish doctor or lawyer, beyond the disapproval of the dreaded Christians.

In order to grow up perfect, a boy had to study: at public school, at *cheder*, at music lessons. Perfect also meant the avoidance of frivolity. Sports and girlfriends, for example, were frivolous and only for the *goyim*.

The role of saviour must have sometimes seemed less than worth it to these downy-cheeked chosen ones, and some were destroyed along the road to perfection, for any behavior unworthy of a firstborn son was immediately punishable. The punishment was often physical. It was in Jacob Horowitz's case. He was beaten regularly, and so that was his young life: study and punishment.

He did have friends. Sammy Asch, Herman Shumlin, Willy Gartenburg, Mike Perlstein. But they were all outcasts, fellow monks whose families considered them too good for play.

In the evening, his myriad studies finished at last, Jacob would retire to the dining room and his library books. He loved histories and biographies and, hidden among them, the Horatio Alger and Frank Merriwell pulp novels.

"My entire boyhood was engrossed in books," he later said. "My parents knew nothing about me."

There were other materials he dared not bring home: the library stocked all the daily newspapers, and before making his withdrawals, Jacob would climb upon a sturdy wooden chair, crossing his legs beneath him. He'd spread the newspapers out on the long table and read of the great professional sporting clubs and their splendid athletes. When a sister saw him at it, he held a forefinger to his lips. She nodded in conspiracy. Like so many boys who had to do their playing this way, he developed a formidable store of sports knowledge, the statistical muscles of the would-be athlete.

One day when Jacob was thirteen, Esther insisted that he walk his sister Mildred to school. He was already an object of derision because he played no sports. To be seen with a nine-year-old girl would destroy his dignity entirely, yet he put on the shirt and the tie and knickers and high wool stockings that had been laid out for him. He picked up his schoolbooks, Mildred fetched hers, and they trudged down Spruce Street, a girl crushed by a big brother's shame. If he but knew how she admired him, how proud of him she was, how wonderful to be walking to school with him. They came to a lot where some of Jacob's classmates had put down their books to play softball. He let go of her hand and she understood. He set his books on the ground and watched the ball as it was pitched. Hit. Mildred eyed him, his fists clenched to restrain his excited spasms. The skinny boy with close-cropped hair and darkening eyes jerked his fists against his hips in ignorant imitation of athletic performance, like a blind man dancing.

"We'll be late," she murmured.

"Sissy Horowitz!"

Her heart froze.

"Please, let's go to school."

"Wanna play baseball, you girls?"

"Who's the *shiksa?*" Because she was blond.

A boy came over and tugged at her hair, and then Jacob heaved his eighty-five pounds at the bully as Mildred covered her eyes, and when it was over he sat on the ground, his clothes torn and soiled, gritting his teeth and blinking his eyes. She looked away to spare him the shame of witness.

"Maybe we should go home; you're bleeding."

There would be hell to pay and they both knew it.

"Gangster, change for *cheder* and throw those beautiful clothes away. They're ruined. People would starve for such clothes."

Jacob started away.

"You're the boy without a limit," Mama said imploringly that evening, and Papa added the usual, "So how can you be such a bum?" Meyer smoothed his mustache and pressed down his beard as he prepared to administer yet another beating. The girls were never beaten because they weren't important enough.

"Whatever he does wrong," Mama told Mildred, "everything is for him. Jacob is our main concern. If his future were at stake, you girls would be *schnell kapuris*." Sacrificed fast. Mildred remembered that bitterly all the rest of her life.

Watching Jacob's beatings through their childhood, the daughters concluded that although Mama was tiny and quiet and only watched while Papa hit, she was the real tyrant. That didn't dawn on Jacob until he was sixty. Then he, too, decided that Esther had been the iron fist in the fur muff. He announced that he would never talk to her again. She was eighty-five at the time and in a home for the aged. He didn't speak to her for three years.

"I have never yet overcome the bigger part of the obstacles that blighted my childhood and from which I suffered a long, much too long hangover," he wrote. "My adolescence ended on my fiftieth birthday, almost to the day. Incredible as it may seem, I spent the greater part of my life blindly following a course that can only be described as suicidal as I tried in vain to throw off a burden of guilt which was securely placed on my back before I was ten years old."

Self-understanding is not self-cure. Harris wrote that in the midst of the three-year silence toward his mother.

"There is a dybbuk in him."

"A what, Papa?"

"Tell your sister what is a dybbuk."

Jacob waited to still the pain from the beating. He tensed his shoulders.

"A dybbuk," he finally said, "is the spirit of a dead person who was wronged in life. This spirit moves into someone else's body. It takes over and it tries to get revenge."

"I think," Papa said, "that Jacob is possessed by such a spirit. There is the devil's spirit in you."

Fortunately, it did not disqualify him from bar mitzvah or high school, but Meyer would ultimately find supporters of this seemingly irrational theory.

◆

Esther stood at the kitchen window and gossiped with a neighbor as Jacob poked in the icebox for something to eat. Little Sylvia played at the sink.

"Look at Eva, the baker's daughter, carrying her own wedding cake."

"If she doesn't hurry," Esther said, "she'll be delivering something besides cake. *Zee schfengat*."

Jacob yanked his head out of the icebox.

"So what if she's pregnant!" he shouted. "Don't you have anything better to do than insult an innocent girl?"

Sylvia nearly toppled from the chair she was crouched on.

"Eva's getting married," Jacob raged on. "You should say a *brucha* for her."

Mama was livid; she glared. She spoke through clenched teeth.

14

"Go to the store and tell Papa what you said."

"But Papa said never to come to the store."

"To the store I said!"

One cognac-soaked dawn, many years later, Jacob remembered. He had gone down the stairs, dizzy with fright, and tried to prolong the walk to the store by counting cobblestones. The blocks flew past anyhow. He'd felt righteous about standing up for Eva until he got a whiff of his father's produce. Then his nerve frayed. The boy had glimpsed the man in himself but he was still a child.

Meyer had his back to the door, which only made him seem more frightening a king of radishes and oats. He turned as if he knew that Jacob was there.

"*Vass vilst du?*"

"Mama told me to come here."

"Outside!"

Not a reprieve. A stay. Jacob waited in the street, watching its business. He picked up a discarded copy of *The Morning Star & Newark Advertiser* and sat down on the curb. Papa had been urging him to keep up with the news, so this might please. At once he was jerked by a hand at his collar and then dragged into the store.

"Now the bum is reading newspapers. There's no hope for him, he's a useless jackass."

Jacob held a skinny forearm to his face for protection. First a slapping with the palm and then with the heel of the hand. Blows that crashed and split on his sweet boy's cheeks, his narrow shoulders, and then he was weeping outside the store, huddled against its wall. He sobbed until, as he remembered so many years later, he understood for the first time that his father was not a great man. Then the skinny youngster with inky eyes pulled himself to his feet. He gulped back his child's tears. He marched into the store and as he marched he scanned the neat rows of baskets with their stores of vegetables and fruits. He climbed the ladder to the second tier of shelves. Pulling the ladder along on its wheels, he yanked down one basket after another, with his free hand sending potatoes tumbling to the floor, carrots and beets and heavy squashes. He threw down heads of cabbage and melons and sent wooden crates crashing into splinters. Fruits and prunes and walnuts rolled and streaked across the floor. Meyer shouted out and the clerks chased after, but Jacob clambered down the ladder and raced through the shop flinging oranges and grapefruits, kicking over barrels and crates and sacks.

After he'd wrecked the store, being disrespectful to his mother didn't seem to matter anymore. Nobody brought it up. He had transcended the beatings. They would continue, but he had begun his escape. He would move into the world of his books, the world of his dreams. In his own mind, this frustrating, painful, and unhappy childhood had ended, if the story he told was true; if the wrecking of the store had really happened. And if not, perhaps his childhood and its unhappiness never ended at all.

THE FIRST ESCAPE

THE HOROWITZES were comfortable enough to be planning Jacob's college education and uncomfortable enough to be worrying about the cost of it. Jacob's friend, tall, sad-eyed Herman Shumlin, had been coming around with college materials all that year, 1916. Herman would spread out the brochures and urge Jacob to concentrate on junior year grades; to get the applications out on time. The Shumlins couldn't afford college, but if Herman seemed to be trying to go vicariously, Jacob wasn't trying at all. School had become boring and he had become inert, afloat, interested only in his books.

His favorite book, those days, was *The Revolutionist's Handbook* by George Bernard Shaw. A lifetime later he would remember feeling comforted when he read the book. His ideas were not, as his parents said, *meshugenah*. "I'm sane and they're crazy!" he recalled thinking.

From then on he devoured Shaw's work, unearthing such exotica as the early novel, *Love Among the Artists*. One day he would personally remind Shaw of that youthful work, to the great man's delight.

For now, he lay reading on the dining room sofa of the Newark apartment.

He was spurred from lethargy when the Asches moved to Florida, taking Sammy with them. Then Jacob abandoned Shaw's Fabian Socialism for a capitalistic plunge. He had a notion that Sammy Asch could buy oranges directly from the Florida orchards and ship them to Newark to be sold to Papa's wholesale customers at a price usually paid to middlemen.

"A produce tycoon we have," Meyer said. "Study your Talmud." Mildred watched Jacob trudge back to the ancient text, adjust his *yarmulke*, lean forward on the table and rock as he read the Hebrew aloud, rock as the men *daven* in *shul*. By evening he had convinced his father to cooperate in the orange venture.

They called on the trade together, for one time close. They would go out after supper and come home cheerful partners. As Jacob suggested, they guaranteed satisfaction and with nothing to lose, Papa's wholesale customers signed up.

The evening calls by father and son overlapped into morning calls that the boy made alone, calls that his parents didn't know about. Jacob was missing a few days of school each week, for a month. At the end, the enterprise produced a profit of a few dollars, small but satisfying.

Then letters began to arrive from Sammy Asch, pressing for a second order. Jacob's interest had waned, but now Sammy wanted to buy a whole carload of oranges and Meyer thought that was a fine idea. Jacob gave in and went back to calling on customers. It would be the last time he would ever listen to his father on business matters, for the carload rolled across North Carolina along with an Arctic weather front and the oranges did not thrive.

Jacob went on a shopping spree with what profits he had left after helping Sammy pay the farmers. Newark's haberdashery pushcarts yielded up a silver-tipped ebony walking stick and a pair of fawn gray, pearl-buttoned spats. Just what a boy needed. He wore the spats over his wool stockings and high black shoes, just below the knickers.

He'd kept a secret. There *was* a college that interested him. He hadn't written for its application, knew nothing of its curriculum, its standards, or its faculty. His idea of it was drawn from a hopelessly undependable source and without a doubt its attraction was symbolic rather than academic. The college that Jacob wanted to attend was Yale. He'd learned everything he needed to know about it from the Frank Merriwell books.

Unfortunately, he had failed third-year French because of classes missed during the Florida orange escapade. He could not satisfy the foreign language requirement.

It was June and well past the application deadline when Jacob strode into the principal's office at Central High School and announced his intention of traveling to New Haven to apply in person for the Class of 1921. He walked out of that office with his transcript in hand and was aboard the New Haven

Railroad the following morning. It was his first trip anywhere since the pleasure cruise from Lemburg to Newark.

◆

"Why should I have been nervous?" he asked the family as they hovered
around the oak dining room table.

"I just knew you'd do it," sang fourteen-year-old Mildred.

"It was the Hebrew," he said, "after I'd failed French."

"How could he fail French?" Mama moaned for the thousandth time.

"Because he's a good-for-nothing bum," Papa said, keeping up with her.

"I suggested Hebrew as my foreign language and offered to take any test
they wanted."

"Do they teach Hebrew at Yale?"

"Yale's *motto* is in Hebrew."

"So they gave you a Hebrew test?" Papa asked.

"For two hours, and I got a perfect score."

"They accepted you?"

"They accepted me, Mama."

◆

Yale's freshman orientation week began in mid-September. Jacob arrived
alone, new black valise and new clothes, off the Jewish island and into the
Gentile sea. He was assigned to room 391 in Berkeley Hall. A desk, a bureau, a bed—a spartan contrast to the European density of his mother's decor. This would prove his introduction to the drier pleasures. Even the grand
and spacious apartments that Jacob was to occupy in the future would be
sparely furnished.

There was a tap at the door and he opened it to find a young man with a
startling scar across the bridge of his nose. It was from the first of a lifetime
of operations that would never quite correct a deviated septum. The stranger
smiled and extended a hand.

"My name is Ray Malsin."

By his own description, Raphael Malsin was "a slow developing young
man," gentle, passive, and easily dominated.

"I'm Jake Horowitz," Jacob said, instantly renaming himself.

"I guess they put the Jewish freshmen on this floor," Ray said. "All seven
of us."

The remark was sardonic. They suspected that Yale had a quota of Jews
for each freshman class, but nobody knew for certain.

"You don't talk like an immigrant."

"Oh, *I* was born in America."

19

"So was I," Jake lied. "Newark." For that matter, he'd told Yale his middle name was Harry when in fact it was Herschel.

They chatted earnestly, outvowing each other's commitment to the study of philosophy. They groused about the required freshman subjects. Jake would be taking chemistry, English, German, and Latin. They discussed the future immediately. Trivia could wait until they knew each other better.

Ray swore he would never go into the family business, but he would. He'd end up president of the Lane Bryant chain of women's clothing stores.

"How about dinner tonight?" he asked.

Jake had little cash. Soon he would be playing bridge for pocket money. The semester's food at the Commons—the school dining room—had been prepaid.

"Actually," he said, "I was curious about the college food."

Ray would have none of that and he soon returned with two of the other Jews in the Class of 1921. Abe Kaufman was an amiable fellow, tall and athletic, with dark and curly hair. Dave Bunim was the opposite, small and slight and unfriendly. They were a couple of fashion plates, Abe in his belted tweed jacket and Dave in knickers and a yellow argyle sweater.

Now Jake was twice an outsider, the only poor Jew at Yale.

He finished plastering down his hair with the matched steel brushes his sister Mildred had given him for a send-off present.

"What gets me," he said, closing the door behind him, "is I've been here a whole day and still don't know the secret Yale handshake. Could we be different?"

They all laughed with fright and strolled across campus swapping jokes and trying to establish themselves, Kaufman with sports knowledge, Bunim with social credentials, Horowitz with literary references. They all tried to impress each other, except Ray Malsin, as they sat down in a family restaurant that served bread, butter and a salad with every dinner. Jake kept buttering bread, then said his stomach was upset and ordered a cup of broth. He could have eaten; Dave picked up the check for everyone.

◆

They huddled together for comfort, these bright boys, against Yale's routine anti-Semitism. Perhaps it had been implicit in the Frank Merriwell stories. Perhaps Yale's Gentile image had even *attracted* Jake, though his disgust with anti-Semitism was steadfast. Midway through freshman year, one of the campus magazines—*The Record*—published an article that began, "When Jews and other scum beyond human ken make Yale fraternities . . . "

That was something Jake wrote about repeatedly, in various memoirs published and unpublished, always in raging detail. He'd dressed and started across campus with the hateful magazine rolled up in his fist. Teary-eyed and dazed, he was stopped by the only senior he knew.

"Wait a minute, kiddo," said Elliott Cohen.

Cohen was a Southern Jew, which gave him a certain privilege since it made him an exotic even among his own. As an editor of Yale's undergraduate literary magazine, he was, moreover, an undergraduate with intellectual credentials. Years later, Cohen would be the editor of *Commentary* magazine.

"What's bothering you?" he asked the distraught Horowitz.

"*This* is bothering me," Jake snarled, shoving the magazine in Cohen's face. "So Jews are 'scum beyond human ken'?"

The older boy scanned the page. "They must be right about you," he said, "because only scum beyond human ken read this magazine."

"I'm going to find the *goy* who wrote this and I'm going to kill him."

Cohen raised his hands in mock surrender. "Don't make me an accessory before the fact. Keep your mouth shut and come on up to my room for a drink. Then you can go about your dirty work."

In the room in Vanderbilt Hall, Elliott opened a gallon jug of hard apple cider and poured out a couple of glasses.

"It seems to me," he drawled, "that if you're going to shoot this fella, whoever he is, you've also got to shoot the editors of the magazine for printing the damned thing. But if you shoot the editors, why you've also got to shoot the faculty adviser and then everyone else around here who not only keeps the publication going but actually supports these particular views."

Elliott refilled Jake's glass.

"And that's taking in a pretty big group of folks. On top of that, have you got the money for the gun? The bullets? Are you ready to buy all that?"

"I was taught to believe," Jake said bitterly, "that the aim of education was to civilize men. Well there isn't a goddamned thing about Yale that has the remotest connection with civilization." He gulped the apple cider. "Can you imagine? We're spending a whole semester on Carlyle's *Heroes and Hero Worship*. They're treating it as if it were a classic. I bet you in twenty years no one will have heard of it."

"Jesus Christ," Cohen said, "you really are a freshman."

"Okay, so I'm a childish idealist. But you're a senior. You're supposed to *help* me. How can a Jew have any dignity around here? Why should I have to go to Protestant chapel every morning?"

Elliott shook his head wearily. "You still judge this place by moral standards, as if it were an institution of higher learning when in plain fact it is a resort hotel. And also, my young friend, I'd thought you wanted to grow up to be a rich Christian like Otto Kahn."

21

The subject of Kahn, the financier, arts patron and Catholic convert, diverted Jake. "Did you hear the joke," he asked, "about Otto Kahn walking past Temple Emanu-el and being stopped by a hunchback beggar?"

"Tell me if you must," Cohen said.

"Kahn gave the beggar a dime and said, 'We're standing in front of Temple Emanu-el. You know, I used to be Jewish,' and the beggar replied, 'You know, I used to be a hunchback.'"

"Don't be bitter," Elliott said. "Few things are worth it."

◆

Jake spent the summer playing violin in the orchestra of a resort hotel, The Clarendon, in Asbury Park, New Jersey. He hoped to save enough money to make his sophomore year less impoverished. Instead, things got worse. The very *lundtsman* who had suggested the grocery business to Meyer Horowitz now urged its sale. He convinced Meyer to buy an old factory in Waterbury, Connecticut, and go into buttons.

"Buttons" meant all variety of clasps, brass pins, glove fasteners, even soldier gaiters. Military contracts, the man said, would make Horowitz rich.

Meyer moved the family into a two-family frame house in Waterbury, at which point, unfortunately, the Armistice was signed.

Mr. Horowitz struggled with the new business while the sophomores at Yale were moved to Welch Hall. Jake still had his own room, but now a door connected it with Abe Kaufman's. The arrangement gave the boys the privacy of singles, the company of a double.

Jake began cutting classes regularly. "My connection with the college curriculum," he later wrote, "had grown so tenuous that I had to ask a friend whether I had signed up for chemistry or geology." In the spring he was suspended from school, not for missing classes but for cutting chapel. It didn't faze him. He took his final exams anyway and did perfectly well, although he only edged past geology and economics.

The friendships held. Ray Malsin and Abe Kaufman kept paying Jake's way and nobody minded except Dave Bunim.

"The guy's a lousy ingrate," he'd growl, and one night the others, too, found Jake hard to defend. He'd slammed through the door to Abe's room crying, "My kingdom for a shirt!"

Kaufman stared at him from several sizes away and Horowitz, grasping that difference, went out and down the hall to Bunim's room. Dave was out of shirts and Ray had gone home for the weekend. Jake stalked the hall trying every doorknob and then trotted down the stairs to find Morris Sklar, class of 1922, heading out of the bathroom. Horowitz followed the boy into his room, strode directly to the bureau, and took a shirt. Dave Bunim, having followed, stood in the doorway and watched grimly.

"I need it," Jake said to Bunim.

"*I* need it," Sklar said too, as if Bunim were judge. "I've got a date tonight."

"The hell with your date," Jake said.

"Come on, borrow somebody else's."

Jake stripped off his sweater and, grinning sadistically, put on Sklar's fresh white shirt.

Sixty years later Bunim was still incensed by the recollection.

"Such a son of a bitch he was, taking that shirt. He didn't know the meaning of compassion. He had no interest in people, none whatsoever."

Resentful memories of Jake Horowitz had rankled Bunim for a lifetime. "He was a louse at Yale, he was a louse outside of Yale, he was a louse all his life."

◆

Long after I had received notice of my expulsion, I was summoned to the dean's office. The dean was a frosty-eyed old fellow named Frederick Sheetz Jones.

"What are you doing here?" he said. "You've been expelled."

"Really? This is the first I've heard of it," I said coolly.

"You mean you didn't get your notice of expulsion? It was sent to your post-office box."

"Do you suppose I'd be hanging around here if I knew I had been expelled?" I had raised my voice. This was not only impudent, it was imprudent—the dean's temper was legendary. He glared at me speechless with outrage. . . . And then . . . a look of bewilderment passed over his features. . . . I walked to the door with the studied casualness of an old-school actor preparing the ground for his exit line. "If I am to be expelled," I said, placing one hand on the doorknob, "I believe I am entitled to written notice. Good morning, sir." . . . If the large inkwell on the dean's desk had struck me in the back of the head, I might have been injured but not surprised.

Absolutely nothing happened, either then or afterward. I never heard any more of my expulsion. . . .   — Jed Harris, *A Dance on the High Wire*

The one class he attended was taught by the head of Yale's Department of Philosophy, Professor Charles Allen Bennett. Much as Jake loved the course, the final exam awed him.

"I don't know where to start cramming."

"You're smart," Malsin said, "and you have a real knack for philosophy. Just write what you think makes sense and don't try to fool Professor Bennett."

The examination's major essay question was about the origins and development of Christian philosophy. Jake had nothing against Christianity, only its abusers. "It is astonishing," he wrote, "how many millions of people in the Western world profess the Christian religion. What is scarcely less astonishing is how few practice it. There is nothing ironic about this tragic state of affairs. If the protracted slaughter, recently concluded in Europe, proves anything at all, it is that this religion, the ultimate flower of an austere, desert-bred civilization, is completely unsuited to the still savage tribes that occupy the continent." After this introductory paragraph, Jake changed the subject. Ignoring the examination question, he wrote about Chinese philosophy and Lao-tzu and earned an A double plus for his work. Professor Bennett returned the examination book with the notation, "For maturity of thought and terseness of style, the best paper I have ever had from an undergraduate." Jake saved the booklet his whole life.

◆

Esther and Meyer Horowitz had always been as prompt with payments as they'd been tight with pennies. The children had once heard Mama arguing with Meyer about economizing on transportation.

"Skipping the trolley and walking to the store," Meyer said, "saves the carfare. Five cents is five cents."

"The shoe leather, you fool! The shoe leather you wear out by walking costs *ten* cents."

What made that particularly ludicrous was that they weren't poor. Things were different now, things were difficult, and the threatening letters that Jake received from the Dean's Office no longer related to his attendance record. They were about dormitory rent, cafeteria charges, laboratory fees, tuition payments. Still, Mama told the girls, Jacob would not be deprived of Yale. Esther didn't know how the fees would be paid, but they would be paid, she said.

Jake apparently decided that they couldn't be. It was time to quit school anyhow. Abe Kaufman had already made up his mind to leave at the end of the spring semester and go straight to law school in New York (bachelor's degrees weren't required at the time). That was a helpful precedent. For Jacob, the Lao-tzu examination paper made it possible to quit with dignity; to quit with an A double plus, and he did. He'd concocted a scheme that, in its blend of the plausible and the preposterous, showed him developing from the businesslike conservatism of the Florida orange deal to the sleight-of-hand of theatrical producing.

The idea was this: Hordes of immigrant Jews in the New York area had left relatives behind in the Lemburgs of Eastern Europe. These villages were so remote, even uncharted, that their inaccessibility, chaotic postal service, and changing national borders made it impossible to send money or goods there with any certainty of delivery. Jake concocted an offer of reliable postal service. He would personally travel to the farms and *shtetls* bringing money, clothes, and food from America. The fees would provide him with enough to cover a European tour after the work was done.

Jake had met Karl Blaustein through Abe Kaufman. Karl was as irritated by Harvard as Abe and Jake were by Yale. He liked Jake's idea, and together they wrote a classified advertisement and placed it in the *New York Times*. The response was so great, and so immediate, that Karl and Jacob sailed within the month.

Exuberant in the first flush of travel, the youngsters decided to see a bit of cosmopolitan Europe before setting out for its farmlands. They rented a tiny apartment on the Boulevard des Capucines in Paris. By week's end there was only enough money left for one of them to undertake the main purpose of the trip. Karl won the coin toss—if winning meant going to Latvia, Poland, and Lithuania instead of remaining in Paris. Jake did his best to appear downcast about it.

A lifetime later he was still recounting his subsequent adventures, but that information is unfortunately straight from the horse's mouth. Were we to take Jake's word for it, as stated in *Dance on the High Wire*, he parlayed his last sou into a substantial sum—"far more than that of a mere French senator"—by betting along with a hustler he met in a Paris billiards hall. A young Frenchwoman named Françoise made life romantic and "So began my ascent to the good life," he wrote. "We dined, night after night, in the best restaurants, saw all the best shows and operas. I tipped like a spendthrift and became a favorite of headwaiters, sommeliers, and doormen. I engaged chauffeured cars to take us everywhere. Sundays we drove out to the country and visited delightful inns for lunch. I encountered well-to-do people only too ready to invite me to join cozy little combines on the Bourse."

Perhaps. Even by his own account, however, Jake had no money left by the time he got to London. He lived briefly on the dole and then tried to get back to America by stowing away on a freighter as had so many heroes of his childhood pulp fiction. Unlike them, he was caught. He paid his fare stoking coal in the boiler room. It was one experience he never recounted in all his years of storytelling. Why? Not snobbery. He reminisced about being in prison while a cross-country hobo. Perhaps the boiler room had been unpleasant rather than colorful. But as far as his tales were concerned, he'd successfully stowed away and that was what he told his sisters when he got back in January.

He had come back to begin the twenties, America's and his own.

WHAT PRICE GLORY?

JAKE HAD NO DESIRE to return to his family, no idea of what work to look for. He went back to Yale and slept on the floor of Ray Malsin's dormitory room. He spent the days in the library. The routine was similar to the one he'd followed as a registered student. When the school year was over, Abe Kaufman asked him to come home with him for the summer, a timely invitation.

Sam and Fannie Kaufman lived with their eight children in a handsome town house at 133 West 118th Street in Morningside Heights, Manhattan. It was a ghetto of upper-middle-class German Jews who felt they were a caste above the East European immigrants swarming all over the Lower East Side.

The Kaufmans were going abroad for the summer. For them, Europe was a place to visit, not flee. They sent all the children to camp except Abe. The two college boys had the house to themselves. In August, Abe's fifteen-year-old sister Bobbie dropped out of camp and became one of the gang. They had such good times that Jake was invited to stay on after the Kaufmans came home. Bobbie insisted that there was no need to inform her father of their house guest; she was sure that Mr. Kaufman would be asleep when Jake got in from late-night carousing and would have long since left for the office when Jake got up. Chancy as the arrangement seemed, Jake needed little convincing. Abe and Bobbie provided his spending money. They never felt they were being used. Jake was good company and that evened things out, they thought.

26

One Saturday in November, Abe borrowed his father's Packard limousine and the three of them bundled into the front seat. They slid back the chauffeur's roof, turned up the heat, and, wrapped in blankets, drove to New Haven for the Yale-Harvard football game. The dormitories were open to visitors after events of such significance, and Ray Malsin was giving a party in his room. There, Jake met Anita Greenbaum.

She was a serious freshman from Connecticut College for Women, a compact girl with short, straight brown hair, a pretty round face, and hazel eyes. She looked quite a bit like Jake's sister Mildred, but Anita was a bohemian, which was proclaimed by her creatively mismatched clothes. The only reason she put up with Connecticut College for Women, she told Jake as she puffed seriously on a cigarette, was because it was a progressive school with its own dance department.

"A Yale education," he replied, "is no more and often quite a bit less than a gentleman's holiday, 'gentleman' being a euphemism for 'illiterate alcoholic.'"

Phil Rich was Anita's date that day. Their romance was complicated by another one he was conducting at home. Phil was trying to hold on to both girls by writing poems to Anita while spending alternate weekends in Philadelphia. One of those Philadelphia weekends, Jake took a train ride up to the Connecticut College for Women in New London.

"I had to know what you thought of the poems," was his defense for visiting Phil's girlfriend. "'Float free in your bower / Sweet angel 'neath heav'n's flowers.'"

"Did Phil read that to you?"

"I wrote it for him. Like Cyrano de Bergerac."

"And I suppose you did it for art's sake?"

"I did it for the money. I told him I'd never written a poem in my life. When he offered a dollar apiece, I said, 'Say hello to Lord Yaakov Byron.'"

That was how Jake and Anita's romance began. When he visited her at home in Bridgeport, he slept on the parlor sofa. When he came up to school he stayed at the Salvation Army dormitory. They never went anywhere, not even for a sandwich, but money didn't matter.

By his own description, Jake had gone to Europe "just barely not a virgin." He had enjoyed a week-long affair in Paris, but that was the extent of his experience. Anita's commitment to free love made him a man, a man at ease with women. Then and ever after, he would talk to them as people. Men would be the ones he sought to hypnotize. Women were his friends, and that would prove the secret of his lifelong success with them.

It was Anita who introduced Jake to the theater too. She told him about Isadora Duncan and Gordon Craig, she introduced him to the plays of

Shakespeare and, as spelled at the time, "Tchekov." Though she claimed to care only for art, the message she delivered was the glamour and excitement of "the show business." And the more Jake heard about it, the surer he said he was that his ache for a special life, an adventurous life, a nervous and surprising life, would be fulfilled in the theater.

He got a job, his first, as a junior reporter for *Billboard*, a theatrical trade paper. He wrote up production plans and casting announcements. Mr. Kaufman remained his innkeeper. Then he moved to the *Clipper*, another trade journal, when he was offered the chance to write theatrical reviews. He was the third-string man but there was plenty to do, with three or four shows opening almost every night that spring and fall of 1921. Anita called him her "dramatic cricket," and he thrilled her with descriptions of opening nights, flossy audiences, and the new plays. The only one that he approved of the whole season was Eugene O'Neill's *Anna Christie*. He scorned the rest.

"They're silly entertainments and stilted dramas presented by philistine producers to infantile audiences. Anyone could do better."

"You could," she replied, and then sat straight up. "Jake, you must become a theatrical producer."

He looked startled, then interested.

"I could put on good shows," he told her. "Not these silly operettas and spectacles. Nothing has gotten the theater into more trouble than artistic pretension. Its greatest strength is entertainment. There's more truth in a comedy sketch or a dance team than any of these biblical pageants. They give people the lowdown on common sense. The theater doesn't care whether you're Jewish or Gentile, white or colored. All the theater cares about is whether your jokes are funny and that you don't drop an orange while you're juggling. You're okay if you can do a time step and carry the tune."

That was how Anita remembered him talking. She didn't always agree with him, considering her own taste more artistic than his, but she was vitalized by the vigor and directness of his young intelligence. Not so her mother. Mrs. Greenbaum complained about Jake's heavy beard. She didn't like his poverty. She didn't like *him*.

"That young man is sinister."

Anita was sure that her mother, who wasn't Jewish, disliked Jake because he was. It didn't matter, she was going to marry him anyway, she decided, and wheedled a proposal out of Phil Rich, hoping to make Jake jealous.

His thoughts were elsewhere. Drinking one night at a bar popular among newspapermen, he had met Maxwell Anderson, a tall, muscular fellow who wrote editorials for the *New York World*. Anderson had lofty ambitions. He wanted to write verse plays and historical dramas; he wanted to become

America's Shakespeare. He already had one play under option, *White Desert*. His new project was a military melodrama, written in collaboration with a fellow journalist named Laurence Stallings. Jake insisted on accompanying Anderson home to get a copy of the script and stayed up the night reading it.

In the morning, eager to catch Anderson at home, he dashed down the stairs, out the front door, and into the arms of Mr. Kaufman, who was stepping into his limousine. It was a scene from a farce as they stared at each other, the dignified realtor and his scruffy stowaway tenant. Then Jake rushed off to deliver his enthusiasm for the play. This was the script, he told Anita, that would launch him.

Anderson, though, considered the play two drafts from completion. Eager as Jake was to get started, he could only wait, and hope that Anderson would honor the promise to give him first crack at producing it.

Events now seemed to be converging on him. The play needed time; Anita was pressing for marriage; Mr. Kaufman had evicted him; the job at the *Clipper* was oppressive and its time clock unbearable. Then Phil Rich made a suggestion that seemed perfect.

Anita had told Phil that she was rejecting not only his marriage proposal but Jake's as well. Phil thought it might cheer up both failed suitors to bum across the country. Flight being an ever-present alternative in Jake's life, he agreed.

The itinerary was vague. They would veer south for warm weather and then ride the rods west, sneaking onto freight trains, first through Delaware and Maryland to Greensboro, North Carolina, and then over the Plains States. By North Carolina, however, Phil's energies were spent and he went home to Philadelphia and marriage.

With only Jake Horowitz to bear witness, the record once again becomes unreliable. He sold encyclopedias to farmers, he later said; dug holes in frozen farm fields. He was seduced by lonely boardinghouse mistresses. "I was," he wrote, "the pampered guest for five days of the fire department in Greensburg, Pennsylvania. I served briefly as a Latin tutor for a feebleminded youth in Peru, Indiana. . . . I spent a week on an Indian reservation. . . . But most of the time I was merely a tramp, and as such I was given free lodging in nine jails all the way from Suffolk, Virginia . . . to Missouri Valley, Iowa."

He did get as far as Colorado, that at least has been verified. He became the editor of an arts magazine there and tried to convince Edward G. Robinson, who was acting locally, to join him in forming a Denver repertory theater. Robinson had made up his mind to try Hollywood and the movies. Horowitz decided to go in the other direction.

Anita, meantime, had left school for Greenwich Village. She took a little apartment on Barrow Street with two roommates, Caroline Francke and Peggy Jacobsen. They were serious young ladies, though of the three only Caroline would ever make a serious career; serious enough, at least, to write a few plays and co-author the screenplay for the Jean Harlow movie *Bombshell*.

Anita anglicized her name to Green and got a job in the advertising office of the Oppenheim Collins department store on 34th Street. Evenings and weekends, the roommates held soirées, Anita the *artiste*, Peggy the flapper, and Caroline the wit. They would put red bulbs in the lamps, candles in saucers, open a bottle of Dago Red wine, and turn on the Victrola. Then they'd whirl and glide about the living room in diaphanous gowns. The boys would sit on the floor and watch, cross-legged and urgent.

As the candlelight and the music and the wine and the frightened yearnings had their effects, the girls became daring. A shoulder strap slipped off a white shoulder and *la danse sensuelle*, as Anita called it, began. The music might be Ippolitov-Ivanov's "Caucasian Sketches" or Ethel Waters singing one of her naughty songs. One evening, Peggy bared a breast. Anita said it was the only time she ever saw Herman Shumlin blush. Paul Streger, another Newark boy, elbowed Herman and giggled, making Herman all the redder.

Then Jake came home.

"I'm going to be very rich and very famous and very tragic," he told Anita, "but I'll be goddamned if I'm going to lead a boring life."

They were leaving the balcony of the Criterion movie theater in Times Square; were squinting into the glare of the Grand Foyer. Anita took Jake's arm as the throng carried them toward the marble staircase. He gazed down on the crowd below and she felt a sudden chill of worry for him.

"How can I possibly find a play that will reach all these different people?"

"Don't think of them as so many," she whispered. "Think of reaching just one of them. If you can produce a play that reaches one, you'll reach them all."

"Well it had better be soon," he said. "I've got to make a million before I'm thirty because I'm going to burn out fast."

Anita's eyes flooded. "Look at that statue," she said, pointing to a marble nude. "Don't you think these movie palaces are vulgar to beat the band?"

She never forgot the subject she'd just changed.

◆

The first chance for Jake Horowitz to become a producer did not involve such heady concerns as had awed the young man staring down upon the movie crowd. The real world was more practical. The opportunity arrived with a clearly printed price tag.

Richard Herndon telephoned to offer a share in his forthcoming production of *The Romantic Age*. Horowitz was not interested in being a mere financial participant, but this project emanated prestige. The author was A. A. Milne, the director the reputable Fred Stanhope, and the stars were to be Margalo Gillmore and Leslie Howard. They were all members of the international theatrical establishment.

Jake made a special trip to Yale and told Ray Malsin about the opportunity. He gave a script to the reserved college senior, along with the warning that it wasn't *War and Peace*. Ray found it a "sweet, mindless play," but he convinced his mother to invest five thousand dollars and make Jake Horowitz a producer.

The play would open in six months to mild, commercially useless praise and close as a dignified failure. The experience would give Jake nothing but experience. He'd try to get Anita a bit part and be brushed off. He would be denied an artistic voice in the production and not even be given billing as an associate producer. He wouldn't let any of it happen again. Everyone has to pay a price of admission, he was to say to Anita. Fine. Mrs. Malsin had paid his.

◆

The Double R was a Brazilian coffee shop on West 44th Street off Sixth Avenue. It was a hangout for theater aspirants, and Jake spent a few hours there almost every day. Anita, whenever she could, dashed uptown from work to meet him for lunch. Jake had promised her a part in the Anderson play and this was the day of the final draft. She hurried into the restaurant and saw Jake sitting at a window table, reading the script. He looked up and said, "It's my play of destiny. It's going to rocket me to success." He handed her the script. "Max is calling it *What Price Glory?* and he said it's mine. All I need is three hundred dollars to pay for the option."

Going home with Anita late that very afternoon, he had his chance to get the three hundred. Murray Graham strolled into their subway car at the 34th Street station. Murray was one of Peggy Jacobsen's beaus. He was an executive in training at Macy's and a timid young man. Jake leaped from the yellow rattan subway seat and pounded Murray on the back. Over the roar of the train he flattered and cheered and said the fellow already looked like an executive. He even offered Murray the chance to become a theatrical investor.

Murray conceded that an executive training program at Macy's probably sounded grand but, he said, the salary wasn't. He had some savings because he was still living with his parents, but hardly enough to become a theatrical investor. About three hundred and fifty dollars.

Why, Jake could hardly get over it. For only three hundred dollars someone could get in on the ground floor of a great show, and that would still leave Murray with fifty dollars in the bank. He could take his mother to the opening night of *What Price Glory?*

Murray looked at Anita with alarm, it seemed to her, but he went along with Jake's enthusiasm. He took out his checkbook and, as the train hurtled downtown, he leaned on his creased and shaky briefcase and wrote out the check. Signing his name carefully, neatly, he tore out the check and handed it to Jake with a brave grin. "It took me an awful long time to save this up," he said. "It's just about my last cent."

"You'll never regret it," Jake said. "It's the start of a wonderful theatrical career."

Anita looked away. She didn't like Jake taking advantage of this boy's timidity. Then, so uncharacteristically that she would be startled by the memory ever after, Jake tore the check in half, saying, "Save your bucks for my next show. I've decided to keep this one for myself."

Anita hugged her young man on the walk back from the subway station. She told him that taking someone's last cent was taking unlucky money and that she was proud of what he'd done, proud of his sympathy for Murray. Had he torn the check up in sympathy? Did Jake have a conscience? Anita never did know.

She tried to cheer him. He insisted he was fine.

"I'll get the option money from Ray's mother," he said, begging off from an overnight stay even though Caroline and Peggy had both gone off for the weekend. Anita understood his gloom.

Jake went straight to a telephone booth and called Peggy Jacobsen at her parents' home in Brooklyn. He asked if she'd go to dinner with him that evening, and as he didn't mention Anita, neither did she. Peggy agreed to meet him at Delmonico's.

She always was a nifty-looking girl, with bobbed hair and long legs and slinky hips, but in her up-to-the-minute batik dress and broad-brimmed picture hat Peggy was stunning. Jake gave her the kind of glamorous New York evening she'd never had before. They made love that night on the sofa of her parents' living room. It must have been his way of punishing both Anita and Murray at the same time.

◆

Ray Malsin had delivered the valedictory speech to the Yale Class of 1921 and then moved into an apartment on Broadway at 80th Street. Jake joined him there, explaining to Anita that the Malsin family was his most important contact. It was not a powerful argument, but he was becoming authoritative and she defensive. She was in a weak position; she knew it and hated it but was helpless to change it.

"I had intended to remain your number one investor," Ray told Jake on the subject of *What Price Glory?*, and with that Jake's heart sank. It wasn't a matter of the *Romantic Age* loss. "My mother is still as impressed with you as I am," Ray said, "but there's a family cash problem. It'll loosen up in three or four months."

"There's a time element," Jake said frantically. "It's just a matter," he stammered, "of . . . only three hundred . . . dollars."

Ray shrugged helplessly and Jake rushed off to ask Anderson for a postponement. It wasn't granted and he wasn't surprised, he told Anita at the Double R, wearily rubbing his eyelids, his cheeks, the stubble of his beard, and smoking cigarette after cigarette. Anderson blamed it all on the *New York Sun*'s dramatic critic, Alexander Woollcott. "Woollcott told Max he'd never heard of me. He said it was important to have an established management. They're giving *What Price Glory?* to Arthur Hopkins instead."

"I'm sorry," Anita said.

"Well, the hell with Woollcott and the hell with Anderson. I suppose it came as something of a shock to me that a man who could write in iambic pentameter could be faithless," Jake said, looking up at Anita and managing a near-smile. "That's what I said to Max. Woollcott never heard of me. God damn. I may never in my life have so sure a chance again, but if I do, I'm not going to be caught without money." Then he whispered, "None of this is going to happen again."

It was the first time she noticed his whisper, a mannerism that was to become a part of his personality, and the first time she sensed what her mother had meant by "sinister."

She leaned across the table and kissed his closed eyes. He had no choice, he said, but to accept a job as an assistant to Claude Greneker, the press agent for the Shubert brothers.

Jacob J. ("J.J.") Shubert and Lee ("Mr. Lee") Shubert were the most powerful figures in the American theater. Their Shubert Corporation owned scores of theaters in New York and across the country; they had affiliation agreements with hundreds more. They produced many of the shows that played in those theaters. Their headquarters in the Shubert Theatre on 44th Street was the power center of the American stage. It was a place to learn the business of show business, and Jake's press agent job would serve other purposes too. The Shubert office was a scene of intense activity; people were going in and out; productions were considered, rejected, or approved; there was argument and gossip. And all this pandemonium orbited the inner offices—the silent, majestic sanctums of the Shubert brothers themselves, the raunchy Mr. Lee and the icily imperious J.J.

The job of assistant press agent to Claude Greneker introduced Jake for the first time to the people of the working theater. It put him in contact with actors, stage managers, directors, and playwrights. The office also gave him access to the best scripts, for plays were submitted to the Shuberts before going to any other producers. One day a gem might be overlooked and he'd grab it.

One of the regulars in the waiting room was a skinny, taciturn, thoroughly Gentile giant, a six-foot-six-inch actor named George Abbott. He'd just returned from touring in *Dulcy* with Lynn Fontanne and between performances had collaborated on a play, *The Fall Guy*, with James Gleason, another actor in the company. Abbott was haunting the Shubert office because he wanted them to produce his play, because he had directing ambitions, and because he needed acting work to support those hopes as well as his bride Ednah.

Horowitz and Abbott got on, different though they were, because of a shared contempt for the current crop of producers and playwrights. They planned to overwhelm the New York stage with modern melodramas. They'd stroll down the street to get a sandwich, Abbott towering silently as Horowitz sounded off.

One morning, Greneker asked Jake to join him in Mr. Lee's office. Jake listened as Shubert told Greneker about a script the office was going to produce. It was a play that Jake had read with some nausea only the night before.

"Jesus Christ," he exploded, "I could pick better plays than you simpletons!" and he was fired on the spot.

Presumably, *The Romantic Age* had convinced Richard Herndon of Horowitz's cleverness and money-raising ability. Herndon was now opening a farce called *Applesauce* for an indefinite Chicago engagement. He offered Jake $125 a week to be the press agent. That was a heady salary, and Jake told Anita that in a year's time he'd be able to save enough of it to begin producing and perhaps be able to get married. She accepted that because her other choices, demanding that he stay or take her along, were not his choices.

He took the train to Waterbury to say good-bye to his family. Papa was still struggling with the button factory, its brass pins, its button fasteners. The town was dreary. The Horowitz apartment looked much like the one in Newark, everything having been picked up from one place and set down in the other. Yet, something about it was wrong. The big oak and leather pieces didn't quite seem right in one half of a Waterbury two-family house. Perhaps it was city furniture.

Not inspired to redecorate, Esther's only change was a wall in the living room that she covered with framed family photographs. These dark or sepia pictures of bearded grandfathers, dour grandmothers in long black dresses, and overdressed infants had been enlarged and then trimmed to round or rectangular shapes. They'd been hung in elaborate wood Victorian frames to cover the wall, a display to establish the past.

The centerpiece of this display was not the traditional picture of paternal grandparents. The dominating photograph on the Waterbury wall was of baby Sylvia perched on a table, flanked by young Mildred and adolescent Jacob.

His arrival touched off a celebration among the sisters, because he hadn't been home for a year and the absence had cloaked him in glamour. He came with tales of Manhattan, its stages and speakeasies. This was a home where life played in Yiddish. It was a home in which even the simple diversion of radio was monitored, when tolerated at all. Jacob was proof that escape was possible. He made time for each sister, time alone to talk of who they were and what they wanted to do and how they could follow him out of this constricted home and into his exciting world. They were eager to become his acolytes.

Sylvia was seventeen and easy pickings for an exciting big brother. She was the family beauty, smart and sensual. While fifteen-year-old Florie sat on the living room Oriental rug and listened agog, Sylvia perched on the leather rocker, her long legs folded beneath her. She was thrilled as Jake wove a glittering narrative linking Flo Ziegfeld with Sergeant York, Jack Dempsey and Sophie Tucker. He wanted to move Sylvia to New York. He would assume responsibility for her education, he said. Saul was eight years old and stood in the doorway. Jake didn't bother telling him anything.

◆

To those who knew him in the Chicago days, Jake was happier and less complicated than he would ever be again. He was free of Anita's marital pressures; he had all the money a single fellow needed; his job was fun, he was good at it, and Richard Herndon was not a boss to exert authority. Jake Horowitz was a young man at the start of the future.

Although he had an office, to those who knew him it was as if he lived on the streets. *In action*. He'd amble along State Street, hands stuck deep in his trouser pockets, a cigarette dangling from his lips, his beard stubble bristling.

He checked into the Congress Hotel. It was hardly elegant but show folk stayed there, it offered theatrical rates, and just across the street was a speakeasy, the Friar's Inn. "The town was in its hey-day," he later wrote, "wide open. Within a week I had a hundred friends on the newspapers and I moved through their city rooms with the assurance of a professional and the nervous energy of a dervish."

He had theatrical friends too: Walter Connolly, an actor in *Applesauce*, and his wife Nedda, who was in a local touring company of *Iz Zat So?* And another pal was a fellow press agent named Richard Maney.

I first met [Horowitz] in Chicago in 1924 when I was publicizing my fifth *Greenwich Village Follies*, and he was the courier for *Applesauce*. He was lean, dark and hungry looking. Scorched with ambition . . . he fumed at the circumstances which prevented him from producing plays in New York. He was convinced he was better equipped than those thus engaged. After listening to him for twenty minutes, I was convinced too. He discussed the theater more intelligently and eloquently than anyone I had met . . . I have met most of the theater's wizards and my opinion still stands. . . . While his mates talked about sniping three sheets, planting layouts and circumventing the drama editor of *The Chicago Tribune*, he carried on about Stanislavsky, Meyerhold and Gordon Craig. While they studied the overnight entries at Jamaica, he rhapsodized over Max Beerbohm's *Zuleika Dobson*.

In Chicago he was known as the "horizontal press agent" because of his reluctance to get up once he'd retired. . . . Charged with industry while vertical, he rarely found time to shave. This omission, plus spontaneous whiskers, contributed to his menace. Shaved or bristled he was acid and truculent. . . . He had one exclusive grief. *What Price Glory*.   — Richard Maney, *Fanfare*

Nobody ever claimed that *Applesauce* was a masterpiece. Jake himself thought it was "harmless theatrical trash." The show was a vehicle for Alan Dynehart and Clairborne Foster, both audience favorites. The ways of publicity were, like the theater itself, rowdier than in later times, and more ingenuous. Jake's first brainstorm was the line, "*Applesauce* is on every tongue." He managed to get the slogan into gossip columns and newspaper photo captions. Nobody thought it wanting in the wit department. Some even gave it credit for keeping the play popular, and the play became very popular. Jake and the world seemed to be the same age. Young.

One afternoon he personally carried a crate downtown, kneeled in the middle of State Street, and released a turkey. There was no connection between a turkey loose on State Street and the play *Applesauce*. The show wasn't about a turkey and, all hoped, it wasn't itself one. Yet, despite this irrelevance, editors, alerted by Jake to the event, sent out their photographers and reporters. The stunt made most of the newspapers and on such bursts of publicity, *Applesauce* ran a full year in Chicago. Jake was earning a reputation as an inventive, industrious, energetic publicity man and a generally bright fellow, a comer.

Nedda and Walter Connolly and Richard Maney spent many evenings with him. They'd meet after the shows and have dinner at Henrici's Restaurant. Nedda thought Jake seemed on top of life. He would bring along a girlfriend named Helena. They'd met at the Shubert office in Chicago, where she worked as a secretary. She was "a brassy, broad-hipped, big breasted dame," Horowitz would later recall, "and I had fallen in love with her."

They'd whirl on the dance floor and he even picked up everyone's check, now and then. The only time Nedda recalled his being in a bad temper was when Dick Maney mentioned that New York had a new smash hit melodrama, *What Price Glory?*

"I'm going to produce a bigger show than that," Jake said. "All these producers are old putzes, Ziegfeld, Herndon, Arthur Hopkins. You don't think Hopkins had brains enough to actually choose *What Price Glory?* Aleck Woollcott chose it for him."

A quiet little fellow had joined them at the restaurant table and was listening intently. He was a friend of Nedda and Walter's named Irving Cooper, and as he later put it himself, he'd done well for a twenty-five-year-old. Irving Cooper was in the concessions business: souvenir programs, candy, checkrooms, sheet music. It earned him a thousand dollars a week. He even had a new car. Walter told Jake about that just before Irving arrived.

"Cooper," Jake said, pouncing, "you know, any smart young guys could walk into New York and take everything away from these old school producers. We could do it. Why don't you come in with me?"

"There's too much noise to talk about it here," Irving said as the big Chicago steaks were set on the table.

"Okay," Jake grinned. "I want to drive that car of yours anyhow. Pick me up tomorrow at my hotel and we'll go for a spin."

Cooper's heart fell. He'd just bought the brand-new Moon roadster a week earlier. It was cream colored and he'd laid out $1,800 for it. When he pulled up in front of the Congress Hotel the next day he was sick with worry.

Jake trotted out of the hotel.

"Slide over, pal," he said, opening the door on Irving's side. Cooper edged over to the passenger seat.

"How do you start this thing?" Jake peered along the instrument panel and then burst out laughing. "Just kidding, kiddo. I've been itching to get my hands on one of these."

Jake started the car and pulled into traffic without looking behind or signaling. He sat all the way back in his seat and drove with his arms extended straight out, gripping the steering wheel tightly. He kept up a running diatribe about the other cars on the road. Finally he came to the subject of producing. Cooper tried to concentrate while sweating out the agitated driving as Jake restlessly switched lanes, honking the horn, braiding through the heavy traffic.

"It sounds interesting," Irving said shakily as they screeched up in front of the hotel. He sighed with relief. "What's your situation with *Applesauce*?"

"It's been running a year. All Herndon had hoped for was four or five months. He's made almost a hundred fifty thousand dollars out of it here. Now he wants to bring it to New York, the sucker. It isn't a New York show. Anyhow, I'm not going back there as a press agent. I'm coming back as a producer, and if you want to throw in with me, you're welcome, only let me know quick."

Jake suggested they share the expenses of a New York office and each come up with an initial investment. Irving could stay in Chicago and Jake would mail him the scripts. Those that interested Cooper he could co-produce. Irving said he'd think about it, and Jake got out of the car.

"Nice jalopy you've got here," he said, patting the windowsill. "You might have the wheel alignment checked."

He strolled into the hotel. It was the end of his Chicago year and it had been a good year. He'd found independence and known exhilaration and developed professional assurance. He came back to New York committed to being a man. His careers were about to begin, the career of a theatrical producer and the career of elbowing in on and dominating other lives.

Weeks later he wrote to Irving Cooper, "Listen pal. New York is wide open for a couple of smart guys like us. The theater is going to boom. What's happened so far is nothing compared to what's ahead. Between your bucks and my know-how we could set this town on fire. Now I've got to tell you I haven't the ghost of a play but I haven't given up hope. If we open an office and start reading scripts, I guarantee you within six months we'll be smoking cigars in *The Twentieth Century*'s best compartment. We'll be making railroad trips just like the rest of those bastards."

BELOVED OF GOD

ONCE JAKE LEFT NEWARK for Yale he never had a permanent home again. He was never to accumulate possessions or stay at one address or live with one woman for very long. This shrinking from connections was incongruously coupled with an apparent inability to be alone.

Returning to New York in 1924 after the exhilarating year in Chicago, he moved in with Anita. He didn't love her, or so he wrote Irving Cooper, but she stood at the open door, eager to embrace him, and he came in.

She had a new place, a floor-through in a Greenwich Village brownstone at 43 West 10th Street. The roommates were gone. As an expectant mother prepares a nursery, this expectant wife had prepared a honeymoon nest for a longingly awaited husband.

Jake told his sister Mildred he was trapped. Mildred had become his confidante. She worked as a reporter for the *Newark Ledger*. She had been invited to some of Anita's soirées and she liked the girl, but she adored her brother.

He took an office, his first, in the Bond Clothes Building at Broadway and 46th Street. It was just a partitioned-off section of a larger suite that booked vaudeville acts, but it was a producing office, it was in Times Square, and it was his.

With Irving Cooper in Chicago, Jake treated the business as his own. The staff he assembled had nothing in common but greenness. Two menbers were old Newark friends, Herman Shumlin, the general manager, and Paul Streger, the casting director and stage manager. They were clever but meek young men; Horowitz sought out those who could be intimidated. He'd bullied Herman since they had been teenagers, and Paul was as timid as Ray Malsin.

But they were also capable. Herman had the mind for figures and the organizational instinct that a good general manager needed. Streger was an actor who knew most of the actors around town. He would be a good casting director if they ever found a play to do.

Jake hired his first secretary, Jean Barkow, the one employee who actually had experience. His strangest choice for the staff was the press agent, a thirty-one-year-old New Englander named Samuel Nathan Behrman, who was as jumpy as a marionette and wretchedly shy. Jake hardly needed another promoter in the house. Behrman could serve other purposes. He certainly wrote well enough to do feature articles for the Sunday papers, and that was a major function of any press agent.

Sam Behrman had drawn himself up from an impoverished childhood in Worcester, Massachusetts to George Pierce Baker's famed playwriting class at Harvard. He'd gone on to graduate school at Columbia. Starting as a clerk at the *New York Times* he had advanced to an editorial job in the book review section. The jobs supported his writing of unproduced plays.

As he said in his memoir, *People in a Diary:*

The American Way brought [Jake Horowitz] into my life. My agent, Harold Freedman, sent it to him in Chicago where [he] was then press-agenting some show. [He] wrote to say that he wanted to produce it and would, as soon as he could raise the money. But he couldn't raise the money. . . .

He asked me to be his play reader and press agent. I knew nothing about this highly specialized vocation. The dean of New York press agents, Richard Maney . . . took me in hand. He tutored me. For a long time afterward, he kept telling people that I had asked him what a marquee was. He explained to me that it had nothing to do with French nobility. . . . No one could have been greener than I, but on the first Sunday I got a lot of stuff in the papers. There were then fourteen papers in New York. . . .

Anita would see Jake over breakfast coffee and then not again until late at night. There were rare dinners at home and few guests. He usually went to the theater after work, but not with her. All the rejection only made her feel more urgent about marrying him. When he finally did come home he would stay up and read and in the dawn hours he'd pad into the living room and make telephone calls.

Behrman wrote:

It was at that time that my telephone phobia began. I have never since been able to dissociate the ring of the telephone from the imminence of danger. . . . [Jake] would call me up at two and three in the morning to berate me for something I had done badly or failed to do at all.

◆

"I don't want to be Mrs. Jacob Horowitz," Anita said one morning, and Jake looked at her as if to say this is just too good to be true.

"I know I sound anti-Semitic, but 'Horowitz' is too *immigranty.* You don't hear of producers with names like that even though some of them must be Jewish."

Jake told her practically all of them were, even David Belasco, who affected the habit of a Catholic priest and wore a clerical collar. "The only vow he's ever taken," Jake said, "is a vow of cheap theatrics."

In a flamboyant era, Belasco certainly was a flamboyant character. At rehearsals, when his stage manager would greet the producer, he would try to see whether Belasco was wearing a real wristwatch or a prop watch. If it was a prop watch the stage manager knew Belasco was planning a tantrum. Soon the producer would be striding up and down the stage, shouting, clapping his hand to his forehead and finally ripping off the watch and slamming it to the floor, smashing it to bits. Jake detested Belasco's using such tricks in productions, but he thought them wonderful in the man and always relished telling the prop watch anecdote.

It was common at the time for Jewish people to anglicize their Russian or Slavic or German surnames. In the theater it wasn't to conceal Jewishness. There, historically, nobody cared what you were. The purpose of a name change in the theater was to make it more euphonious and memorable. If a certain defensiveness could be read into this sense of what was a euphonious name, and into the desire to appeal to mass (that is, Gentile) audiences, it was a complex defensiveness.

To Anita's suggestion that he change his name, Jake replied that he'd already decided to call himself Harris. There was an established producer named Sam Harris, one of the few Jake admired.

She liked the ring of "Anita and Jake Harris," but he said he was changing his first name too. He wanted something altogether new and original, a name nobody in the theater had ever had before, and said he remembered an Old Testament tale about a change of name. It came from the Second Book of Samuel, chapter twelve. The Talmudic studies had stayed with him. Verse twenty-five. God told the prophet Nathan in a dream that he wanted to prove with a new name how much he loved King Solomon. The new name was to be "Jedidiah," the "iah" being an abbreviation of "Yahweh." The name meant "beloved of God."

"My name is going to be Jed Harris."

41

"I never heard of anyone named Jed."

"I'm the first."

He never would change his name legally. Many years later, when everyone knew him only as Jed Harris, his passport still carried the name of Jacob Horowitz. He was surprised when Mildred told him she'd changed her name, legally, to "Harris." "How could you do such a thing?" he asked her. "I was born Jacob Horowitz and I'm going to die Jacob Horowitz."

◆

Jake once told Anita that when a producer wants new plays all he has to do is pull the bed quilt over his head and mutter that he is interested in scripts. The next morning a stack of unsolicited manuscripts will be piled high on his desk with more pouring in through the transom. On this particular summer's day in 1925, however, the script arrived under George Abbott's arm. The lanky actor-writer who used to haunt the Shubert office had enjoyed a 176-performance success with his play, *The Fall Guy*. He stuck out his long arm for a handshake with the physical forthrightness of an athlete.

"Hello, George," Jed whispered.

Abbott sat down and put *Love 'Em and Leave 'Em* on the desk. He'd written it with a poet named John V. A. Weaver. It was based on Weaver's popular volume of slang poetry. Abbott thought it was a solid piece of farce, though he had no illusions about being a great writer. He considered himself a play carpenter who needed a collaborator to invent plots, just as did his model, George S. Kaufman.

The young producer paid attention. He seemed to Abbott a "hypnotic listener, if there is such a thing." He gazed into Abbott's eyes, occasionally nodding. Everything the actor said seemed to be of tremendous significance to him. His whispering had become habitual by now, a mannerism designed to pull people in physically—make them lean forward—and to entrance them. Any conversation with him seemed to be important.

Abbott didn't think what he was saying merited such concentration but was excited by this intensity. Jed nodded eagerly, earnestly. He waved off all outside interruptions and phone calls. His comments were warm, understanding, reasonable, and direct. He hunched over, leaning on his elbows with his cheeks cradled in the heels of his palms. In his right hand a cigarette was tucked against the webbing between his index and third fingers. When he inhaled he practically kissed his palm while squinting through the opened fingers and the smoke. His eyes, voluptuous and inky, swallowed Abbott. The actor felt he had not been mistaken about the conversations they'd had at the Shubert office; not been mistaken about bringing *Love 'Em and Leave 'Em* to Horowitz.

"Not Horowitz," Jake said. "Jed Harris."

As Abbott recalled, Jake—Jed—leveled with him. "You're a man of the stage, George, and you hate baloney. That's a rare combination in this town. Most stage people are full of it. They're still doing cheap tricks. I think there's a place on the stage for realism and action, for intelligent playwrights, a place for melodrama that has the spirit of today, the fast rhythm of a machine gun. They're all idiots, the guys producing now. They turn down the good scripts and produce the junk. The door is wide open and we can walk right through it. I think we ought to work together as a team. I produce," he said, "and you write and direct. I trust you, George."

"And I trust you," Abbott replied. A Calvinist from crust to core, he had a reverent attitude toward trust. "I think we can do everything together."

Harris laughed. "We'll do 'em all! You direct 'em, I'll produce 'em."

"I'm serious about this, Jake."

"Not Jake; Jed Harris," was the whisper, "and I'm serious too."

◆

George Abbott's *Love 'Em and Leave 'Em* was not the first play to be billed "A Jed Harris Production." *Weak Sisters* opened on October 13, 1925. Irving Cooper was uninvolved because Jed had found a money man—Leonard Blumberg—who was willing to be just a money man. Blumberg invested $9,000 to finance both plays. Cooper had always said he would participate only in those plays that he agreed to do and so there seemed nothing objectionable about this. It should have been plain to him, though, that Jed was not going to share anything if he could help it.

Three days after *Weak Sisters* opened to mixed reviews, the twenty-five-year-old Jed Harris sat down for his first newspaper interview. The reporter was from the *New York World*.

Interviewing me is a lot of bunk. I wouldn't stand for it at all if I didn't think it might help my show a little. I could get you interviews with the actors, or bunk stuff about myself, but what's the use of your asking me silly questions with a perfectly straight face and expecting me to answer them seriously?

There's no art in the theater, never was. It's a business, like selling butter and eggs. Everybody's an "artist" in the theater nowadays. Joe Cook, Fanny Brice, George Kelly, all of them. So-called critics and reporters go to a show and if they like it they say it's artistic. If they think an actor or a producer or a comedian or a dancer is clever they call him an artist. What does it mean? Nothing.

I didn't produce *Weak Sisters* for you or any reviewer or critic, but because I thought it was a play that people would pay money to see. There's no use saying anything else. I enjoy putting a play together; working with the author, picking the cast, the scenery, the lighting, the costumes, pointing the scenes, trying the play with one scene out, risking it with a bad scene in just because it has some quirk or line I like.

But after that it's boring. Don't ever think it's glamorous or artistic. It's an outlet for one's energy, a trade like any other trade. If you're good you're good, but don't drag art into it. In the modern theater, with so much money involved, there is no chance for real art. Anyhow, real playwrights and actors don't think of themselves as artists. They're clever and skillful and know what they're doing.

See what the critics did to Charlie Chaplin by telling him what a great artist he was?

Although the interview didn't rescue *Weak Sisters*, it did introduce the New York press to a colorful new face in the show business. He would always be quotable, unpredictable, outrageously sensible. For his part, he seemed to understand that the press was becoming God-like in its creative power. He was, after all, a former press agent. In the years to come his name would be in the papers almost daily, and that would play a major role in his self-invention.

The most effective approach to this, he apparently realized, was to become more important to the press than in need of it. Harris cultivated a mystery, an elusiveness, a shadowy glamour. The whisper and the unshaven face became his trademarks and a sardonic wit his style. He would always talk to reporters, but they had to find him first. He made sure they did.

Meanwhile, Anita wept. She had been the unconventional one, the believer in free love. Now she was too old for free love, and feared becoming a spinster. The pitiful scenes made Jed nasty and one night he walked out of the apartment and stayed out until the morning. He came back and said they would get married.

On December 11, 1925, Anita and Jed hailed a cab and headed downtown to City Hall with their witnesses, Peggy Jacobsen and Herman Shumlin. No religious ceremony for these modern young atheists. The mood was like the day, cloudy and cold. Anita chattered, but it was nervous babble. Jed's silence hardly disguised his gloom.

On the street outside City Hall, he was stopped by a beggar, a sorry young man who grasped him by the elbow and said, "By God, it's Jacob Horowitz! Don't you remember me? Charley McIver from the boiler room of that old bucket of a freighter."

"Good Christ, of course I remember you! You helped me stow away."

Herman, Peggy and Anita watched, waited, and listened.

"I wasn't much good at it," McIver said. "They found you, didn't they?"

"And made me a stoker too," Jed laughed. It was the first time he'd laughed all day. He laughed hard and then stopped. "Things bad for you?" McIver shrugged. "The whole world's rich," Jake said.

"Not me. I'll probably sign aboard another crate. You look okay."

"I'm getting married," Jed snarled. He took out his wallet, tucked a twenty-dollar bill in the fellow's breast pocket, and without another word turned on his heel and climbed up the steps of City Hall. Anita, Herman, and Peggy followed.

The taxi ride uptown after the ceremony was more funereal than festive. Peggy kept an eye on her friend. She still considered Anita her friend even after having slept with Jake. "Sex is above morality," the pretty flapper liked to say, "and beneath discussion."

Anita knew that only emotional blackmail had forced Jed to marry her. To Peggy she looked as though she wanted to jump out of the cab and kill herself. The silence was oppressive. Jed broke it cruelly.

"Well you got what you wanted. Doesn't it make you happy?"

Anita stared out of the window, her round eyes wide and wet.

They went out, the four of them, and got drunk. When Jed left the table for the men's room, Anita told Herman and Peggy that during the wedding ceremony she felt "as if I was drowning. The water came up over my head and I was sinking, sinking, sinking . . ."

◆

Jed got away from married life by putting every minute into the production of *Love 'Em and Leave 'Em*. He left Anita at home during the out-of-town tryout engagement. He worked hard there in Atlantic City and even helped George stage a crapshooting scene since Abbott didn't know much about gambling. Then, just before the opening, he became nervous. He told Abbott to fire Joseph Bell, the leading man, and play the part himself.

Abbott refused, telling Jed that he would never act again, and Bell was kept. An uncomplicated and unflappable man, George Abbott considered Jed Harris's panic a flaw in a producer. Bringing a show to New York can be a frightening experience, he knew that, but the producer has to reassure everyone, not add to their nervousness. Joseph Bell was given fine reviews and when *Love 'Em and Leave 'Em* opened in New York on a wintry night in February 1926, it was, if not a bombshell, certainly a success. Jed and his financial partner, Blumberg, made a few thousand dollars each from the six-month run. Anita went out and bought a dining room table and chairs.

"Let's give a dinner party."

She had been thinking about it for weeks and had finally worked up the nerve to make the suggestion. They were in bed. Jed was reading, his glasses pushed down to the tip of his nose. Not glancing up, he surprised her by saying that it sounded like a fine idea. He suggested inviting Herman and Paul and Sam from the office, and Jean Barkow too. To balance things out, boy-girl, Anita would ask her old roommates, Caroline and Peggy. And, they agreed, George and Ednah Abbott.

Anita remembered it all going beautifully, and after dinner, Jed poured brandy. Everyone pulled chairs around as he told stories of being young in London and Paris. He whispered and chuckled as if hearing the funny parts for the first time. He turned to the subject of Yale and stated a theory that he would repeat in his memoir, *A Dance on the High Wire:*

According to the Ape Theory, any normal, reasonably healthy baboon could achieve passing grades in any arts course at Yale, but a trained chimpanzee would graduate with honors. This doctrine had won me small notice, but it did not go unchallenged. A graduate student in zoology wrote me a letter deploring my ignorance of primates. He even took the trouble to draw up a list of eminent baboons. Among these he named fifteen United States Senators, five German theologians, nine faculty wives, and the entire student body of the Sheffield Scientific School.

The living room filled with laughter as Jed manipulated his audience. "But what in the world is the Ivy League coming to?" he asked. "I understand that Morey's, the Yale club where poor little lambs get stewed, I hear that they *haff in dees pless six fragrant wiolations from de boad of helt rules.*"

Everyone roared. Yiddish dialect was the rage of New York. Everyone was doing it. The fad had been started by the newspaper cartoonist, Milt Gross. His *Nize Baby* stories were repeated all over town after running in his weekly column in the *Sunday New York World.* Gross was working on a complete Yiddish dialect version of *Hiawatha* and after that he planned to do *'Twas the Night Before Christmas.* Nobody could wait.

"*Dee helt wiolations mitt Morey's iss noddink,*" Jed said soberly. "*Sotch a dollink baby, dott Jatt Herriss.*"

◆

Sam Behrman brought Philip and Virginia Dunning's *Bright Lights* to Jed. "While in many ways I found the play offensive," Behrman later wrote, "it sure was theater and it made everything else seem old-fashioned."

Harris passed the oilcloth-bound script to his secretary. "Jean," he said, "when Anita stops by after work, tell her I can't make it for dinner. Ask her to take this home and read it."

He went off to the theater with Streger and at the intermission, as usual, said he was too bored to stay.

"I'm only halfway through," Anita said when they came in, "but I can tell you right now, this is the worst thing I have ever read."

They all sat down in the living room. Jed opened the script. From time to time Anita would shake her head to remind him of how bad the play was but he remained immersed in it.

At last he closed the script.

"These people can't write."

"What did I tell you?" Anita cried triumphantly.

"But it's going to be a great hit. We'll give the Dunnings their five hundred for the option and get George to do the rewrites. I want to be in tryout by July."

"And where are you going to get the five hundred dollars?" Anita asked.

"Since you were so intelligent in judging the play, you ought to be equally useful in suggesting ways to raise the money."

Jed turned to Streger. "Tell Jean to send a copy of this off to Cooper in Chicago. I want that option money by return wire. This isn't going to be another *What Price Glory?* Aleck Woollcott may never have heard of Jacob Horowitz, but he's goddamned well going to find out who Jed Harris is."

◆

Abbott told Jed he hadn't the time to even read *Bright Lights*. He was in the thick of two plays already. Having gotten a second draft of a comedy, *Norma's Affair*, from a Southern schoolteacher named Ann Bridgers, he was also rewriting *Spread Eagle* with a newspaperman, George Brooks. Jed thought they might walk over to the Automat for lunch anyhow—he had a mania for the baked beans. As they started out he stopped at Herman Shumlin's desk.

"What's that?"

"I'm cleaning up the *Weak Sisters* account. There's some unpaid overtime and a bill from those kids who hauled the set away."

"Fuck that."

"What do you mean?"

"I mean the show's past history, it lost every penny. Who knows where they all are?"

"I do."

"You're a stupid man," Jed whispered and Herman froze. "I only let you work here because of old times and Newark, so what happens? I give you a trivial job and you can't handle it. Why didn't you go to college, Herman? Good Christ, you're stupid."

Herman turned toward Jean Barkow as if for help. The secretary cringed with embarrassment, and long later Abbott remembered being nauseated by the sadistic exhibition. Harris picked up the checkbook ledger Shumlin was working on, ripped out the page, and tore it up.

"I said fuck 'em. Come on to lunch, George."

Meanwhile, Irving Cooper was calling from Chicago.

"Mr. Harris just went out," Jean told him.

"Tell Jed that I read *Bright Lights* and I think it's great. G-R-E-A-T, you hear me?"

"Great, Mr. Cooper."

"Tell him I say let's do it, let's do it now, and if he disagrees tell him I'll produce it myself, you hear?"

"I hear, Mr. Cooper."

At the same time, Paul Streger was streaking towards the office with the most amazing story. Streger had gone home to New Rochelle over the weekend. They were a close family, and Paul was the first of the five brothers to have moved out. The youngest of the boys was eighteen-year-old Milton, "my fat kid brother," Paul called him.

Milton had a twenty-five-dollar-a-week job but he also had, which was more important, a genius for shooting craps. He exercised this genius every Saturday night, and on Sunday mornings he'd pass on a share of the winnings to his big brother Paul. Four or five extra dollars could always come in handy.

This particular Saturday night, Paul was in the kitchen and hadn't heard his brother come in. He looked up from his cookies and milk and there was fat Milton.

"Hi, kid. How'd you make out?"

"Come upstairs."

"Why are you whispering? Everyone's asleep."

"Come upstairs," Milton repeated urgently.

Paul followed him up the three flights of stairs to the boy's attic bedroom, kidding his brother about being so mysterious. Milton let Paul into his room and then pushed the door shut tight behind them.

"Well? What is it?"

Milton pointed to the cot he slept on and there, to Streger's astonishment, spread out in two neat rows, were eight one-thousand-dollar bills and a stack of hundreds. Milton practically wept as he spoke.

"I broke the professional craps game in White Plains. I won sixteen thousand dollars. Mom and Pop are going to kill me."

Paul gaped. What, he finally mumbled, was the kid doing to do with it all?

"I don't know," the boy said desperately. "After Mom and Pop kill me they'll commit suicide and I suppose the cops'll take the money. For God's sake, take some of it off my hands."

Streger reached out as if toward a box of snakes. He snatched a thousand-dollar bill.

"That hardly makes a dent in it," Milton said, on the brink of tears.

Paul took a second thousand-dollar bill and carefully folded the two of them small enough to hold in his fist.

"Be careful, kid," he said in a dramatic whisper.

Milton responded with a shudder and a stifled sob. Paul opened the door, shut it softly behind, and tiptoed down the stairs. He didn't dare go back to New York immediately for fear of provoking his parents' curiosity. Monday morning he borrowed ten dollars to buy the train ticket rather than attempt to pay for it with a thousand-dollar bill and get arrested himself. He ran all the way from Grand Central Station to Times Square and saw Jed chatting with George Abbott in front of the office building. Gasping for breath, he called out to Jed as he stumbled the final steps.

"For Chrissakes, are the cops after you?"

"I hope not. Come on upstairs," he panted. "Got to talk to you."

"Can't George be in on it?"

Streger shook his head and Abbott said his good-byes. Skipping the elevator as usual, Jed trotted up the stairs while the exhausted Streger tried to keep up.

"What is it?" Jed asked over his shoulder. "What was so important?"

"If you'll stop I'll tell you."

And in the darkened stairwell of the Bond Clothes Building, Streger opened his fist. Harris stared.

"Where did you get that? . . . I don't care. Open a bank account and get a certified check for five hundred dollars, made out to Phil and Virginia Dunning. My boy, you're going to have a piece of the show that's going to take the American theater out of the stone ages."

JED HARRIS
PRESENTS BROADWAY

JED'S LUNCH WITH George Abbott at the Automat had been even better than baked beans. The director had gone over the possibilities and problems of *Norma's Affair* and *Spread Eagle*. He was trying to sell Harris on the two plays in the only way he knew: directly and without guile. Harris was so absorbed he let the tea grow tepid.

The Automat was always noisy. Jed still whispered. George spoke up loudly about Lee Tracy, a young actor he'd seen in a flop play. Jed liked the actor too, but not for *Norma's Affair*. Tracy was an "off the streets guy," Harris said. He had a strong stage personality but not enough technique to pass as a Southerner. On the other hand, Tracy would be perfect for the lead in *Bright Lights*.

"The Dunnings modeled that hoofer on Roy Lloyd," Abbott protested. "Even the character's name is 'Roy Lane.'"

"Roy Lloyd can understudy."

Abbott sipped his milk.

"Let's call it *The Roaring Twenties*."

Jed looked up and grinned. "I thought you hadn't time to read it."

By the time they pushed out through the revolving door, the two had agreed to do all three plays together. *Spread Eagle* was never a question, but Jed wasn't sure about *Norma's Affair*. He'd rejected it a year earlier, but now

George was rewriting the comedy into a drama with the new title, *Coquette*. Harris told Abbott he'd go along with it.

No terms were discussed because theirs was a relationship between friends, but Abbott assumed that the arrangement on these plays would be the same as it had been for *Love 'Em and Leave 'Em*, the standard two-thousand-dollar director's fee and a royalty of one percent of the gross receipts. They'd been speculating about tryout dates and locations when Streger came staggering down the sidewalk clutching the thousand-dollar bills in his fist. Yes, lunch had been better than baked beans.

Jean Barkow didn't enjoy the afternoon as much. Jed told her he was busy if Irving Cooper called and Cooper kept calling all afternoon. With business better than ever, Irving had not merely the option money to wire but all eight thousand dollars needed to produce the Dunnings' play. Now, Jed didn't want Irving's money because, thanks to fat Milton Streger, he didn't need it. He wanted a strictly financial partner who would share neither authority nor credit. He asked Sam Behrman about Crosby Gaige.

According to Behrman:

> Gaige was a partner of the Selwyns, who had two theaters on Forty-second Street and one in Chicago. Crosby had a paneled office and a pornographic collection in the drawer of his Sheraton desk. He was tall, affable and enigmatic. Jed and I often wondered about his being in the theater at all; his chief interest was in real estate and I suppose that was why the Selwyns found him useful. He was bookish; his hobby was collecting first editions by living English authors. He had "contacts" with them, among them Arnold Bennett and Liam O'Flaherty. He had a beautiful country place, Watch Hill Farm, at Peekskill on the Hudson. Alexander Woollcott, Franklin P. Adams, Arthur Krock, George Kaufman and Moss Hart, the Lunts, Gregory Kelly and his wife Ruth Gordon, actors, actresses, newspaper publishers, were steady weekend guests—you could meet almost anybody at Watch Hill Farm. . . .
>
> Hilda Gaige was lovely and very dear. She was slender, with questing, blue-green eyes and shimmering chestnut hair. There was a sympathy and affection between us always, and on her side an unwavering belief that I would emerge from press-agentry. She had a wonderful laugh. She was elfin—an adorable elf with a shadow over her. . . . It came to me one day; it was her husband, it was Gaige. She was afraid of Gaige.
>
> I brought Jed and Gaige together. Gaige read the script, though Jed said that Gaige had no equipment for reading a script, that his enthusiasm for it was simply an echo of his own. They made an arrangement to produce the play together, each to put up half the production cost.

Jed described Gaige to Anita as "a dilettante and not so terribly bright." Even straightforward, easygoing George Abbott considered the man "a not very talented amateur."

When Sam brought Jed up to Watch Hill for a weekend of selling Crosby on the play, Hilda was herself sold on the dynamic, bright and sexily arrogant young producer who was seventeen years younger than she. There is a contempt and a bitter jealousy evident between these lines of Behrman's:

Jed liked Hilda and she adored him; she worshiped all creative genius. She took him to a tailor to dress him up to his new-found station. He was, she assured him, very handsome and it would be apparent to the world once she had provided him with some decent clothes. He had always been a genius, but henceforth he would be a well-dressed genius.

While Hilda dressed Jed, Anita decorated the apartment. She put up curtains in the sunny kitchen to complement the wood cabinets. She loved the look of the fold-up wire toaster at the ready on the stove. She poked around in secondhand stores until she found just the right pictures for the little corridor between the bedroom and the bathroom, and she constantly changed bedspreads. Bedspreads, she later mused, must have been sexual symbols to her. Every time she replaced one of them she was probably fantasizing about Jake. "He undressed the moment he came through the door," she remembered, "and stayed undressed all the time he was home . . . when he was home."

◆

Phil Dunning stared at the rehearsal script. The start of his first production should have been thrilling, but the neat black binder carried an unexpected heading:

THE ROARING TWENTIES
By Philip Dunning and George Abbott

The play's title had been changed so many times that Dunning probably would have been surprised to see the same one twice. Plainly, he was gaping not at the addition of George's name, but the deletion of Virginia's.

Abbott and Harris explained that if three authors were listed it would clutter up the program and make the play seem to have been written at a meeting. They said that Phil's wife would understand. They had not sought Virginia's opinion on the matter. Dunning acquiesced in silence.

The play's leading character, as Abbott described Roy Lane, was "a typical song and dance man with his coat off, sleeves rolled up." As promised, Jed came through with Lee Tracy for the role and Roy Lloyd became the understudy. Harris was a strict believer in type casting. He thought the ideal actor for a given part was someone exactly like the character being portrayed. Few actors would ever convince him that they could play anyone but themselves.

There were no casting surprises. Jed and George tended to agree, and when they couldn't think of anyone, Paul Streger came up with sensible suggestions. Two actors were cast for odd reasons. Ann Bridgers was given a walk-on as a cigarette girl. The author of *Coquette* had no stage experience. Harris and Abbott thought that if she was on tour, the rewriting of her play could continue. The other casting exception was Eloise Stream, who was hired to play one of the chorines. Eloise was Gaige's current girlfriend.

As the rehearsals began in New York, Abbott took one look at Eloise and winced. "Bad," he said, "really bad." Jed said they had no choice. Eloise came with Gaige's share of the production cost and Gaige's half of the production cost—which Jed had inflated to $16,000—was of course the whole thing.

"I put up my half right away," Crosby kept saying to Behrman, "but so far your friend Jed hasn't put up his. Not a penny so far from him."

The Roaring Twenties was supposed to open an Atlantic City tryout on July 5, 1926 and, if it went well, the company would be given the summer off. The show would then play Asbury Park and Hartford before coming to New York in the fall.

The day before leaving for Atlantic City, Jed sat down to a good luck lunch with all the fellows. As Streger and Abbott reconstructed the scene many years later, Jed said, "The theater you see nowadays has outlived its usefulness. It's popular, sure, but that's because audiences love a show so much they'll see anything that's on a stage. These hammy Shakespeare revivals . . ."

"And," Abbott added, "the farces overplayed with muggings and double takes . . ."

"Ridiculous," Jed said. "Do you know what's in the air? A more realistic type of acting and writing. Show folk and audiences want the energy that vaudeville and the musical comedy shows have, and that's what Broadway's going to have now."

He stopped, and he stared so dramatically that they all turned toward him, Phil Dunning and Paul Streger and Herman Shumlin and Sam Behrman and Lee Tracy and George Abbott.

"That's what Broadway's going to have," he repeated, whispering. "Our play isn't going to be called *Bright Lights*, and it isn't going to be called *The Roaring Twenties*. There's only one title for it."

They stared. He paused. They waited.

"The play is going to be called *Broadway*."

Now the dramatic pause was not Harris's and it was not contrived.

"*Broadway*," Abbott finally repeated.

"*Broadway*," Dunning beamed.

53

Jed's whisper burst into pride.

"We're presenting *Broadway*," he said.

◆

Anita begged Jed to let her come along to Atlantic City. A woman given to fantasy and manageable hallucination, she believed that if she didn't go with Jed now, the marriage would be over. She thought he sensed it too and didn't want such an ending either. That, she felt, was why he agreed to her coming, though she never really knew.

She got her ticket and boarded the train at Pennsylvania Station. He wasn't there yet, although Sam Behrman was, and Herman and Paul and the company. The train lurched and she peered anxiously through the window. At last he came striding down the platform, hands plunged into his jacket pockets. He lengthened his stride as the train began to chug, and then broke into a trot.

He sprinted along until he leaped and caught the railing of the last car. He tried to yank the back door open but it wouldn't budge. It was a "blind," as he'd learned in his hobo days; a fake, decorative door.

The train was plunging down the track, through the tunnel. Jed hammered on the back of the car as it burst into daylight. He couldn't be heard over the clacketing wheels.

He climbed onto the roof. A taut horizontal rope sailed toward him and he ducked it. Then another rope whooshed overhead, and still another. The ropes were an alert for an approaching tunnel. He lay flat on the roof, spread-eagled as he inched the length of the car and then climbed down. The end doors, however, were locked and he beat frantically on the glass window. When Anita reached the car she got a porter to open the door and let him in as the train shot into the tunnel.

Rehearsals continued in Atlantic City with George pressing for the tempo that Jed kept talking about. "Like a machine gun, that's how this should play," Jed would say, pacing the floor of the rehearsal hall and, later, the Apollo Theatre. He'd approach the stage snapping his fingers. "Tempo!" he'd whisper urgently, and Abbott knew that Harris was right. They both wanted the show to come across like neon lights and cigarette smoke.

Crosby's girlfriend, Eloise Stream, had come a long way from her original incompetence—according to Abbott she was now only terrible. Even the lineless part of the cigarette girl seemed too much for Ann Bridgers. Walking on stage in front of nearly a thousand people is not a natural part of the human repertoire. Stage nerves are instinctual, like a fear of snakes, and being on stage was reducing Ann to wreckage.

These were not cataclysmic travails, and on July 5 *Broadway* was ready for its first audience. The curtain rose to an audible gasp. The setting was the garish lobby and backstage area of the Paradise Night Club. One door led to the cabaret room, another to the business office, a third—with the speakeasy peephole—to the street. A set of spiral metal stairs rose to the performers' dressing rooms. There were a couple of slot machines. Lil was banging away at the piano while the master of ceremonies, Roy Lane, was rehearsing a dance number with some of the chorines: Mazie, Grace, Ruby, Pearl and Anne. Eloise Stream was playing Pearl.

It was a world that Phil Dunning knew from his stage-managing career. With the pinwheel lighting (rotating multicolored filters), the flashing neon sign, the smoke, and the dancing, the stage picture was gaudy, tough, and vividly contemporary. The sound of it matched the sight. "Go fry an egg" and "Ah, shut your face" and "lay dead" peppered with "nix" and "kibitzer" and "do-ray-me" and "no kid."

The audience hushed for the story. Lane, cocky and naive, is soft on Billie Moore, one of the chorines. "I and her are fixing up a little act." Billie is being wooed by Steve Crandall, presumably a businessman but in fact a bootlegger. His competitor, Scar Edwards, stops by to complain about Crandall muscling in on his Harlem territory and Crandall croaks him with a shot in the back.

Billie won't dine—"tie on the feed bag"—with Roy because of a party that Crandall is throwing. "Pardon while I laugh," Roy sneers, holding open his jacket sleeve and laughing into it. "You got talent, kid, when I bring it out . . . why I can see our name in lights now: 'Roy Lane and Company.'"

Dan McCorn of Homicide turns up asking Crandall whether he's seen Scar Edwards lately—the murder news is out. A confrontation is avoided as Roy and the girls set up for the floor show. Taking his place on line, Roy tells Billie, "Even if a jane I'd put my hope and trust in was going to hell, I could still go out and give 'em my best . . . There's the cue." He takes the straw boater hat and cane. "Give it to 'em. Cut 'em deep and let 'em bleed. Here we go. Here we go. Let's mop up."

Lee Tracy danced out behind the chorus line as the curtain fell on the first act, and a roar, a crowd of whistles and huzzahs, exploded from that Atlantic City audience. At the back of the theater Anita and Sam grinned at each other. Backstage, button-bright Paul Streger and his roommate Herman Shumlin shook hands and did a dance step. George Abbott was in the lobby, too nervous to watch, but hearing the roar of the audience he opened the door and let that joyous noise wash over him. Crosby Gaige, elegantly tailored as ever in his Wetzel suit, turned and pounded him on the back.

Jed was leaning against the side wall of the auditorium, watching the performance, watching the audience. His pale and bony face glowed in the reflected stage light, his pomaded hair aglisten.

Although gangsters and gunshots and hoofers were new to the stage, the Philadelphia critics who had come down to see the Atlantic City tryout were less than enthusiastic. Harris was not dispirited. That's what tryouts were for. He sat down with Dunning and Abbott and told them he wanted to make the play leaner. He wanted to cut out any cheap comedy, all extraneous gags and pratfalls. He thought the best humor in the play, such as Roy Lane's absurd conceit, worked because it was related to character. Now he wanted to set the humor and the musical aspects against the play's melodrama. This syncopation, he said, would give *Broadway* its rhythm.

Atlantic City was a good place to work. It was one of the fashionable resorts. Anita could hardly keep from sighing each time she entered the hotel suite. This was her first taste of luxury, and she loved the flavor. Artistic people especially, she felt, could appreciate satin upholstery and lush carpeting and velvet drapes because "we're so tactile." She bought a parasol and a straw hat with flowers and she strolled along the boardwalk. Sometimes she even strolled with Jed, and she was sorry when it came time to go home. The West 10th Street apartment would be more depressing than ever.

The show was playing a matinee on the Sunday they were leaving and so Jed checked them out of the hotel in the morning. He parked the suitcase at the concierge's desk, a glass-paned octagonal mahogany affair in the middle of the lobby. When they returned, late in the afternoon, the desk was closed.

Jed advised the hotel manager that he was an imbecile for not having a goddamned key to the goddamned cage and then he quieted down. He strolled to a brass urn and withdrew the doorman's oversize umbrella. Returning to the concierge's desk, Jed pulled over a side chair, stepped onto it, and then up on the wood ledge surrounding the big desk. He peered over the frosted glass enclosure, basking in the stares of guests and employees.

Swinging a leg over the top, rather nimbly for a non-athlete, he held the umbrella by its tip, leaned in, and lifted up the suitcase with the handle. Grabbing the bag with his free hand, he brought it over the glass top and dropped it to the floor with a thump.

A round of applause was provided by his audience. He leaped lightly to the floor, smiled, tipped his hat, and extended an arm to Anita. To still greater applause they strolled grandly through and out of the lobby, into the waiting auto, the rear and the valise brought up by an equally proud bellboy.

"You're never going to forget me for this," Jed said to Anita when they were alone in the car. It was redundant. She was already enthralled.

◆

In the months that lay before the play's next engagement, Anita pressed
Jed for attention. She knew she was pressing but couldn't stop herself. She
reminded him of the part he'd promised her and said she would settle for the
cigarette girl.

"Even I can tell that Ann Bridgers isn't long for the part."

He waved her off. She told herself his nervousness made him irritable; his
nerves were why it didn't feel like being married. Still she wept.

He was remote to Leonard Blumberg and Irving Cooper too. Blumberg,
who had financed *Weak Sisters* and *Love 'Em and Leave 'Em*, insisted that he
had an oral option to finance *Broadway*. He would sue over it and win a
$5,000 settlement. Cooper's was an even more substantial claim, but he wasn't
the suing type. Jed offered him the play's souvenir program concession and
Irving accepted it. He didn't complain, but Jed did. Jed said he was always
being victimized by the Irving Coopers and Leonard Blumbergs of the world.

◆

An audience of overfed, sun-dazed vacationers filled the raftered summer
stock theater in Asbury Park that warm August evening in 1926. Yet when
the curtains swept shut on the first act, their buzz and chatter exploded even
before the house lights went up. This animation held throughout the intermission and trailed the audience back down the aisles, muffling to a hush
and then covering over as the lights went down and the curtain was lit for
the second act of *Broadway*.

Melodrama resumed at the Paradise Night Club. Roy Lane is planting a
fake telegram to rescue Billie from Crandall's attentions. "I'm no prude," Roy
says of the protective efforts. "I'm for light wines and beer," and then he
proposes marriage because "it would be better for the act." Conceding that
her heart beats faster whenever she sees him, Billie feels they're too poor to
talk about marriage. Roy, ever touchy, reads that as an interest in Crandall's
money.

Now Eloise Stream's role of Pearl becomes important. Detective McCorn
tells her he knows she was Scar Edwards's spy at the club. She and Scar
were supposed to get married. McCorn hasn't the heart to give her the news
of Scar's murder, but, as she is getting ready for the pirate number, Crandall
does tell her. Eloise wails, faints, and slides down the stairs. (Abbott told
Streger he had to give the girl credit: "Good scream, good faint.")

Crandall is now in a black mood and turns on Roy, "possibly the greatest
living song and dance artist who never played the Palace." Yet he expects
Roy to emcee a party he's throwing for some Chicago pals. "I wouldn't stay

and entertain your gang of goofers if you kissed my foot in Macy's window at high noon."

"Why you dancing tramp . . ."

"It's guys like you give New York a bad name."

The audience was cheering his brass and, standing at the side wall, Jed shook his fist triumphantly. Then Crandall pastes Roy in the mouth and the audience was stunned silent. Could anyone remember a knockdown in a play?

Crandall's pistol is square in Roy's face. The hoofer is rescued only by Detective McCorn's sudden entrance and then Roy is flabbergasted to find himself holding the gun that Crandall dropped. Everyone covers up for the hood, even Billie. "I'll kill you if you touch her," Roy shouts. "I will, God damn you!" but McCorn yanks him toward the door. "Oh, God, Billie!" Roy cries as the second act curtain closes on honky tonk music.

The once sluggish audience burst into cheers.

As the final tryout began in Hartford, with barely a week left until the New York premiere, Jed announced that everything was wrong with the third act. Abbott and Dunning disagreed. As Abbott remembered, he told Jed, "It's the goddamned realism of the thing that's making it work and in the last act it all comes to a head. These out-of-town critics are accustomed to broad playing, whether in farces or Shakespeare." The Asbury Park local reviewers had been neither enthusiastic nor dismissive, probably intimidated by the big city Philadelphia reviews.

"But the audiences will have no problem with it," George said, "and neither will the New York critics. We've got no exaggeration, either in the comedy parts or the melodrama, and that counterpoint is working. The third act, just as it is, brings that mixture to a boil and I'm not saying it just because I'm the director."

"You may not be the director much longer," Jed whispered ominously, and he went on to complain about the constant entrances and exits of Roy and the chorus girls. Monotonous, he said. Abbott kept himself from pointing out that Harris had urged more of those entrances and exits because they gave the production its machine-gun tempo. Jed suggested they take the whole last act out of the nightclub lobby and set it in the office. It would give the audience a change of scenery. George insisted that this would ruin the sense of an insular world. The idea went against everything he'd ever learned about the theater.

"Maybe you haven't learned everything about the theater," Harris whispered. "A change of directors might make sense. I've been considering Hugh Ford."

Abbott felt queasy. This play meant more to him than anything he'd yet done. He considered going along with the resetting of the third act.

Then, the usually meek Dunning spoke up. "The show doesn't need a change of scenery," he said quietly to Harris, and recalling it years later, Abbott smiled with remembered admiration. "It's a poor idea," Phil said to Jed. "You're too nervous. George is doing a wonderful job and it would be a mistake to try and get by without him. Come on, George."

He took Abbott by the elbow and walked him out of the office. The subject of rewriting the third act, or of replacing Abbott, never arose again. It had been panic, and Jed's panic would swell. On the morning of the New York premiere, he told Anita that he wasn't going to attend. He was certain that the show would be a success, "but I'd be bored to death sitting through it again."

He told her to go with Sam Behrman and was already in his pajamas when Anita walked out the door on September 16, 1926. Sam was standing beside the cab's opened door as Anita gathered the skirt of her new red evening gown and slid in. She was still wondering whether she should have stayed home. She pictured Jed walking to his bed and lowering himself on shaky legs; pulling the blanket up under his chin and, as he stared at the ceiling through the darkness, sliding under the ice floes of worry.

◆

New York usually knows when a hit play is coming to town. It braces itself for the excitement. With a popular new show in town the city revives, proud of itself and of the crush for tickets; proud of the brokers sending their office boys to buy up the good locations; proud of the restaurant crowds, the drinking crowds, the taxi crowds. A new hit in town gives New York City fresh energy, and the city needs that.

No such anticipation preceded *Broadway*, and George was worried as he turned from the bureau mirror so that Ednah could knot his bow tie.

"Keep your fingers crossed," he said, tilting his chin toward the ceiling while she stretched to reach his neck, "and maybe we'll be okay."

"Can't cross my fingers and knot your tie, dear."

"Then forget the tie."

There was similar tension in the tiny West Forties apartment that Paul Streger shared with Herman Shumlin, but a more mundane concern prevailed among the Horowitzes. Mildred felt that her parents ought to wear formal clothes. Papa refused. The sisters were wearing evening gowns. Saul wasn't going.

As Sam helped Anita out of the cab in front of the Broadhurst Theatre on

West 44th Street, Alexander Woollcott stood there chatting with the beautiful actress Ina Claire. The critic was short, soft, and elegantly androgynous. His beady eyes darted through thick spectacle lenses.

Sam told Anita that he couldn't sit with her, hadn't the calm for it. Perhaps it didn't occur to him that she might resent his giving the seat beside her to Hilda Gaige, or that Hilda too might feel uncomfortable. George climbed the stairs to the balcony, from which he preferred to watch the performance in anonymity. Herman and Paul were in the wings, Jed was home in bed, and Phil Dunning wasn't there at all.

> Dunning didn't see the curtain rise on *Broadway*'s opening. He had to get the curtain up at the New Amsterdam Theatre where he was stage manager for *Sunny*. Outraged he couldn't see the opening of his first play, *Sunny*'s stars chased Dunning out of the theater at nine o'clock. The stars? Marilyn Miller, Jack Donahue and Clifton Webb. Rarely has a stage manager been routed by so celebrated a trio.
> — Richard Maney, *Fanfare*

As the Broadhurst Theatre's house lights went down for the third act, Anita took a deep breath and sank into her eighth row seat. She'd been chatting with the Yale boys she hadn't seen for years, Ray Malsin and Abe Kaufman and even Dave Bunim, as bitter as ever. She made excuses for Jed's absence and said as little as possible to Hilda.

She finally met the Horowitzes. Mildred introduced her. They smiled.

She'd seen Sam during the intermission. He'd been standing at the back. He said everyone thought, so far so good. But, he added, if the play faded in the third act, the audience wouldn't remember the first two acts if they'd been *Hamlet* and *King Lear*.

"Here's God's little gift to the nightclubs now," one of the chorines wisecracks and with Lee Tracy's entrance the theater rocks with applause. Up in the balcony, Abbott was thrilled, never having heard of a hand being given an actor in mid-play. He was glad Lee had business to do—collecting his gear—while the cheers resounded.

Roy Lane is quitting the Paradise, "this bucket of blood." He is angry with Billie too, though she tries to convince him she slept home with her mother in Trenton. He's certain she went to Crandall's party. Everyone in the floor show is hung over from it.

"I'll tell you something else," Billie says. "The reason I went to my mother's was to ask her, if a girl was terribly in love with a person, so much it was like regular love at first sight, was it all right to marry 'em even if they was poor, that's what. Now how'd you like to go to Hell?"

The club manager is begging Roy to stay and save the show.

"I might fake a Mammy song at that."

"You'll be the whole show tonight."

"I am every night. If you don't think so, you're crazy. On the level, boss, I don't know what you'd do without me."

The audience roared over the little guy's egotism. Comedy from character, as Jed had been saying, and the counterpoint between comedy and melodrama moves up another level with Crandall's nervous entry. For somebody had taken a shot at him.

"How'd you like to break in your act with Billie?"

"No," Roy tells the club manager. "The act is split, it's off, it's all busted up."

"I didn't say I wouldn't," Billie pouts. "He don't want me anymore."

Roy gives in, grudgingly, but "just to keep the show going." He takes a few warm-up steps. "I used to think," he says to Billie without looking at her, "we'd make about the best combo I could imagine . . . there's our music. We'll finish in a blaze of glory."

The two of them dance off-stage and into their act, leaving Crandall to sweat. Then he confesses the murder of Scar to the club manager and Pearl overhears. She takes a revolver from her purse.

The audience held its breath.

"Turn around, rat!"

Eloise Stream was playing the hell out of the role.

"Good girl!" Streger whispered aloud in the wings.

The *thrrrppp* of the gun's silencer sends Crandall lurching offstage.

"He's dead all right. Right through the old pump," Detective McCorn says, and rules it a suicide. Roy and Billie finish their act and are offered a couple of engagements by a vaudeville booking agent who happens to be in the club. Pearl is collapsing in a chair. Billie is throwing her arms around Roy's neck.

"Gawd, you must love this guy."

"There goes the gong, girls!" Roy shouts, breaking out of Billie's embrace. "All ready! Come on, Pearl. Gee, I'm happy. Our names will be in bright lights soon. Roy Lane and Co."

The chorines danced through the wings and offstage as the Broadhurst's curtain came plummeting down and oh, what a roar went up. The audience rose to its feet, a wonderful creature. The curtain soared and fell, rose and fell again and again, with bows for everyone and a huge, billowing ovation for Lee Tracy, and then George and Phil were dragged on stage for more great cheers.

"Don't miss the point of this, Clifford." It was a young actor named Harold Clurman on the steps down from the balcony, talking excitedly to his roommate, a serious, aspiring playwright, Clifford Odets. "This is more important than a 'meaningful' play. This is of these times, it *is* these times. It's all this laughing and drinking and Wall Street craziness. It's the hysteria, the wildness and shoot the shoots. It's the America where everybody's going to make a million dollars in the next half an hour. And the realism. It's just what Stanislavsky was talking about."

As Clurman remembered it, Odets wouldn't be convinced. "These are first nighters," he said skeptically. "The reviews will be different."

Reaching the bottom of the stairs they elbowed past Sam Behrman, who was standing at the head of the aisle scanning the critics' faces for telltale signs of reaction.

"There's Woollcott," Odets murmured.

"He's short enough to be superficial," Clurman quipped as the critic paused to whisper in Behrman's ear; this Woollcott who had never heard of Jake Horowitz.

Now Jed was home alone as Woollcott paused to tell Sam what he thought of *Broadway*.

7
THE METEOR

THE MANAGER of the Broadhurst Theatre smiled formally and said good night as he locked the front doors behind the last of the opening nighters. Then the ushers in their black dresses and lace collars swept across the rows of empty seats in search of trash. Black seagulls swooping for discarded programs.

The house lights were switched off, the lobby, the lounges, the balcony, the corridors, the walls, the ceiling. The well-wishers and backslappers left, and Lee Tracy was alone in his dressing room with George Abbott. Tracy dabbed the spongy pad in the jar of cold cream and scrubbed at his makeup. The throng had been crushing, but he'd hardly minded. Under the circumstances, he said to George, a drink was in order, no?

"Sure, kid," the director said. "You deserve it," and Tracy poured himself a bourbon.

Abbott was a conservative man and he had been cautioning everyone to delay celebration. The audience had been enthusiastic, ten curtain calls, but the reviews wouldn't be out until six in the morning, and then just the morning newspapers. Herman Shumlin said that George was so pessimistic he wouldn't celebrate his own birthday until he was twelve, but Abbott knew it was bad luck to call yourself a hit before there was a line at the box office.

Irving Cooper dragged Sam Behrman to a telephone to call Jed with the news of Woollcott's remark. Sam would only agree to stand by while Irving made the call. Anita answered. Jed was still sleeping. Behrman took the phone.

"Woollcott said, 'Jesus, this is the greatest.' He said, 'Wait till you see the papers.'"

Then, like a good boy, Sam handed the telephone back to Irving.

An ecstatic Anita rushed off to rouse Jed. She made Irving repeat Woollcott's remark.

"How can you trust a critic," Harris responded, "who hardly knows whether he is a man or a woman?"

Irving's excitement couldn't be deflated and he even suggested coming over to celebrate. Behrman shook his head desperately, yet he went along. Everyone else had other plans. George Abbott was anxious to get some sleep. Phil Dunning was having midnight supper with Virginia, who hadn't even gone to the opening night and was hardly about to make an appearance now, least of all in Jed Harris's apartment. Since Paul and Herman had long ago made plans to go on a tear with Lee Tracy, the only ones available to celebrate with Jed were Cooper, who'd been cheated out of co-producing the play, and Behrman, whose relationship with the man was so complex and wretched.

Harris greeted them at the door. He was naked. Cooper looked everywhere but straight ahead. He tried to lighten the mood with a champagne toast, but Jed's nudity just wasn't conducive to partying. The man wouldn't even cross his legs.

The telephone rang. It was after midnight but the hour is no barrier to a gossip columnist. This one asked if it were true that Harris had slept at home through the premiere of his own show. How could he possibly have done it?

"It was really quite simple," Jed replied. "I took off my clothes, got into bed, and closed my eyes."

The effort at gala was maintained for another half hour and then everyone gave up and went home.

The morning newspapers, one rave review after another, confirmed it: the show wasn't merely a hit. It was a hit of hits. Percy Hammond wrote in the *Tribune*, "*Broadway* is the most completely acted and perfectly directed show I have seen in thirty years of playgoing," and Hammond was generally considered the best and toughest critic in town. But of course it was Woollcott whose review meant the most to Harris.

"The official hat of this department," the critic wrote, with quote advertisements in mind as usual, "which has almost forgotten how it feels to leave the departmental head, is hereby sent into the air for *Broadway*."

Woollcott fulfilled Harris's every fantasy of vindication. To cap it all, the critic would write an effusive preface to the published edition of the play.

Harris relished the turnaround but chose not to remind Woollcott that he'd been responsible for the loss of *What Price Glory?* Revenge was not worth a critic's hostility. Instead, Jed cultivated the critic and, as a man responsive to celebrities, Woollcott would prove not only an ally but a devotee.

"Why don't you face it, Aleck," Jed once told him. "You are in love with me."

"I am afraid," Woollcott replied, "that you suffer from delusions of grandeur."

The quip was clever but also revealing of a truth that must have been satisfying: Alexander Woollcott might have told Maxwell Anderson that he didn't know who Jake Horowitz was, but he certainly now knew who Jed Harris was. And Jed knew who he was too. There is no success so exhilarating, so momentous, so explosive as that of a smash hit show. Harris couldn't separate himself from that success. "His self-belief was hypnotic," Sam Behrman said. "He simply knew that he was destined for mastery, that his success with *Broadway* was merely the first rung of a career that would be omnipotent. And it was so. For a long time it was so."

JED HARRIS PRESENTS
"BROADWAY"

It wasn't his show. Crosby Gaige owned half and had paid for the whole thing. Phil and Ginny Dunning had written the original play. George Abbott had revised and directed it. Sam Behrman had brought it to Jed's attention, and Paul Streger had provided the option money. As general manager, Herman Shumlin had done the line producing and Irving Cooper had pushed Harris to do the play. The production belonged to all of them and still it was true:

JED HARRIS PRESENTS
"BROADWAY"

For the style of the production, the kind of theater it was, the rhythms that characterized it, were Harris's style, his rhythms, his kind of theater. With *Broadway* he was initiating a tradition that would ever after be associated with the place, Broadway. It was to be a theater in his image: clever, tense, urban, dynamic, and above all, contemporary. He was, therefore, presenting not just *Broadway* but Broadway.

There were other producers. Belasco and Hopkins, Winthrop Ames, Flo Ziegfeld, Max Gordon, Henry Miller, Sam Harris and, first of all, the Shuberts. There were playwrights, directors, song writers and many great stars, all of them making up this new and brashly American kind of theater. They all played parts in its creation but Harris seemed to personify the phenomenon. He was Broadway incarnate.

◆

An acclaimed new show is called a "hit," even a "smash hit." This is not merely in apposition to a "miss." A hit show connects soundly, as a bat does with a baseball, and its impact, too, seems physical. In life, no individual ever wins such resounding approval as a hit show does. Being part of such approbation is a share in a child's dream, for a hit is the world crowding your doorstep; it is the telephone ringing without stop; it is love come crashing through the window and under the door and breaking through the walls. And another thing so lovely about it is so often this love comes in the form of money.

Jed Harris's office shook from the impact of such success the morning after *Broadway* opened. Companies had to be formed for other cities and abroad. A movie sale was to be negotiated. Directors and actors crowded the little place, eager to be near victory, knowing that now other plays would be done by this producer.

They were right. Jed had decided to do not only *Coquette* and *Spread Eagle* with George, but also Charles MacArthur and Ben Hecht's *The Front Page* and *The Royal Family* by Edna Ferber and George S. Kaufman. These four plays, he had Sam announce, would be presented within eighteen months.

While the whole world funneled into his office, he stayed in bed. Herman and Paul were detouring to 44th Street on their walk to work. They had to see the line at the Broadhurst's box office. A few of the grips were lounging outside the stage door on the balmy September morning. They provided Herman and Paul with a different view of the success story. They were distant, even hostile. Shumlin and Streger were no longer part of the gang. Now they were capitalists.

The five-hundred-dollar option money that Paul had provided, thanks to his high-rolling brother, guaranteed him two and a half percent of the show's profits. Paul had gotten that from Jed in writing. Herman didn't have a percentage of the production, he was still on salary, but he knew that he, too, would share in the bonanza.

The cost of producing *Broadway* was recovered in two weeks. Within a year there would be six companies touring the country and productions in Rumania, Hungary, Italy, Bulgaria, Germany, and Austria. The play would become the first American show to be bootlegged by the Soviets who, being no party to the international copyright agreement, refused to pay royalties. Everyone else paid, though, and in the next year and a half Harris and Gaige would make nearly a million dollars each on this play alone.

Harris proved to be as uninterested in money when he had it as when he hadn't. He did not rush to buy things. On the other hand, Gaige, though already wealthy, promptly spent his new money in ostentatious ways. He rented an enormous Fifth Avenue apartment and had Hilda furnish it grandly. The living room was paneled in walnut, from floor to ceiling. Every inch of the walnut could be covered with drapes drawn the length and width of the room.

Taking Sam through this new showplace, Hilda gloomily drew the drapes and then lit the lamps to demonstrate how the room would look at night. Then she plopped into an armchair and stared at her young and bookish friend.

"I can't," she said. "Do you think I'm terrible? I've got to leave Gaige. Haven't you known it?"

"I didn't know it was as serious as that."

"You'll be my friend, won't you? You'll see me through it, won't you?"

Recalling this conversation in his memoir, *People in a Diary*, Behrman was too discreet to specify what "it" was. There is an implication of a love affair between Hilda Gaige and Harris. If that is in fact what happened, apparently Jed did not return her feelings. For Hilda returned to her husband.

Jed never threatened to leave Anita. His cruelty was cold. He saved his heat for bystanders. She first saw that in a taxi cab outburst.

The driver seemed just about to miss the rhythm of Seventh Avenue's traffic lights. Jed urged the man to hurry. It was not for fear of being late but simply because he was drawn so taut. As the next light was about to change he ordered the driver to turn east and go over to Sixth Avenue. The cabbie asked him to relax. Jed said he would relax if there was a driver at the wheel. The man slowed to a stop at the next traffic light and slid shut the glass between himself and the passenger compartment. Harris pounded on the partition until Anita became frightened. She begged him to stop but he kept pounding until the driver pulled over and told them to leave. Anita was embarrassed, but Jed simply opened the door, got out, and flagged down another cab.

She took it as an isolated incident. He'd been sweet lately, he had even spoken about having children. He used to say that nephews and nieces were better than sons and daughters because you could make wonderful birthdays for them and not have to see them again for another year. One night, though, he mused on the possibility of a son.

"If I ever had one I'd name him Jasper Bugaboo Harris."

Anita was thrilled. She wasn't facing up to reality. This was no marriage. She spent her days, and most of her nights, alone. The opening night of *Broadway* was the first time she'd met Jed's family, except for Mildred. Of course he didn't visit them either, and hadn't since he'd helped them move back to Newark when the Waterbury business collapsed. Anita reminded herself that she wasn't close to her own parents, but the rationalizations were of little comfort.

Unhappily, then, she spent her way through the lonely afternoons. Jed couldn't give her anything but money.

"I discovered auctions," she recalled, many years later. "They had people and excitement, they were theatrical and I could come home with something to show for my day. I knew nothing about auctions and at the beginning, anyway, made foolish mistakes. Once I bid against myself. Another time I bought giant plush red velvet drapes for the three big windows in the living room. I bought the matching valances too, red velvet valances decorated with gold braid. Probably from the ballroom of some old hotel and not my taste at all. I bought a slipcover for a sofa. The cloth looked like a nun's habit and it couldn't possibly fit. I knew you don't buy slipcovers without having them fitted. I even bought a silver pie knife engraved with someone else's initials. I didn't know what in the world I was doing or why."

More in need of company than acquisitions, she shopped at Oppenheim Collins as an excuse to visit with old office friends. When Jed saw the boxes he told her to go to the better stores, Bonwit Teller or DePinna or Bergdorf Goodman. This store snobbery was doubtless learned from Hilda Gaige, who continued in her role as Jed's finishing school teacher. Now, with the fabulous success of *Broadway*, she decided that the Bond Clothes Building office was inadequate to his present status. She boldly convinced her husband to give Jed a suite in the Selwyn Theatre Building. Crosby may or may not have suspected an affair, but he was irritated with Harris anyway. Although he was getting some $13,000 a week for his half share in the show, it still rankled him that Jed had never put up the original investment. Perhaps he felt guilty about his own philandering. Perhaps he was frightened of losing his wife. In any case, Gaige and Harris were still business partners and so there was some sense in providing office space in the building.

It may not have been as posh as Hilda wanted, but the suite was certainly more impressive than the old oversized cubicle. Jean Barkow sat in the big waiting room, managing traffic, for there was a horde of job seekers, hangers-on and success scavengers. It was, she recalled, like a clown act, with people virtually hanging from the window ledges.

"Fuck 'em," Jed said, the first time Jean asked what to do about them all. He said it, she felt, to impress the men who were with him in his office. He was, as usual, sitting with feet up on the desk, leaning all the way back into a pillow of cigarette smoke. He was announcing, declaiming, proclaiming, promoting, while the cigarette kept going in and out of his mouth.

The secretary didn't know who the men were, though she suspected they were gangsters. When they came out on their way to lunch the men struggled and pushed for the privilege of helping Jed on with his coat. Their appearance created a tumult in the outer office. Lost in the roar, waiting to see her brother, was Mildred. Jed looked skinny to her, and seemed engulfed in the camel's hair polo coat the men were draping over his shoulders. If those men squeezed together, Mildred thought, the shield around Jed would become a vise.

They forged through the room like a military formation, Jed seemingly oblivious to the eager hands, the people groping to ask or plead or beg favors. He didn't notice his sister and she wept there, surrounded by the shouting actors and directors and playwrights.

◆

Forty-second Street was glittery and exciting, hardly imaginable as the sleazy avenue it would become in fifty years. Walking east to Times Square from his office on the north side of the street, Harris would have passed the Apollo Theatre, where *George White's Scandals* was playing; the Times Square Theatre with *Gentlemen Prefer Blondes*. Across the street at Wallacks Theatre the marquee assured customers that *Laff That Off* would provide "A Clean Laff Every 29 Seconds."

That September of 1926 there were flops at the Eltinge Theatre (*Ghost Train*) and the Liberty (*Happy Go Lucky*), yet the inane *Abie's Irish Rose* was a great success at the Republic Theatre. On the corner of Broadway, the Rialto featured a stage and screen show, *Kid Boots* starring Eddie Cantor, "Plus Himself in Person." Phil Dunning was still the stage manager for *Sunny* at the New Amsterdam. It would be a couple of months before he would work up the courage to quit.

Harris relished telling about one such stroll along 42nd Street when he was stopped by a young man very like himself, dark, wiry, and unmistakably Jewish.

"You're Jed Harris, aren't you?"

"Yes," Harris whispered with a smile.

"I'm George Gershwin."

"I know. I've seen you in many theater lobbies, Mr. Gershwin. I think you're a wonderful songwriter."

"I am," Gershwin said, "aren't I?"

"The best."

"There's a question I've been wanting to ask you. How old are you, Mr. Harris?"

"I'll be twenty-seven in February."

"Shit," Gershwin said. "I'm twenty-eight."

"In a philosophical sense," Harris later mused, "Gershwin was much, much older than that, for he was only going to live another twelve years."

◆

Jed's first priority was a London production of *Broadway*. Perhaps he was seeking to replace his impoverished experience there with a first-class edition. Perhaps England represented prestige, civility and culture to him. Or else it was just an excuse to travel.

Roy Lloyd, Lee Tracy's understudy, was at last going to play the role that had been written for him. Rehearsals began in New York and the Strand Theatre was booked for a Christmas Day opening.

Two weeks before the company was to sail, Jed decided to replace Lloyd. Always mad for vaudeville, he had impulsively stopped in at the Shubert Riviera on upper Broadway. An act called "In The Park" was on the bill, a song and dance sketch about a couple of sailors on shore leave. One of the sailors was played by a feisty hoofer named James Cagney, and Jed left the theater determined to have this fellow play Lane in London.

James Cagney's manager was a clever and beautiful nineteen-year-old, Jean Dalrymple. A performer herself, she also ran a management sideline for two acts, Cagney's and "A Woman Pays" for Archie Leach (later to be known as Cary Grant).

The Riviera house manager gave Harris her telephone number and Jean was thrilled when he called. The newspapers were filled with *Broadway* and its twenty-six-year-old producer. Jeanie herself had producing ambitions, and she was eager to meet this dynamic, successful, and therefore sexy young man.

They had lunch. He leaned across the table and looked intently into her Episcopalian blue eyes. He needed a shave, and she thought that was sexy too. There was an almost erotic contrast between her marcelled blond straightforwardness and his exotic complexity.

He wanted to know where she was from, where she'd gone to school, what she was reading, what her politics were. He talked to her about classical and popular music, and they went on about Jerome Kern's latest, *Criss Cross*. It wasn't another *Sunny*, they agreed, but it was still Kern. Jerome Kern and the lyricist Otto Harbach were as important to Jed as Coolidge and Dawes and, he added, "they're definitely smarter."

When he finally got to the point—Cagney—Jean did not gripe about the threatened cancellation of bookings. To the contrary, she agreed that it was a casting brainstorm. Jimmy was brash, vulnerable, and he really was a song and dance man. As for *Broadway*, she said she thought it was the first play of the modern American theater because it brought real life to the stage—the facts of life and the energy of life. Give him Cagney? That was only the beginning.

When Jed told George Abbott he was replacing Roy Lloyd with a vaude-villian, the director thought it was more of the same old panic. He remembered being urged to step in for Joe Bell in *Love 'Em and Leave 'Em;* being threatened with replacement as the director of *Broadway.* He said he thought Roy Lloyd would be just fine, and in hope that Jed would calm down, changed the subject: *Broadway* was now in its third month. George had been paid his directing fee but he was supposed to be getting one percent of the gross receipts and the show had been playing to packed houses. He'd received none of the royalty payments.

Jed lighted a cigarette, inhaled deeply and whispered, "Crosby says he never heard about any royalty for you."

George was stunned. He said there had been a handshake on it. Jed didn't deny that, but he kept blaming Gaige. He pointed out that he'd paid George the proper director's royalties for *Love 'Em and Leave 'Em,* but Abbott said that only pennies were involved there.

Jed liked to exhale smoke in fancy patterns; thin streams that whistled through his lips or curled into his nostrils. He spread his fingers over his face, inhaling, and busied himself with these filigrees. George knew the intention was to exasperate.

"You fellows are cleaning up," he said bitterly. Jed smiled with his lips pressed together and whispered that he was sorry, but on account of Gaige there was nothing he could do.

"You're the producer."

"You'll get your co-author's royalty. That's going to be a lot of money, pal."

"Don't you 'pal' me," Abbott snarled, standing up. "You're a common cheat."

"You still sound like an actor," Jed hissed. "We should have fired you in Atlantic City. I had to rewrite and direct the whole damned thing myself. Can you imagine what would have happened if we'd taken your advice about the third act? Consider yourself lucky."

Abbott straightened to his full height and looked down from six feet six inches of disbelief. "You've got me, there's no contract, but don't you ever ask me to direct anything again. Not *Spread Eagle,* not *Coquette,* not any of the companies of *Broadway,* and that includes London. You are an unscrupulous man and I can't work for a liar."

Harris looked straight at him and smiled as Abbott turned and stalked out of the office. A few days later the Harrises and the Gaiges sailed ahead for

London. The others would follow. Paul Streger took over the directing of the London company. Roy Lloyd accepted, a second time, the loss of a role that was based on him. He would stay on as Lee's understudy.

Then, at a Wednesday run-through, Paul faced the agonizing fact that Cagney was not up to the part and they were sailing on Saturday. Without calling Jed he decided to give Roy Lloyd a crack at it that evening.

It would be the first time Roy went on. Lee Tracy was not an ungenerous man but, like many actors, he couldn't bear to have anyone else play his part. Insecurity and ego and the identification of one's existence with a role can overcome anything as trivial as illness. Throughout stage history, the mere mention of an understudy has prompted medical miracles.

It was the only performance of *Broadway* that Tracy would ever miss. He watched it from the back of the theater, along with Streger and Shumlin and Dunning and even Abbott, and Lee was the first backstage to congratulate Roy. They all thought he would be wonderful in London, and only then did Paul call Jed.

Harris took the news with equanimity. He told Paul to sail with the company and rehearse Roy on the ship.

"I don't even have a passport."

"Get it tomorrow. You don't sail till Saturday and while you're at it, tell Cagney."

Streger spent that Friday doing everything but telling Cagney. Before going to the passport office he stopped by to give Roy the good news. The actor's joy abruptly faded. He had no valise, nor the money to buy one. Paul found someone in the New York company to lend an old woven straw bag with a broken lock. Roy thought it was funny; said he'd tie it with a string. Paul just stared at him, amazed by the similarity between this actor and the role he was playing.

The bad news for Cagney had been delayed so long that Streger was left to deliver it at the bon voyage party the New York cast was hosting at Sardi's. Only hours remained until sailing. The crowd was in an upstairs, private dining room of the popular theatrical restaurant. The place was filled to overflow with wives, friends, and backstage people. The actors gave Paul a wristwatch. As stage manager he was the one member of management who worked with them in daily performance. As casting director he'd been responsible for hiring many of them.

He finally got drunk enough to deal with Jimmy. It was two o'clock in the morning. He stumbled into the men's room and found the actor at a washbasin. As Cagney looked at him in the mirror, Paul said, "You aren't going to London." Silence. Jimmy turned around and asked if it was a joke. They were both short and beady eyed, though Streger had none of Cagney's jittery energy.

"You'll get two weeks' salary."

"But my bags are already on board."

As if they would change their minds because his bags were on board.

Tears ran down his cheeks. He begged for an explanation. Paul had prepared one. Years later he remembered the speech as if it were a poem memorized in childhood.

"You're a hoofer, Jim, and you play the part like a hoofer. Lee is an actor and he fakes the dancing so that it doesn't interfere with the dialogue of the play. With you, the show stops while you do the dance because you're a real dancer. You're too good. It upsets the whole rhythm of the play."

Paul clenched his fists and his teeth, hoping that Cagney would buy it. The kid fled.

◆

While waiting for the company to arrive in London, Jed was entertained by John Balderston, the *New York World*'s London correspondent. Balderston had just become a playwright too, and a successful one. He'd dramatized an unpublished Henry James novel and, as *Berkeley Square*, it was running simultaneously in London and New York. The Harris charm was working utterly on him, and the playwright-journalist introduced Jed to the British theatrical and literary establishments, from Noël Coward, Gertrude Lawrence, and Max Beerbohm to Edith Sitwell and Arnold Bennett. But the only notable Harris was eager to meet was George Bernard Shaw. Balderston arranged that too and they went to the great playwright's country home for lunch.

At seventy, Shaw was radiantly healthy. His most recent play, *Saint Joan*, had been acclaimed as a work of his prime. Harris, during his final television interviews, reminisced about the visit.

He was absolutely adorable and very hammy indeed. He came on exactly like an actor. His boots were polished, his beard was carefully combed, his hair was immaculate, his complexion was pink and he walked up and down his drawing room like Tarzan. Beating his chest with both fists he said, "As you see I am frail and brittle." I said, "Hear, hear." He stopped, fixed me with a frown and then gave me the most dazzling smile. He was "on"—he was "on" as an actor. He was just a dream of a fellow, he put on a whole performance for me.

At one point I said to him, "Does it strike you that the plays of yours that have been the most successful are the ones where you had very little to do with putting them on?" That exasperated him. He said, "You're a Jew, aren't you?" I replied, "So far as I know there isn't so much as a single taint of Gentile blood in my veins." He roared.

73

I told him I'd heard a story about how he directed. That he inflected each word, every line in a play, and gave that to the actors so they had to learn exactly his way of pronouncing every single syllable. He said, "That is a damnable lie!" and I said, "I'm very glad to hear that, Mr. Shaw."

I'd heard he was very hard on a character actress in one of his plays. I said, "There was a story you'd sat down during a performance in the front row, unmistakable in your beard, there at the footlights. And you studiously watched the performances and afterwards bounded up the stairs. You walked up to each actor and said 'Splendid,' 'Fine,' 'Couldn't be more pleased;' and then you came to this character actress that you'd given such a hard time to and you said, 'My dear, you get worse and worse!'"

Shaw screamed with laughter and said, "That's an absolute lie. I'm incapable of anything like that," and of course he was telling the truth. It was just a phoney story. He was the soul of kindness and a man capable of great sentiment.

I loved him. I wished I could sit around with him forever. I felt like saying to him, "You don't know how much you did for me. You made amends for a perfectly lousy childhood that I had. This sanity of yours . . ." But I never got a chance to say it.

We got into furious arguments.

Harris always managed to provoke fatherly types to anger and he never seemed to understand why he was doing that.

◆

He loved London more than ever. He told Sam Behrman, "I think of settling down in England. And you know, if I did and I went into politics, I think I could have the same career Disraeli did."

Behrman thought this was so ridiculous he repeated it to John Balderston. Instead of laughing, the journalist gravely replied, "I have no doubt whatsoever that Jed could."

◆

Hilda Gaige assumed responsibility for the company's London accommodations. She insisted that the cast stay at the Savoy, a first-class hotel, if not quite in the same league as the Berkeley, where the Gaiges and the Harrises were. Hilda even oversaw the actors' registrations. When Roy Lloyd swung into the lobby with his straw suitcase, she shook her head in disapproval. "That isn't right for the star," she told Streger, "tied with a string. I'm going to treat Roy to a splendid new grip."

When Roy was ready to go to his room, one of the elegantly liveried bellhops picked up the ratty valise and held it at arm's length as if it were infected. He carried the bag with the tips of his fingers all the way to the room. Opening the door, he lowered the repulsive object to the floor and asked Roy dryly, "Shall I cut your cord, sir?"

The story became part of *Broadway* lore.

Behrman writes:

Broadway opened at the Strand Theatre. . . . The house was full, the audience dressy. I sat with Jed's wife, Anita. I saw Siegfried [Sassoon, the poet] and Edith Sitwell. . . . I saw the Balderstons. I saw Arnold Bennett, a hero of mine. . . . *Broadway* is a gutter play about the lowest forms of human life, set in a degraded cabaret frequented by rival bootlegger gangs with guns at the ready. I wondered how this genteel audience could relate to it. . . . The vision of life offered by this play would make you see the bomb as a cleanser. . . .

I saw Siegfried and Miss Sitwell in the intermission. Miss Sitwell said she was having a lovely time. Gaige [and] Hilda . . . joined us. . . . Jed was threading the lobby, eavesdropping on comments. Hilda waved to him. He waved back but did not join us.

For Anita that opening night was a "literary, theatrical and society spectacular. What surprised me most about it was that the staid British weren't satisfied with just yelling and cheering. As if that weren't enough, they stood on their seats and clapped their hands over their heads as if they were trying to reach the rafters."

As Behrman continued in his memoirs:

At the party everyone felt the play had gone very well and would be a hit. Balderston telephoned [*The Observer*] and had St. John Ervine's notice read to him. "It's a money notice!" he announced. At one in the morning Jed said he was leaving and asked me to come to his suite with him. . . . When we got there he called room service and ordered coffee. He was quite amiable.

"One thing about you I'll never understand," he said, "how you can spend so much time with the Gaiges."

"I like them very much," I said. "Gaige has always been very kind to me. I love Hilda."

"A lot of good that will do you."

He was smiling. He had anticipated this conversation. . . .

"I've bought a play. *Coquette*. I'm putting Helen Hayes in it. That'll give you a nice little job when you get back."

"Not me. I'm quitting."

"Hecht and MacArthur are working on a terrific play for me. Chicago newspaper life. *The Front Page*. What I've seen of it is terrific. . . . You'd be very foolish to quit. I've read your plays. You'll never get anywhere with them. They're thin."

"The [Theatre] Guild doesn't think so."

Jed looked at me pityingly. He was silky.

"Poor deluded boy. Why do I call you boy? You're at least ten years older than I am. I don't like to break it to you. But I'd better, to keep you from making a mistake. You know I'm a master of espionage. My spies are everywhere. I know what's going on in every office. The Guild will never do your play. They have other plans. You'd better stick with me."

This was the fully developed Harris, putting knowledge to cruelty's purpose. The Theatre Guild had just decided against producing Behrman's play.

His agent had cabled the disappointing news only days earlier. How had Harris known?

"There's one thing you don't understand about me."

"There are many things I don't understand about you." Jed sipped his coffee. "Your devotion to the Gaiges, for instance."

"You keep harping on the Gaiges. It slips your mind that Gaige has financed this whole production. You never put up your share. Is that why you hate Gaige?"

"You're a stooge for Gaige. You're in love with Hilda. Just because she hates Gaige doesn't mean she'll give you a break. Get on to yourself."

"I'm on to you."

He got up, walked over to me and said quietly, "If there was no penalty for homicide I'd kill you."

I couldn't resist quoting a line from *Broadway*. "Ain't you the brave guy, though?"

I left. . . . I went back there [to the Gaige party] and rang the doorbell. Hilda opened the door. . . .

"Party's over. Gaige has gone to bed. . . . Sit for a minute and talk to me. I feel sort of—what did Jed have to say?"

I followed her into the drawing room. I sat wondering how I could edit Jed's remarks to make them presentable. She sat opposite me in a big armchair, her hand over her face.

"Oh, he's very high. Full of plans. . . ."

. . . Hilda wasn't listening. She was crying.

THE LONE EAGLE

Paul Streger, Herman Shumlin, and Sam Behrman had long fantasized about when and how they would abandon Jed. "It was a dream the three of us shared," Behrman wrote. "We lived for the moment when we'd give up our jobs."

But despite regular abuse and dismay, Streger and Shumlin had not yet mustered up the nerve to quit. Behrman was now sailing away from London and Harris but it was not as they'd planned. He had quit defensively, inflamed by hurt. Harris could hardly feel abandoned.

As if to inspire Streger to leave Harris too, Gaige asked him one day whether the royalty checks had been coming in all right. It was January of 1927 and *Broadway* had been playing to sold-out houses for four months. Now it was a hit in London as well.

Paul had received nothing. Crosby gaped in exaggerated shock through his fashionably hexagonal steel-rimmed glasses.

"I've signed about forty thousand dollars' worth of checks for you," he said. "Maybe you ought to ask Jed about it. I gave them to him."

On the return voyage to America, Paul and Herman balanced profit-taking against quitting. The positions were different. Jed might have been withholding Paul's checks, but that was only a tease. He would have to pay ultimately. Streger had a contract. Herman's right to a share of the *Broadway* profits, unfortunately, was only a matter of justice.

As the general manager, Shumlin knew—it was his job to know—that Harris was now making twenty thousand dollars a week, personally. Herman, personally, was making seventy-five dollars a week. He was older than Jed. They had grown up together in Newark. That made the disparity humiliating, and for an extra dig, Harris sent Shumlin to Port Washington to pick up his new yacht. It was a forty-foot cruiser with a flying bridge, *Marlene II.*

Soon afterward, Paul looked up to see an ashen-faced Shumlin emerging from Jed's office. Herman walked as if in a trance. He opened the top drawer of his desk and stared into it. He turned to gaze at Paul through unseeing eyes.

It came out later. Herman had been subjected to games and evasions. Don't sit in this chair; is the sun in your eyes? Jed fiddled with cigarettes, blew smoke rings, gazed out the window. He asked how *Broadway* was doing. He was startled to learn how little Herman was being paid. He talked about production plans, about the movie sale of *Broadway*, and then he gave Herman a raise.

"A raise, he gave me," Herman croaked.

Broadway was making Harris a millionaire. It was making Gaige a millionaire. George Abbott and Philip Dunning would earn almost a half million dollars each as co-authors. Paul would get more than a quarter of a million for his two-and-a-half-percent interest.

"He said such terrible things to me," was all that Herman could say in the office before sliding his desk drawer shut. He took nothing. He floated past Jean Barkow and out the door.

As Streger reconstructed the scene some fifty years later, claiming total recall, he knew it was his turn. He wasn't frightened. He could always work as an actor. He strolled into Jed's office and said with a smile, "Crosby told me he signed forty thousand dollars' worth of checks for me."

Without hesitation Harris replied, "They're safe in my desk," and he patted the top of it.

"I'd feel a lot better," Paul said, patting his stomach, "if they were safe in *my* desk."

Jed smiled, opened the drawer, and tossed out a handful of checks. If he had been caught at any impropriety, he didn't act it. *But why had he kept the checks?* Paul gathered them up, feeling as he had when fat Milton had pointed to the row of thousand-dollar bills on the bed. The money had no reality for him.

"Thanks," he said, and then added, "for everything. I'm quitting you, Jed."

Harris looked straight into his eyes, then rose to gaze out the window.

Streger turned amiable. He said he thought Jed was the most brilliant producer and manager in New York, "and I know you want to direct."

Harris seemed surprised by that. He'd never mentioned an interest in directing.

"I'm sure you will be a genius at it, in fact I agree with you about your being a genius in general. But you are a complicated, difficult, neurotic man. You demand everyone's total engrossment in your career. You won't share the spotlight with anyone. Nobody else can get any credit. Everything we did, you did. You did everything. Well, we took it, all of us here, and we laughed because it was you and you were a oner. But I guess it finally became, after all the meanness and abuse, just too much of a chore."

Streger felt better, now that he'd begun. He was an actor and he was warming to the scene.

"But that isn't the reason I'm quitting. The reason I'm quitting is the same reason that Sam and Herman quit. It's because," and he took a step closer to Jed so that he could surely be heard; the actor in him concentrated on diction, pronunciation, projection and conviction. ". . . it's because you are about as objectionable a human being as you can get."

Streger walked out. He emptied his desk and said good-bye to Jean Barkow. She sat in the quiet office. Sam was gone, Herman was gone, now Paul was gone. Dick Maney, who had replaced Sam Behrman as publicity man, clattered away at a typewriter.

◆

There was a tremendous outpouring of national affection and joy when Charles Lindbergh returned after his record-setting solo flight across the Atlantic. Of all the ticker tape parades that honored one hero or another, none was more spectacular, none more adoring, than the one New York City gave for Lindy.

Jed stayed home that day. He didn't go to the office. A puzzled Anita watched him grumble around the apartment until he finally revealed what was bothering him. "They'll never give *me* a parade," he said.

Yet he was angered by an obsequious letter from Yale that should have made him gloat. His name was listed high on the letterhead. It was a request that Jed, as "one of Yale's most eminent alumni," lend his name and perhaps some tickets for *Broadway*, to help attract contributions.

His reply began with a reminder that having missed his senior year, he was not an alumnus, "eminent or otherwise." He noted that there were few pleasant memories any Jewish student might retain of the college. And he concluded with a demand that his name be removed from the letterhead as well as all lists of Yale alumni. Any request for tickets, he added, should be directed to the appropriate box office.

◆

George Abbott, to his own amazement, agreed to direct *Spread Eagle* after all. He wanted it understood: he would never work with Harris after that, and wouldn't direct *Coquette* under any circumstances. But *Spread Eagle* was already booked into the Martin Beck Theatre for an April premiere and rehearsals were beginning immediately. There wasn't time to find a new director and, as usual, George had become a credited co-author.

Jed sat in the back of the theater while George rehearsed, and if the director noticed, he didn't show it. He arrived promptly at ten, called a lunch-break at noon, and broke at five, as if it were an office job. If Jed wanted to talk to the cast, give them notes afterward, that was his business.

Spread Eagle was a political melodrama about American military involvement in Mexico. Osgood Perkins played the lead and, in the bit part of an Indian, complete with body makeup and loincloth, was young Harold Clurman. The future director and critic would remember Harris's talks to the cast. "I don't think that Abbott was so thrilled about Jed's being there," he said, "or talking to us, but he acted as if he weren't aware of it. I told my roommate Clifford [Odets] that Harris was as keen in his observation of acting as anyone in my experience. His notes showed a very sharp eye."

Clurman was then courting the beautiful actress Stella Adler. The Adlers—Jacob, his wife Sarah, and their children—were the Barrymores of lower Second Avenue, where the Yiddish Art Theater was thriving. Jed seemed to feel that he was the bridge between the international commercial theater and the Yiddish culture that was in his bones, and for which he had such affection. He had brought Noël Coward and the Lunts to the Lower East Side to meet the revered actor, Maurice Schwartz, and the newspapers had given much space to the meeting. However different the sophisticated comedians might have seemed from the East European tragedians, they all shared an actor's spirit and Harris doubtless appreciated that.

Now he motored with Harold Clurman to pay homage to Jacob P. Adler at the family retreat in Lake Saranac, New York.

As they were ushered into the living room, the normally jovial Clurman removed his hat in respect. Adler was, after all, a patriarch of the Yiddish stage.

Young Harris, however, had ambled into the room, plopped down on the sofa without invitation, stretched out his legs and hoisted them onto the coffee table. Then, just as one might guess he had with Shaw, he proceeded to banter with Adler, to disagree and challenge and finally argue with the great man.

Perhaps Shaw had indeed been refreshed by Harris's brash candor. We only have Jed's word on the visit. The Adlers, however, were not refreshed. They were appalled. They watched Harris's antics as if he were a ruffian in the synagogue and then they struck. Yiddish theatricality plays like the elements. The considerable Jacob P. Adler was made, or had made himself, in the raging and unforgiving image of the Hebrew God, the Jewish father. If Shaw had, as one might speculate, seemed to Harris a father to provoke, Adler was the paradigm of fathers.

He rose from the overstuffed armchair, as if from a throne, and filled the room with a roar that Clurman feared would blow the patterned flowers from the wallpaper. Harris seemed to be fighting a gale to gain his feet.

"Out!" the old man bellowed, and his sons Luther and Jack picked Jed up by the elbows.

"Get him out of here!" Adler roared, pointing to the door like the rabbi Jed had seen in the Newark Yiddish theater. And inexplicably, as Luther and Jack carried him off with feet flailing the air, Harris cried—to whom?—"I told you when I was twenty-six I'd be a millionaire. Well I am!"

◆

He would catalogue the weaknesses of those he knew and capitalize on those weaknesses. When *Spread Eagle* failed despite good reviews, he set out to change Abbott's mind about not directing *Coquette*. George watched pennies. Harris offered a thousand dollars for each company of *Broadway* that he would observe and approve. Abbott said he would not oversee any company, but that he would watch a performance of each, and Jed said that was fine. "I told my wife," Abbott remembered, "that I would do it to protect the property but I said, 'Ednah, if Jed thinks it means I'm taking back what I said then he doesn't understand me at all.'"

Harris did have to find another director for *Coquette* and hired George Cukor because he thought the fellow would work well with Helen Hayes, the show's star. Jed had once feared that with the comedy *Norma's Affair* having been refashioned into the tragedy *Coquette*, Hayes might be wrong for it. But he changed his mind.

> I had regarded Miss Hayes . . . as a very "cute" actress. But then she suddenly appeared in Barrie's *What Every Woman Knows*, and her subtlety and power astounded me. I decided that she was the only actress in the world to play *Coquette*.
> — *A Dance on the High Wire*

Harris's view of the play as tragedy more than made sense. His theatrical senses were acute and impeccable. "A gay, well born girl," he said, "gets into the family way because of a hillbilly. Her father murders the boy and she kills herself. It's that simple." Then, he confided to Anita, "if anyone finds out it has elements of Greek tragedy, we're dead. This girl is going to die for what began as a harmless flirtation because when women flirt they don't realize what male forces they're provoking. There ought to be capital punishment for teases. . . . I tell you, Anita, this play is going to make us a fortune on the hankie concession alone."

Coquette was to open in November, a scant six weeks ahead of *The Royal Family*. Three days into rehearsal, Helen Hayes telephoned Abbott.

"If it's about *Coquette*," he recalled telling her, "I don't want to discuss it."

"But it's your play."

"I won't work with that man," George said. ". . . Are you having troubles?"

"Please meet me for lunch. If you have any feelings for me at all—any respect for me as an actress—please meet me for lunch."

As they sat down in the restaurant she poked at her hair, fixing and refixing the comb at the back.

"Mr. Cukor is quitting. We've just been rehearsing a few days and he's quitting. I think Jed's a little nervous."

"Jed isn't nervous. He's crazy."

"These two shows at the same time, us and *The Royal Family*. It's too much."

"I won't work with him."

"Darling, the audience is going to sit on its hands for three hours. For the sake of your play and yes, for my sake, *please*"—and she looked imploringly into his eyes — "*help*."

Abbott tried to be reasonable about it.

"I'll take it over for a week and then we'll see, but you have to personally assure me that I will never see Jed's face. I don't want him in the theater."

She pressed his hand and smiled, blinking her Irish blue eyes.

"You have my word. Bless you, George."

Jed had put her up to it. George realized it too late.

◆

A certain amount of contact between the men was inevitable. There was casting to be reconsidered, scenic designs, costumes. The exchanges were curt. At rehearsal, Harris kept to the agreement, although now and again George spied a shadow in the balcony. He liked having made Jed Harris into a sneak.

At the Atlantic City tryout, the audience did not seem to appreciate the play. On opening night the applause rang out like a pair of sea gulls idly flapping their wings.

"We've got to work on this script," Jed said.

Abbott wasn't interested in talking.

"Listen, the show's in trouble."

"Give it time to settle. You're always panicking."

"For Chrissake, it's a mess."

"If you know so much," Abbott said coldly, "why don't you direct it yourself?"

Harris decided to do more than that. As Abbott and Miss Bridgers had constructed the second act of *Coquette*, the heroine has been devastated by her father's murder of her lover. The family lawyer appeals to her to save the father by testifying that he was protecting her honor.

"All right," she snaps. "Go away, just go away!"

Now, as the authors watched a performance some days later, they were startled to hear their character cry, "No! I hope they hang him! I want him to die!"

They pressed up the aisle at intermission to confront Harris, who had been watching from the back of the theater. Who, they demanded to know, had changed their line? Jed told them who had.

"You know perfectly well," Abbott said, "that you are not permitted to write anything into a play without the consent of the author."

Harris suggested that they complain to the Dramatists Guild, knowing that authors do not close their own plays, however rewritten by others.

Recounting the incident, Harris's recollection was twisted by gratuitous cruelty and darkened by spite. "Having decided to get rid of Abbott, I found the decision painful." There was no mention of the director's refusal to work with him or the why of it. Harris added, "Though we had little in common, [Abbott] was honest and hard working. And although he was parsimonious and almost phenomenally dull, we had been friends for a long time. He always carried my instructions out to the letter."

Nasty as these remarks were, they were made pathetic by fate. For Abbott, by the time they were written, had become the grand old man of the theater, "Mr. Abbott," and had not spoken to a forgotten Jed Harris for fifty years.

◆

At a "still virginal 37," as Harris tactfully put it, Edna Ferber was quite a bit older than he. (More than he realized. She was actually forty at the time.) The product of a well-to-do Jewish family but a shy and rather plain woman, she applied her romantic nature to her writing. Her novel *Show Boat* had been an immense success and was to be produced as a musical. Now she was at work on *The Royal Family*, collaborating with George S. Kaufman.

Miss Ferber traveled to Philadelphia to see *Coquette*. The audience reaction was still sluggish. Miss Hayes was rumored to be seeking a way out in order to do a new play by her husband, Charles MacArthur. The producer of that play was said to be Jed's own partner, Crosby Gaige, who had already asked to be relieved of some of his *Coquette* investment. Harris bought out the share.

George Abbott was gone. Jed was directing now. Rehearsals continued between performances. Meantime, Harris revised the script. Then rehearsals resumed with the new lines.

As the curtain rose on *Coquette* [that Philadelphia opening night] I was cursing myself for having worked the company so hard. . . .

Within ten minutes I knew that all would be well. . . . The audience was no longer watching a comic entertainment that would turn confusingly harsh and bitter, but were almost from the first moment absorbed in a drama. . . .

After watching the play for fifteen minutes from behind the orchestra, I walked into the box office, sank into a chair and fell asleep. I awoke in time to see the curtain fall. . . . Soon I could see Miss Ferber coming up the aisle, the bosom of her plum-colored silk dress showing dark, round stains like huge polka dots. Her eyes were red as she took my hands.

"It's a masterpiece—the whole thing," she said.

— Jed Harris, *A Dance on the High Wire*

Coquette opened in New York on November 8, 1927 at the Maxine Elliott Theatre. Miss Hayes was rhapsodized, and the play became a great success. The interest that Gaige had sold back to Harris was ultimately worth one hundred thousand dollars.

If Jed had been glamorized by *Broadway*, his meteor was sent arcing still higher and brighter by *Coquette*. Between the two productions—there now were six American companies of *Broadway*—his income had soared to one hundred thousand dollars a month.

He exchanged the seldom-used *Marlene II* for a fifty-foot sloop with an auxiliary inboard motor. He hired a full-time crew, a cook, a mate, and a dimwitted captain whose first act aboard ship was losing a pillow in the engine's innards. He took the new office staff—Whitaker Ray had replaced Shumlin—out to the ship for weekends at sea. Maney, Ray, and Harris played cards while the sloop was moored in the City Island marina.

The office in the Selwyn Theatre Building, hectic before, now threatened to burst apart, exploding actors, playwrights, and directors in a blast of scripts and glossy photographs. With personal relations tense and the partnership all but severed, Gaige probably wanted Jed out of the building, but the two were still associated with *The Royal Family*, which was in rehearsal and booked into the Selwyn Theatre downstairs. Crosby had to wait.

◆

The Royal Family introduced Jed to George S. Kaufman, who was the theatrical editor of the *New York Times* even though he had already established himself as the co-author of *Beggar on Horseback* and *Dulcy*. Kaufman was a tall and skinny young man who would have looked ordinarily bookish were it not for his hair, which stood on end as if electrified. Otherwise he was crumpled, with a bony and bespectacled Jewish face topping a stretch of shapeless clothes. Kaufman had the soul of a performer, and just as his grouching misanthropy was an invented persona, so this bizarre hair-style and careless appearance was a costume. He and Jed shared a certain solitariness, and, Harris said, they became friends.

The Royal Family is about an acting dynasty and depends for its humor on the public's perception of theatrical egotism and eccentricity. It is set in the plush apartment of a great actress who is temporarily idle and therefore willing to hear out the marriage proposal of a former beau who has returned more ardent, wealthier, and more conventional than ever.

Descending upon her, too, are an aunt who is also a great lady of the stage, and a flamboyant brother who has deserted the theater for Hollywood. Harris himself summed up the script as "not a conventional play with a plot but a series of sketches of a family of actors . . . a fond spoof of the more legendary aspects of the Barrymores."

Edna Ferber knew the Barrymore family and was a close friend of Ethel Barrymore's. She was naive enough to suggest that Jed actually engage the Barrymores to play themselves. The idea was wonderful in its hopelessness and certainly worth a try.

Hardly daring to submit the script himself, Jed let Edna send it to Ethel, who, as he later wrote with glee, "regarded the play as a deliberate insult to her family and threatened us with a suit."

That was never more than a threat and it appeared to be the only trouble *The Royal Family* would ever have.

[The] meetings I had with Kaufman and Miss Ferber were like holidays. Unlike the authors of my earlier plays, they were accomplished professional writers. Ideas for scenes, lines, jokes, and bits of stage business flew around the table while an old player piano banged out Jerome Kern's "Who" over and over again. . . . There was never so much as a strong difference of opinion among us, except for the old lady's death scene I had once suggested. The deeper we got into the play, the more unnecessary and even meretricious that idea seemed to me. But they were convinced from the very beginning that it was a brilliant suggestion, and they clung to it to the end.

When the time came to put the show on, I tried to avoid rehearsing that death scene as long as I could—an experience I would repeat with that utterly fakey moment when Nora slams the door in Ibsen's *A Doll's House*.

— Jed Harris, *A Dance on the High Wire*

Perhaps *Coquette* had satisfied Harris's 1927 quota of problems. Perhaps he was restlessly idle, then, the November afternoon he asked Kaufman to come over with the latest revisions. As usual, Jed had taken a hotel suite for the purpose of rewriting sessions. This time it was the Buckingham at 101 West 57th Street.

The room clerk sent George upstairs. The playwright knocked at the door. The producer opened it. He was naked. Kaufman did not blink. He handed the manuscript over as he strolled into the room and sank into an armchair. Harris sat opposite, crossed his leg horizontally, put on his glasses, and began to read.

After a protracted study, Jed removed his glasses and asked, "Now what do you think of this?" He scribbled a few words in the script, rose and walked the few paces to George's chair. He handed over the script, his genitals staring the playwright in the face.

Kaufman read Harris's suggested change. "Seems fine to me," he said, rising to leave. Jed walked him to the door and opened it.

"By the way," Kaufman said, turning toward him, "your fly is open," and he shut the door behind him. Before the day was out the story was the hit of the Algonquin Round Table.

◆

The Ferber-Kaufman collaboration proceeded smoothly and rehearsals of *The Royal Family* began under David Burton's direction. As might have been anticipated, Jed could no longer restrain himself now that he'd had a taste of directing. Burton would no sooner have his company running through the comedy when Harris would be up from his seat and down the aisle, offering advice and making suggestions.

He seemed strong and confident. Two hits on Broadway are the closest thing to a health restorative. Then, with the opening night approaching, he panicked as usual.

. . . my vitality was at a low ebb.
Very much against my will I permitted [Whitaker] Ray to take me to a doctor . . . diagnosis and prognosis: that my physical energy was all but depleted, and I was living on the rapidly dwindling resources of my nervous energy. . . . unless I agreed to drop everything immediately, at once and forthwith, and to undertake a long rest under the strictest medical supervision, he could not be responsible for my future. . . .
. . . I decided to fire the whole cast and start all over again sometime in the distant

future. My office paid each member of the cast two weeks' salary as they were dismissed. I was in bed in a complete state of collapse. A nurse fed, bathed, and drugged me, and my servant looked after me when she left in the evening.

— Jed Harris, *A Dance on the High Wire*

By "servant" he presumably meant Anita. Neither she nor anyone else in his family is mentioned in the memoirs. One would think he'd been manufactured.

Kaufman and Ferber came by to visit Harris in the hospital. They were of course distressed for him, but also for their play. They told of an offer by the producer Winthrop Ames to buy the scenery, regroup the actors, and proceed with the production. Harris telephoned Ames. The offer was legitimate.

Ames's offer had a salutary effect on Harris's health. Whatever had caused the panic, another producer's interest resolved it.

I slept for sixteen hours and awoke the next day feeling much better. . . . Within the hour I phoned my office and ordered [Whitaker] Ray to round up and reengage the company . . . rehearsals were resumed the following day. . . . Five days later I was on my feet, still a bit rocky, and back at rehearsal.

— Jed Harris, *A Dance on the High Wire*

Harris was always too vulnerable to see through his own pretenses. He did not notice the humor in this Lourdes-like recovery.

The Royal Family had its tryout in Atlantic City as scheduled and opened in New York exactly as first announced, on December 28, 1927. By New Year's Eve Jed had yet another hit to run alongside *Coquette* and *Broadway*.

The combination was exhilarating: two plays hitting the jackpot within six weeks of each other while the cheers for *Broadway* were still ringing round the world. Three hits in barely fifteen months and each unique: a melodrama, a tragedy, a high comedy. Jed Harris was the man of the moment.

HE KNOWS IT TEASES

EARLY ONE SPRING afternoon in 1928, Harris strolled into Sardi's Restaurant for a luncheon appointment. As he was led to the table he saw Sam Behrman dining with Ina Claire. It had been a year since that last, terrible scene in London.

The men greeted each other. The year had been good for Sam too. He'd had his first Broadway production—*The Second Man*—with the glamorous Alfred Lunt and Lynn Fontanne in the leads. He'd been celebrated as America's first writer of high comedy.

Sam introduced Jed to Miss Claire and the beautiful actress extended a languid hand for the producer to kiss.

"I'm sorry," she smiled, "I didn't catch the name."

Ina Claire didn't have to remember names. Everyone remembered hers, she would say; they could tell her theirs.

"Jed Harris," Sam repeated. "The producer of *Broadway, Coquette, The Royal Family, Weak Sisters.*"

Ignoring the bitchiness, Harris complimented the actress on her work in *Our Betters*. "You're giving a finer performance," he said, "than I would have thought possible in Mr. Maugham's little play."

"It isn't *Hamlet*, is it? But you know, I'm not a great actress. My gifts are modest."

"Smart comedy," Jed responded on cue, "is as difficult to play as Lady Macbeth or any of the *Three Sisters*." He turned to Behrman, who said he was completing a dramatization of *Serena Blandish (or The Difficulty of Getting Married)*. The novel had been anonymously written under the pseudonym "A Lady of Quality." Its author's identity remained secret. Harris asked to read it and left for his lunch date.

Dick Maney was waiting at the table with a reporter, discussing the next Harris production, Ben Hecht and Charles MacArthur's *The Front Page*. Jed sat down and started to talk for the record about George S. Kaufman's directing debut.

You can see from his plays that he's a born director. He puts the action right into the script. He'll be perfect for the boys to work with and they're going to respect a fellow playwright. *The Front Page* is a cross between a courtroom play and a melodrama, but it's not going to be like anything ever seen before. It's rough and no holds barred and it's going to be faster than *Broadway*. You know, there isn't a single scene in *Broadway* that runs longer than four minutes. That's what gives it the machine gun tempo, that and the entrances and exits. Nobody goes around counting except me but the average play has about fifty entrances and exits. *Broadway* has about three hundred. That's action and *The Front Page* is going to be even faster.

He'd forgotten demanding that George Abbott cut back on *Broadway*'s entrances and exits. He moved on to a most straightforward, sensible and concise description of the producer's purpose in commercial theater.

I think it's a mistake to make a world shaking skirmish with destiny out of a plain, straightforward melodrama. I produce plays for the purposes of entertainment and not to persuade people into thinking the way I do about things in general . . . maybe I'm nuts but it seems to me that the business of a producer in the theater is to put on a show that will attract cash customers and not undertake to sell an intellectual bill of goods which nobody wants to buy anyhow. Me, I'm sordid and commercial. I like being that way.

The modesty was charming but disingenuous. Harris well knew that magnetism was the theater's first purpose, he knew the challenges of presenting professionally entertaining plays, and his standards were stricter than most other producers'. He also knew how meanings and messages could overload a play. He enjoyed working on *The Front Page* because MacArthur, Hecht, and Kaufman were brainy men applying their intelligences and gifts to the tough, public arena; they were clever collaborators as well as potential subjects for the Harris charm. MacArthur was a textbook newspaperman, solidly married but available for the occasional all-night binge. Ben Hecht had quit journalism to write novels, and they were acclaimed at the time: *Erik Dorn* (1921) and, five years later, *Count Bruga*.

Over the next few years Hecht and his wife, the writer Rose Caylor, were to be objects of Harris's machinations. At the same time, Hecht observed and recorded Harris's behavior with the acuity of a superlative reporter (which he had once been). He watched as the producer attempted to separate wives from husbands and husbands from wives, seeking to divide and dominate not only Rose and Ben Hecht, but Bea and George Kaufman, Helen Hayes and Charlie MacArthur, Mildred Harris and her husband Cappy. Jed's parents had not been quite right about his being possessed by a dybbuk. *He* was the dybbuk. *He* sought to possess others.

Hecht seemed almost mesmerized by Harris. "He purred when he spoke," he was to write about Harris in a biography of MacArthur called *Charlie*. "His skinny jaw jutted. His eyes were dark and slightly upturned, as if listening to some tender inner music. He had the grin of a sorcerer. . . . He entered the room as noiselessly as a snake."

Hecht's feelings about Harris, a mixture of fascination and hatred, filled a whole novel called *A Jew in Love*. Its main character, Jo Boshere (né Abe Nussbaum), is a millionaire publisher and megalomaniac whose explosive success earns him the epithet "The Comet." Boshere is a thinly disguised Jed Harris, "The Meteor."

And yet not everything in *A Jew in Love* damns Harris. Hecht appreciated the man's joy in ideas, his athletic use of language, the fresh routes of his nimble mind. This was no commonplace or predictable intelligence. Here is Boshere/Harris:

> What's wrong with communism is this: it's attacking government, it's attacking something that . . . is obsolete . . . sentimental theories for its change or improvement or even overthrow are automatically absurd . . . an industrialized world doesn't need governments. . . . Lenin was just Henry Ford wrapped up in red tissue paper. . . . The underdogs will own nothing in Russia. . . . I don't give a damn about art. I'm interested in myself, in human relationships. . . . The true progress of man is in our feelings . . . to feel and analyze our feelings and little by little, century by century, pull the human idiot out of the swamps into which he was born. We don't serve governments or charities or theories or factories. What we serve is evolution.

The style of that speech, its language and thoughts, are Harris's.

Hecht saw sexual hunger as only a pretext when Jed wooed women. The fundamental intention of Boshere/Harris in *A Jew in Love*, whether toward man or woman, "was that of a deeper and more inner seduction, a Dracula-like hunger for the life blood of his victims."

If that sounds florid, those were times of floridity, of vamps with panthers on leashes, of Rudolph Valentino and Bela Lugosi. Feverish though Hecht's images may seem to a modern ear, in 1928 it was not so odd to view and even live life in purple.

◆

George S. Kaufman was a writer of less gaudy stripe, although in his way he was colorful too. At first meeting the two precocious young stage professionals, Kaufman and Harris, seemed to be psychological brothers. Hadn't Kaufman once told a cab driver, "It's not your fault that it's taking a half an hour to go five blocks. You can't help it if you're a goddamned fool." That could have been Harris enjoying the risk of a fight.

One day in March, the two of them were walking on West 44th Street when Kaufman waved to a young woman who was standing near the Shubert Theatre. She was as small as Anita, or Jed's sister Mildred; she had pin bright blue eyes set in a round, healthy face and her hair was short, straight and red under the wide-brimmed straw hat.

Waving back at them with a great grin, she started talking before they were even in earshot. Ruth Gordon would always be audible in a theater.

"She thinks," Kaufman said, "that I'm the greatest man on Broadway."

"Wait till she gets a load of me."

Kaufman introduced them, but Jed and Ruth had met before. She had been up for a part in *Weak Sisters* and had decided to take a stand on getting featured billing. Jed had refused even to discuss it. He'd simply left the room and Ruth lost the part. She was established now, co-starring with Humphrey Bogart in Max Anderson's *Saturday's Children*.

A few days later Kaufman telephoned Ruth and asked her to dinner. Jed was coming, too, he said.

Harris met beautiful actresses every day. His aura and power lured them, and it was hardly possible, or desirable, or logical, to ignore them. There were so many actresses, in such farcical availability, that the romantic side of his life began to resemble a comic opera.

It must have been Ruth Gordon's brains, as much as anything else, that made her attractive to him, and he boasted about her wit. "There was once an actor named Eliot Cabot," he told a newspaper interviewer. "I was having lunch with Helen Hayes and Ruth, and Helen said, 'You know, Eliot Cabot's writing his autobiography.' Ruth said, 'That should be a pamphlet.' Helen said, 'I mean his life in the theater.' Ruth said, 'That should be a throwaway.' So quick. Just like that."

Their affair began as Ruth was preparing to take *Saturday's Children* on the road and *The Front Page* was in rehearsal. Jed was enjoying the work, al-

91

though there was some friction with Ben Hecht. The writer wasn't willing to play lamb to Harris's shepherd, but fundamental to the quarrel, too, was Jed's impatience with Hecht's literary pretensions.

So he fought to keep *The Front Page* fast, melodramatic, funny, and straightforward. During the few weeks of rewriting he sought only to make its dramatic arc strong and thrusting. "What you have now," he told Hecht and MacArthur at the start of work, "is like a clock with the minute hand moving steadily while the hour hand never moves at all."

He pressed them to strengthen a single line of action. That line of action, he said, should be "the effort of Hildy Johnson to get out of the newspaper business. At the end of the first act he is temporarily held up by Earl Williams's escape. At the end of Act II he is again held up by Molly Malloy jumping out of the window. And at the end of Act III, having finally gotten on the train to New York with his prospective bride and mother-in-law, he is going to be brought back by some crooked device we will invent. And this will provide us with the theme of our show—once you get caught in the lousy newspaper business you can never get out again."

Chicago was considered to be a bad theater town, but *The Front Page* was tried out there because it was set in Chicago and its authors had been Chicago newspapermen. It made publicity sense.

Perhaps the town reminded him of the *Applesauce* days and brought out the press agent in him. The opening-night audience may not have been as feral in its enthusiasm as he reported. "When the curtain fell at the end of the first act, the roar that rose from the auditorium sounded like the bellowing of a herd of wild animals." But the reception was certainly positive and there seemed little reason to worry about the play. There were other things to worry about. Ruth's disconcerting fertility, for instance.

As she would later recall in her memoir, *My Side*, the young actress made the arrangements herself. She was capable, and it wasn't her first abortion. Jed was a wreck. It was his first, and he was still married to Anita.

Ruth had recently been widowed. Her husband, Gregory Kelly, a thirty-six-year-old actor, suffered a fatal heart attack while on the road in Pittsburgh. Ruth's abortion was performed without complications.

◆

Show people are notoriously superstitious. Backstage luck is always the subject of some theater magazine article or other. The compulsively perverse Harris chose August 13, 1928 for the premiere of *The Front Page*, although for reviewing purposes, the opening was on the next night. It would become habitual, opening on "wrong" dates. Ruth called it "a superstition about superstition." In any case, the show was a triumph.

As for Jed Harris, he was now more than triumphant. He seemed to know a secret. To have presented four popular and critical hits in two years was of course exciting, but he seemed positively infallible. He seemed to be success itself.

The meteoric image was clinched. As Moss Hart wrote in *Act One*, "he continued to light up the theatrical heavens with an unerring touch that had something of the uncanny about it. Production after production, whatever play he turned his hand to, was catapulted into immediate success, and his vagaries, his flaring tempers, his incisive way with a script were already a legend and fast becoming Broadway folklore."

Naturally, then, this perverse man announced that he was quitting the theater. The office, he told Dick Maney, would be closed in a few weeks. Then he disappeared. He took the train to Miami Beach. His yacht followed. He seemed to love boats more than he loved boat rides.

While the sloop sailed toward Florida, he basked in the poolside sun at the Roney-Plaza Hotel. He was not away from the Broadway theater crowd for long. At dinner the first evening, the hotel's owner seated him beside Judith Anderson. The throaty actress was as celebrated for tragedy as Helen Hayes and Ina Claire were for comedy. Her current triumph was in Eugene O'Neill's psychological marathon, *Strange Interlude*, but a case of pneumonia had sent her south.

She was delighted to meet the man who was the talk of New York, the man of whom her friend Noël Coward had said, "He's a one man theater. There is nothing in it he can't do . . . I've passed out over him."

Judith Anderson was tiny, vivacious, and smart, with thick black hair and a magnificent figure. She asked Jed to join her on a day trip to Nassau and he said he would be delighted.

Before boarding the private airplane the next morning, they were asked to make out their wills. It was not a joke. They donned leather caps and goggles and Miss Anderson was helped onto the wing. Her weight, less than one hundred pounds, tilted the plane.

Small planes bump and shift on the least hint of air current, and Miss Anderson remembered that short hop and its bumps, lurches, and sudden drops for years afterward. When they finally rolled to a stop in Nassau, Harris leaped from his seat, ripped off the cap and goggles, jumped to the ground, and dashed off across the little airstrip. Miss Anderson and the pilot laughed out loud. They didn't see him all afternoon, certainly not for the return flight. He must have taken a boat back.

Jed and Judith saw a lot of each other in the next days, until she regained her strength and had to return to the O'Neill drama. Harris took her to the

Miami railroad station and escorted her to the roomette. She told him that he might call her "Meg" (her real name was Margaret Frances Anderson). They grew so cozy that she worried about his getting off the train before departure. He didn't. He stayed on all the way to New York.

◆

His retirement was brief. Maney had been wise to keep it secret. Jed returned to find his income at forty thousand dollars a week.

◆

He told Anita he was moving out. She wasn't surprised but she was stunned. She still found the scene painful as she reconstructed it at the age of eighty. He'd said, "We both know I never wanted to marry you. I only did it out of guilt. It would be absurd to stay for the same reason. Tell my attorney what you want."

He pulled a black valise from the closet, flipped it open and then shut. "The hell with it," he said. "I'll buy whatever I need. I'll be at the Buckingham."

She fell on the bed. She'd known it was coming and had probably known it from the start. When she looked up he was gone. She went to the window and watched him walk out the front door, look for a taxi, stroll up the middle of West 10th Street. She remembered weeping for much of that day.

◆

On September 3, 1928, Jed became famous from one end of the country to the other, famous as no other theater person had ever been. There on the cover of *Time* magazine he made Broadway a national phenomenon. He looked out from the magazine's margins through sparkling, serious eyes, strong and confident. When he'd been shown that picture he said, "People say I look like a Spanish don, or Rudolph Valentino. Before I was famous they just thought I was ugly."

He did look exotic, there on the cover. His eyebrows were arched, with just a trace of skepticism veiling his smile. He was close shaven and his pale skin was drawn tight across a bony jaw and marble cheeks. His hands were characteristically thrust into his pants pockets. His jacket was buttoned and with the vest beneath he seemed sturdy rather than skinny. The picture on the magazine was of a fellow who had mastered the system.

"Goddamn that cover," Harris shrieked to Maney.

"But sire," the press agent pleaded. He thought it was funny to speak that way. "The royal portrait is magnificent."

"What the hell is that caption supposed to mean?"

The caption beneath the cover picture was, "Jed Harris. He knows it teases." The story inside read:

He has a way of hurting people's feelings, especially those of the people who work for him, by showing them how their jobs ought to be done. If on such occasions he did their work clumsily, it might make him unpopular. He does it well, and then, with an obtuseness common to most intelligent and sensitive persons, forgets to apologize.

His face is likely to be covered with short bristles, a condition which, as he is doubtless aware, teases and annoys.

Jed Harris attends to the details of producing plays with a strange, irritable, creative fervor so that you might think he had written them.

Did that suggest he usurped others' credit? *Time* was five years old and not yet inclined to the snideness that would characterize some of its later years. Maney felt that the story was heaven-sent. The coordinating editor, Noel Busch, had taken Harris's word for everything. The article fulfilled its subject's wish to molt his family as snakes do their skins. It had him born in Vienna, with no mention of Lemburg or Newark, or parents, or sisters or brother or wife. No mention, in short, of Jacob Horowitz. The article confirmed his self-invention. He had not existed until becoming Jed Harris. That was all of his life that seemed to matter to him and that was all of it that was in *Time* magazine.

Still, he was furious.

"Drop everything you're doing and bring Busch to my hotel immediately," Jed rasped. . . . To my surprise, Busch agreed to the rendezvous. I . . . took him to Jed's suite at the Buckingham. I rang the bell. No answer. I pushed open the door. The living room was empty. Bidding Busch be seated, I entered Jed's chamber. Prone, covered by a single sheet, he fixed me with a maniacal glare.

"Mr. Busch is without, sire."

Jed eyed me accusingly for a good two minutes. "Take him away," he whispered hoarsely. "I can't trust myself. Were I to face him, I might do something I'd regret all my life."   — Richard Maney, *Fanfare*

These were the routines that tickled Maney. He appreciated baloney when it was showmanlike baloney.

Harris finally moved out of Crosby Gaige's partnership and office building, going across the street to a suite on the top floor of the Sardi Building. From there he could look down on the roof of the Shubert Theatre, occasionally seeing Mr. Lee Shubert sunning himself there.

"Jed Harris?" Mr. Lee said. "He'd fuck anything. If you got hold of a snake he'd fuck it."

One evening, Jed stopped by at Henry Miller's Theatre, where Ina Claire was doing the Maugham play. After the performance he went backstage and invited her to midnight supper at Child's Restaurant. It was an odd choice, a moderately priced chain restaurant geared to unescorted matrons, but he had a thing for the macaroni, just as he had a thing for the Automat's baked beans, the roller coaster at Coney Island, the first base box seats at Yankee Stadium. He had a delightful zest for the details of New York life, but Ina was not charmed by it. To her, macaroni was macaroni.

He stopped by three times that week, each time taking her to Child's after the show. On the fourth night, as she remembered, she told him "I'm not going there again."

"But the macaroni is marvelous."

"The place is too common."

"Fancy places are common. They're filled with social climbers. We don't need the kind of cheap publicity a restaurant provides."

"I haven't had a good meal all week. If you want to talk to me tonight you'll have to talk to me at '21.' I've already booked a table in your name."

Once they were seated, Jed said, "No more of these drawing-room comedies for you." He talked to her of range, of stretching her talents.

"I wish I were as confident of my ability as you are. Some of these plays you talk about sound as if they were for college professors."

"You're wasting yourself on cheap plays," he whispered, gazing at her with intensity. "Like this Maugham, for instance. You're like a little girl dressed up in her mother's clothes. The play is too old-fashioned for you."

There was some truth in that, she felt, but she couldn't have made that many mistakes and become the star she was. Why wasn't he impressed by her? She looked at the brash, conceited, impudent, not very nice (she'd heard) but fascinating young man across the table. What was he saying? What did he want?

He wanted to do classics on Broadway. He'd originally planned a repertory company that would be housed in his own theater on Central Park South. That idea had been thwarted when his crucial actor, the great Holbrook Blinn, was killed in an automobile accident and William Randolph Hearst withdrew the backing. Otto Kahn had offered alternate financing, asking whether Jed would do the works of Strindberg. "I asked for your money, not your advice," Harris snapped, and that was the end of Kahn. Jed was mad about the works of Strindberg.

He had now devised an alternate plan. He would present the classics as commercial ventures, casting them with star actors for box office appeal. He wanted to do von Kleist's *The Prince of Homburg*, Schnitzler's *Professor Bernhardi*, Gerhart Hauptmann's *Hannele*, Pinero's *The Magistrate*, Feydeau's *A Flea in Her Ear*; plays by Molière, Ibsen, Chekhov. And Strindberg's *The Dance of Death*.

The best he could get Ina to agree to was *The Gaoler's Wench*, a new play by a minor literary name of the time, Edwin Justus Mayer. Although the strain of simultaneously preparing *Coquette* and *The Royal Family* was still fresh, he was going to try another combination. Jed had once told Behrman his plays were thin and would never be done. Now he decided that *Serena Blandish* was not so thin; would in fact make a splendid vehicle for Ruth Gordon. This, then, was the plan: Jed would direct Ina's play, trying it out in Brooklyn and Newark while David Burton staged *Serena Blandish* for a Philadelphia shakedown. The shows would come to Broadway one after the other, at the end of January—if Sam and Jed could get Enid Bagnold's approval of the script.

Sam had never met her. He had only recently learned that she was the author of the original novel, the pseudonymous "Lady of Quality." He asked Noël Coward whether he knew Miss Bagnold.

"Indeed I do. Enchanting creature. You will fall in love with her. She unfortunately at the moment is in love with Jed. He read your play aloud to her. He's a very good actor and the reading did the trick. She's on the hook."

"Well it's not surprising. Jed has great charm when he wants to exert it."

"No. Not a bit surprising. But mark my words, it'll be the usual process: first the high temperatures, then the rash."   — S. N. Behrman, *People in a Diary*

The Harris office, as usual, was thick with hopefuls, people without appointments, most of them without specific projects in mind. It seemed to Jean Barkow that Jed pushed through the urgent bodies as if at some stockyard, scowling toward the safety of his office and pulling her along with him. He pressed his door shut against the herd.

"There's a fellow out there who says he's an old college pal."

Dave Bunim was buttoned up in a business suit and a starched collar. Summoned at last, he congratulated Jed, still calling him "Jake." He talked about the hit shows and the old days at Yale. He was sure Jake could, if he wanted, pick up an honorary bachelor's degree. Harris kept smoking with his fingers outspread and later Bunim remembered thinking that Horowitz smoked that way to cover his homely face.

Dave got down to business.

"All these successes must have money blowing in over the transom."

Jed said nothing. Bunim was working for Peck and Company, a Wall Street stock brokerage firm.

"Why kid ourselves," he laughed, stepping behind the desk to clap Jed on the back. "You're a famous fellow. It would be a feather in my cap to bring in a client like you. Remember when we used to help each other out? This wouldn't cost you anything. You say Morgan Guaranty handles your finances. You must be the only man in America who doesn't have his own broker."

Jed remained expressionless. He picked up a script and began to read it.

"We'd give you solid, conservative advice but of course you could instruct us to buy whatever you wanted. If you have a man over at Morgan who's buying for you, he could do it through us. The commission is the same no matter which broker they buy through."

Jed kept reading.

"What do you say?"

Harris read several pages before looking up and smiling. "Oh," he said, "I can't pay much attention to such things." He turned back to his reading and then added, "You were always such a hanger-on."

He said no more. Enraged, Bunim had no choice but to leave.

Jed called Jean on the intercom.

"I want you to buy me a thousand dollars' worth of Banavium Copper."

She pleaded with him not to get heavily involved in the stock market but he ordered her to set forty thousand dollars aside for investment and told her to buy a ticker tape machine. Minutes later he called back and told her to make it a quarter of a million dollars. "And find us a reliable stockbroker."

The man's name was encouraging, Harry Content, and he had a swaggering approach that appealed to Harris's sense of showmanship.

"At tomorrow's market opening," Content said, "I want to buy you five thousand shares of English G.E. I will sell your shares before three in the afternoon. If you have not made a considerable profit, take your account elsewhere. If you have taken a loss, of course I will absorb it."

Jed made twenty-five thousand dollars on the transaction.

◆

The Gaoler's Wench was named for a Salomé of the lower depths, a jailkeeper's daughter who slept with the guards at London's Newgate Prison. Ina Claire had built a career playing sleekly coiffed, fashionably dressed women in sleek and fashionable drawing-room comedies. This role was a novelty for her.

As Jed had predicted, the change was invigorating for Ina, but, as he ought to have known, it was not invigorating for her audiences. Theatergoers like to see their stars as they always have. It is a hedge against their own aging. Their disappointment seeing Ina Claire in rags made a poor play seem worse. Jed lost interest in both Ina and the production after it opened to desultory notices.

When it moved to Newark for the final week, the Shuberts suggested to Ina that they might take over the show and bring it to Broadway themselves.

She worked on it with the company, trimming the three-hour play by a half-hour.

"All my friends would come backstage," Miss Claire recalled, "and they'd say, 'What's this we hear about not bringing it in? Darling, it's wonderful.' And I'd say, 'But what can we do? It belongs to Jed and he hasn't come near us.'"

On the Thursday matinee, he did. He was evidently curious to see what had interested the Shuberts. At the second intermission he went backstage and, knowing that Ina's entrance came ten minutes into the third act, he waited for the curtain to rise before tapping on her dressing room door. Before she responded, he pushed it open. She glared at his reflection in the mirror over her dressing table.

"How *dare* you enter my dressing room without permission?"

"The play isn't any better now than it was in Brooklyn."

This insult was unimportant now. The breach of etiquette so infuriated her that she rose and pushed him. Surprised, he retreated and stumbled over the doorsill, falling down on one knee while clutching the doorknob. Stagehands were just outside. The contretemps seemed to be all over New York before Harris pulled himself upright. Everyone in town giggled over the beautiful actress who had—kicked, it was now—the notorious producer with whom she'd surely been having an affair.

She suspected that Jed had somehow torpedoed the Shubert interest in her play. The frustrated cast took Christmas consolation in congratulating her on the fisticuffs. "By God," one of the actors said to her, "you're the heroine! You knocked that son of a bitch down!" And indeed, to the theater world, striking Jed Harris seemed the height of daring.

Playwright Marc Connelly, otherwise a gentleman, couldn't resist needling Ina about the incident. "I hear you had quite a night with Jed."

She slapped him, knocking the glasses off his nose, and then reached across the restaurant table and raked her nails down the back of his neck. Connelly had a lifetime scar to show for his twitting of Ina Claire.

◆

The flop of *The Gaoler's Wench* didn't mar Jed's reputation any more than had *Weak Sisters* or *Spread Eagle*. Perhaps there was an urge at the time to believe in infallibility. Behrman wrote, "At that time Jed was considered a kind of magician who couldn't produce a failure."

Preparations for *Serena Blandish* were intense, revisions with Sam a daily affair over three meals a day. There was a resumption of the middle-of-the-night telephone calls. The play and Jed Harris became Sam's entire life. As Anita said, "Even when Jed was just working with playwrights on scripts, it would make the writer's wife or family and friends crazy because they'd have no time or thought or feeling for anyone else or anything but this relationship. And of these people—gosh, scores of them—Sam was the tightest caught."

Serena finally went into rehearsal, and in January, 1929, we all embarked for Philadelphia where we were to open at the Broad Street Theatre. I don't think that ever again has the offstage scenario been so intense, so complicated and so unsolvable as in this production. It was a never-ending vortex of misunderstandings which engendered lifelong enmities.   — S. N. Behrman, *People in a Diary*

The offstage scenario that Behrman was referring to included Harris romances—more comic opera—with not one but two actresses in the company: Ruth Gordon and Constance Collier, whom Behrman described as "the high priestess of stage deportment and speech." Jed had met the beautiful Miss Collier when she'd been playing second lead to Ina Claire in *Our Betters*.

The Philadelphia opening went well. The only negative notice came from the *Inquirer* and four out of five reviews wasn't bad. What was bad was that the *New York Times* had a policy of printing one out-of-town review of an incoming show and the source it used in Philadelphia was the *Inquirer*.

George Kaufman still worked as the *Times's* drama editor, and when Harris heard that New Yorkers would be reading a pan of *Serena Blandish* he telephoned George. Dick Maney tried to stop him, saying that Kaufman hadn't the power to alter *Times* policy; that there was an arrangement with the *Inquirer*. But Harris had already committed himself to the attempt. He whispered a greeting to Kaufman and then, with dire cordiality, asked George to kill the *Inquirer* review. Kaufman said he couldn't do that.

Those who saw Harris in rage claimed that his eyelids would lower and become hooded; his lips would slip into a thin and joyless smile; a controlled and focused malice would tighten his skin; and his face, they said, would go black.

By several accounts, what he said was vicious, not only to George but about Bea Kaufman as well. While there is no record of the exact words, they were doubtless similar to what Harris said about Kaufman elsewhere. "There's a smell of dried apples about him." "He and his wife Bea have been referred to as that fat Jewish whore and her withered cuckold of a husband." (In *A Dance on the High Wire* Harris rather deviously put these words into other people's mouths, attributing the "dried apples" remark, for instance, to Edna Ferber.)

Among those at hand and cringing when Harris spoke to Kaufman were

Maney ("This created a schism that was never bridged") and Behrman ("George understandably never forgave Jed"). Kaufman later said that when he died he wanted to be cremated and have his ashes thrown in Jed Harris's face.

Harris wrote, long afterward, "As I look back on that phone call it seems ludicrous to me that I could have been that concerned." Yet as if compulsively, he added, "I never knew a woman I'd give two cents for who was attracted to Kaufman. They were mangy, neurotic women. The only one who wasn't was Beatrice, and she wasn't in love with him."

Anita had warned Jed about making so many enemies. "It won't do you any good," she'd said. "It'll only hurt you." "I know," he replied, "but I can't help it."

These weren't the only travails in Philadelphia. Having had a taste of directing and having always believed he'd been making creative contributions, Harris couldn't sit still for David Burton's staging *Serena Blandish*. Harris unnerved the cast and the director with revisions and rehearsals between performances.

By the time we got to New York the mythology of grievance had proliferated in the company. Constance Collier said that Jed called her in her apartment just as she was leaving for the first performance at the Morosco Theatre to tell her she was playing the part all wrong and that she had no equipment for it in the first place. Whether Jed did or didn't, he had created an atmosphere in which Constance felt he might have said anything. L'affaire Collier took precedence over such trivial matters as whether the play had gotten over. . . .

When I went backstage to see Constance Collier the room was full of her friends, thick with an atmosphere of euphoria. Constance embraced me. "You realize, don't you, that you have a world success!" I didn't know about the world; what worried me was New York. I felt that at no point had the play seized the audience. I went home and to bed, depressed and unhappy.   — S. N. Behrman, *People in a Diary*

In an eerie column for the *New York World*, William Bolitho wrote that Harris's "character and destiny" were the real issues on that opening night, and not Behrman's play. Another columnist noted that "A wave of chill dislike for someone permeated the house." There must have been something of the sort in the air. That is the only explanation available for so well-written and well-received a play running out of audience in a matter of months.

It was just as well. Ruth was restating her fertility and this time she decided to have the child. She simply informed Harris of the decision. Moreover, she told him that she wanted her friends to know about it.

Publicity-sensitive, even in fear, he was appalled by the possibility of this becoming public knowledge. He kept telling Ruth that she looked pregnant. He closed *Serena Blandish* because of it, he said, though the truth was, business was bad. He even convinced her to leave the country and have the child among as many strangers as possible. Berlin, or someplace.

Why had she decided to allow this pregnancy to come to term? Harris said, "She willfully did it—it was part of being an actress and having a child by a famous director." It fed on one of his core fears: helplessness at the hands of women.

Having an illegitimate child was a daring business. One didn't have to be a religious fanatic to consider it scandalous and even in sophisticated theatrical circles, such a birth would have been sensational news in 1929.

Ruth went to Paris, not Berlin, to have the child and Jed concocted an elaborate scheme to get Mildred over there. He wanted her to keep Ruth company during the pregnancy because if he himself was there the news would be out. That wasn't all. He did not incline toward restricting himself to Ruth.

For reasons that are buried with him and probably never were clear (he seems to have been compulsively devious) he did not choose to tell Mildred that Ruth was pregnant. Instead, he devised a scheme to get her over there; sending the whole family to Europe, all three sisters and Mama. Meyer Horowitz said, "I wouldn't even spit on Europe" because of the virulent anti-Semitism, and so Jed was sending him to Palestine.

It was not a good time for Mildred to leave. Her marriage to Arthur Caplan—"Cappy"—had always been strained by her attachment to Jed. With her first front-page byline at the *Newark Ledger* she'd changed her name to Mildred Harris and she still called herself Mildred Harris. Now she pleaded, "I want my marriage to work out. Cappy can't get a passport and if I go to Europe without him, that'll be the clincher. Please, Jed. Don't make me go."

"I'm not making you go," he whispered on the telephone. "I'm asking you to help save my career and perhaps my life. If you can't do it and I've killed myself because of it, all right."

"Don't put it that way. What's so important about all of us going to Europe?"

"If you can't take my word for it when I say my life is in danger . . ."

"Okay, okay," she yelled, slamming the telephone down.

When Jed announced that he was quitting this time, he announced it publicly. The critic Percy Hammond bade him farewell in the *Herald Tribune*, that April of 1929. "Mr. Jed Harris," he wrote, "has discharged his troupe of assistant experts, shut the doors of his atelier and taken an abrupt departure from the scene of his successes . . . just when all of us were depending on him for much of our next season's happiness. . . . Mr. Harris should not be permitted to thus slink in privacy from the hippodrome he has glorified so satisfactorily."

But Harris was intent on slipping from the hippodrome, and Ruth's decision confirmed his intention. Not mentioning that, of course, he told an interviewer:

I'm quitting because the theater is the short pants of the arts. Some people outgrow them. It is like children playing in the nursery. I have put over a great hoax on the whole business. I came along in the theater knowing nothing about it and saw George Kaufman and George Abbott doing clever work and I got them to work for me. They made a lot of money and so did I. Anyway, it's all a hoax and I'm going away and have a long laugh over it.

THE BOY WITHOUT A LIMIT

RUTH GORDON was the first girl Jed ever brought home to meet his parents. His sisters had met her backstage at *Saturday's Children*. Her father, Clifton Jones, had been there too: *Captain* Jones, a sea captain. Her real name was Ruth Gordon Jones.

The Captain had enchanted Sylvia and Florie. They wished mightily that Jed would marry his daughter. Mildred had conflicting allegiances since Anita had become her friend.

Jed was not yet divorced, and so for the sake of appearance, Alexander Woollcott came along as Ruth's escort. The three celebrities arrived by taxi at 136 Spruce Street in Newark.

Women leaned from the windows, resting on their elbows. Husbands stood in the shadows, to watch but not be seen watching. The children were not ashamed of their curiosity. They gathered around the taxi cab and cheered as the stars emerged: Ruth Gordon, Alexander Woollcott, and Jacob Horowitz.

Mrs. Horowitz served roast goose and creamed soup and, as Mildred remembered, Woollcott sponged up the gravy with dainty bits of challah bread. "Jacob," Papa said, as if it were a complete sentence. "Jed," Mama Horowitz corrected. She patted the head of her famous son and smiled at the famous critic and actress. "He's the boy without a limit."

Now Ruth was halfway across the Atlantic to Paris to have his baby and he was terrified of its being found out. But why? He would not have been punished for fathering an illegitimate child. Ruth's career might have been damaged, not his. Of what was he terrified?

With Judith Anderson on tour, Connie Collier in London, and Ina Claire still testy over the *Gaoler's Wench* fracas, Jed stopped by to see Anita. She remembered holding her breath the whole time he was there.

"Don't you think you need a car?"

"It would be lovely to have a car."

"Well, then, what'll it be? I can afford anything, it doesn't make a difference."

"How about one of those LaSalle roadsters?"

"Whoa! That's pretty steep."

"You don't have to get me a car."

"That does it. A LaSalle is what you asked for, and a LaSalle is what it's going to be. . . . How are things?"

"I get by."

The next day he arrived in a two-tone green LaSalle roadster with a spare tire in the fender and the top down. A crowd collected on the narrow Greenwich Village street. A LaSalle was still a novelty, the Cadillac people hadn't yet manufactured many, and Anita beamed as Jed opened its door for her to slide behind the steering wheel. Once they were moving he promised to increase her weekly checks so that she could maintain the auto. Then he asked when the divorce papers could be filed. She stopped the car in the middle of the avenue and stared through the windshield until he got out.

◆

The office remained open until Harris completed all of the arrangements for maintaining his current productions. *Coquette*, *The Royal Family*, and *The Front Page* were still running in New York and there were *Broadway* companies all over the world. As he strolled into his office, Jean Barkow followed with the mail and messages. He shuffled through the pile, discarding all but two items. One was a memo from Harry Content, informing him that his three million dollars was now worth five "and going up." The other was a telephone message from Judith Anderson inviting him to midnight supper with Noël Coward.

Judith—"Meg"—lived at 128 Central Park South and the gown she wore to supper was royal purple. The table was set for three and candlelit. Coward didn't bother with the pretense of a table partner. His homosexuality was no secret. In public, the morality of this presumably reckless era required a certain discretion but he hardly had to pretend among friends. Jed had once engaged him on the subject.

"I've always been curious. What is it about women that so offends you homosexuals?"

"But my dear Jed, I just adore women. Gertie Lawrence is my dearest pal and of course there's Meg Anderson."

"Yes, you seem to enjoy their company, but why don't you like them in bed where you're supposed to?"

Coward laughed. "All that open plumbing absolutely revolts me. I can only imagine that being in bed with a woman would be like feeling the skin of a snake."

Now the three of them adjourned to the piano. Coward sang "If Love Were All" and they all did "World Weary." At Jed's request, Coward sang "A Room with a View" and they joined in.

A room with a view—and you,
With no one to worry us,
No one to hurry us—through
This dream we've found.

Jed and Meg didn't know all the words so Noël carried on alone and they stayed until sunrise, these three at the time of their lives, gathered with cigarettes around a white baby grand piano overlooking Central Park.

When Jed mentioned that he was closing the office and would be living in Europe for a while, Noël played "I'll See You Again." Jed and Meg's romance had involved impulsive trips from the start; jittery flights and amorous train rides. She said summer was a wonderful time to be in Paris.

◈

Harris was so secretive about Ruth's pregnancy that he not only sent her ahead, alone; he insisted that she stay in her ship cabin all the way across. He was sensitive to details, at least. He arranged for a chauffeur and limousine to meet her at Cherbourg and then drive her to Le Havre, where he would meet her.

The car was a blue Lincoln and its driver's name was Victor. Her baggage was to be sent on to the Hotel George V in Paris. Victor was to drive Ruth to the Hotel Frascati on the Cherbourg waterfront.

There she waited alone, with the letters of introduction to a Paris obstetrician.

A few days behind, Jed walked the decks of the Ile de France. A nineteen-year-old Smith College sophomore detached herself from her mother. She was determined to have a shipboard romance, had scanned the passenger list and chosen Jed Harris.

She introduced herself and he promptly began talking politics. He said he meant to become a British citizen and then get elected to the House of Commons. The Smith girl said a Jew would never be elected in England, but Jed thought he could be another Disraeli. That was what he said to her, adding that he seldom met Jewish girls. She should be proud of her Jewishness, he said. "There have always been bad times for Jews and worse times are coming," he said in bed in his cabin.

The Smith girl was going to take the boat train to London. He would be going to Paris first and then take a place in London for the year, making regular trips to the Continent. They made a date to meet at the Grosvenor bar. He'd be awhile in London, he said, showing his sisters the city. Then she would come to Paris with him; she could surely arrange it; she needn't worry about expenses.

She would stay at the Hotel Raphael, he would be at the Chambord, Judith Anderson would be put up at the Crillon, his mother and Mildred at the D'Iena, and unless Ruth had found an apartment by then, she would be at the George V.

As the Ile de France tied up in Le Havre, Jed and the Smith girl said not good-bye but *au revoir*. The girl did not know that Ruth was on the deck, gazing up at them. She only knew that she was being embraced by the brainy and glamorous Jed Harris. But Ruth caught his eye. He gestured for her to leave the deck. In a solitary rage, she returned to the limousine.

When he finally got around to Ruth, he acted as if nothing had happened. He offered no explanation, made no concession to her feelings. He told her to find an apartment in Paris and she certainly did: twelve expensive rooms in one of the city's most elegant sections, at 67 Boulevard Lannes, overlooking the Bois. She was alone, that June of 1929, and would be alone in the apartment until she came to term. Yet she took this huge and magnificently decorated place.

Well, why not?

Jed had hired a second limousine and chauffeur to drive his mother and Mildred through the Polish countryside in search of relatives; a long, shiny black Cadillac rolling through the *shtetls* of Eastern Europe. Meantime, Florie and Sylvia were in London with him. He took them to the Ivy Restaurant, very big with celebrities at the time, and Jed was a very big celebrity. Augustus John came up to say hello and Charles Laughton sat down to chat. It all seemed perfectly natural to Jed, as Florie recalled. Just cozy and everyday.

He took his sisters to the parties and the plays, he introduced them to everyone. In Poland, the peasants stood in the mud, staring in at Mildred and Mrs. Horowitz, surrounding the Cadillac limousine like children on Spruce Street in Newark.

The driver returned the big car to Vienna. From there, Mildred and her mother took the train to Paris. They waited in the hotel room. Mama was afraid to go outside or be left alone and so they ate in the room. On the third day there was a tap at the door. Mildred forgot the wait and hugged Jed while Mrs. Horowitz, never demonstrative, watched.

As Mildred recalled many years later, it was while she helped Jed unwrap the presents that he told her Ruth was in Paris too.

"What a wonderful coincidence! Why don't we all go out for dinner?"

"Maybe not tonight, but she did ask me to invite you for tea this afternoon."

"That will finally get Mama out of this damned hotel room, thank God. It's a lovely thing for the two of us to do."

"Mama isn't invited. Just you."

◆

Ruth's maid opened the great wooden doors and Mildred stared in. The place was glorious, lighted by the sun and glowing with flowers. Then Ruth and her belly appeared and Mildred forgot about the apartment and the sun and the flowers.

"When I was able to think I thought of my darling brother who had given me no warning at all. Why I didn't go into shock and fall down dead I'll never know."

Strolling into the sitting room, they talked about the apartment and the building and how different it was from living in New York. Sitting down, they talked about French food and French fashion and what you could buy at a French grocery.

"So," Mildred said. "When are you due?"

Ruth lowered her eyes, then looked up and smiled.

"October."

Opal birthstone, Mildred thought. What a stupid thing to think of. What's wrong with me?

When she got back to the hotel she flopped onto the bed and wept.

"Darling, was Ruth mean to you?"

"No, no, no, Mama."

"Then what, what is the matter? Is she pregnant?"

Mildred's silence was answer enough.

"Your father will kill himself."

"That does it!" Mildred exploded. ("The tears froze on my face.") "There's a baby coming into the world—our baby—and Papa is going to kill himself. All you're thinking about is yourself. If that isn't typical of this family. Well goddamnit, if Papa is going to kill himself, tell him to go right ahead. This baby is coming. It doesn't have a mother. It doesn't have a father. It doesn't have a country. It doesn't know where the hell it's at, this baby, and it's *our* baby."

"You're perfectly right, darling. We'll go buy it a present."

They went to Fairyland, the expensive children's shop on the Faubourg St.-Honoré, and bought a pink sweater set for the infant who was going to have Ruth's last name for a first name. For Jed would always have a flair for original names and this time he had come up with the notion of using Ruth's family name for the child's Christian name. It would be "Jones," then. They were certain it would be a girl.

◆

The situation smacked of sophisticated comedy, but the actors were slamming doors as if they were in a farce. Judith Anderson checked into the Hotel Crillon in a fury. Jed hadn't met her boat. "I had half a mind to join Grace on the train to Antibes," she remembered years later. She'd sailed over with her friend Grace Moore, the opera star.

The telephone rang. "Meet me at the bar downstairs," he whispered and hung up.

These singular women somehow believed such treatment. Jed could, when he chose, stay at the apartment with Ruth. Other times, such as this, he would leave her to wonder who was sharing his bed at the Chambord. It wouldn't be Judith Anderson tonight. He sat down at the bar, told her about Ruth's pregnancy, and, unamused, Meg left on the midnight train for Antibes.

◆

He sat down to lunch with Mildred and Ruth at the Boulevard Lannes apartment and suggested an abortion. Ruth was in her eighth month. The women just stared at him.

"For the record," Mildred said, "because I know it's too late to do a damned thing about it, why are you having this baby in the first place?"

"My gynecologist told me I had to," Ruth replied. "Because of all the abortions. If I didn't have this baby I might never have any."

"Save it for Belasco," Jed said.

Mildred herself thought it was a bit much, that explanation. It seemed to her that Ruth was simply crazy about Jed and eager to have his child.

"Now let me ask *you* something," Ruth said to Mildred. "Do you think that having a child out of wedlock is immoral?"

"There's no such thing as an immoral or illegitimate baby," Mildred replied. "I'm not so crazy about bringing a child into this world without a full set of parents, but there's somebody else involved: this kid, who hasn't done anyone any harm, a kid with two of the brainiest, most talented parents in the world, and you're both acting like a couple of jerks. So why don't you get married even if it's for only a week, just to give this kid a name and then get your divorce so you can give other people headaches. Why lavish all this stupidity on each other?"

"Because I told you, Anita won't give me a divorce."

"Let me take care of that."

"What does that mean?"

"It means, my darling brother, who never is able to see me except when he needs my help so desperately he's going to kill himself, it means that suppose I can convince Anita to give you a divorce?"

Jed jumped from the sofa and shook Mildred violently.

"How? What do you know?"

Ruth cried out for him to stop.

"Never mind how. Would the two of you agree to get married for the sake of this innocent baby?"

Jed and Ruth looked at each other.

"Well come on," Mildred said impatiently. "If you take much more time to make up your minds the kid is going to join the discussion."

"Okay," Jed said.

"Okay," Ruth said.

◆

Mildred sailed on the *Bremen*'s maiden westbound crossing and was miserable the whole trip. Anita had confessed to a lover taken in despair and revenge. She believed that Jed would have left her in any case, but being rejected for Ruth had given the desertion a crunch.

By the time the *Bremen* docked, Mildred was resigned to betraying her friend. It was, she told herself, for the child's sake. But which child, Jones or Jed? She took a taxi to Newark where she was supposed to meet her husband Cappy at the Horowitz apartment. She hadn't even thought, these past weeks, about her own troubled marriage.

The questions began as she came through the door. Is Ruth healthy? Is Jed taking care of her? The questions kept coming, veiled so that Cappy wouldn't know family business. He still hadn't spoken privately with his wife when the phone rang with a cable from Paris.

Hanging up, Mildred muttered, "Only Jed would do this. He wants me to come back right away on the *Bremen*. I'll set a record. Maiden voyage both ways."

She urged her husband to come along, but, he said, everyone didn't have a job like hers. The Harris connection had made Mildred a privileged reporter for the *New York World*. Besides, Cappy had never gotten his American papers. He would need a "League of Nations" passport, which would take time.

"I've got to see his lawyer and then go. Will you get your goddamn passport?"

The attorney accepted Mildred's information with glee. The law winked at a man's philandering, but a wife's adultery—even after abandonment—was grounds for divorce. Mildred left the law office weary of the whole business.

In Paris, Jed was on the telephone to Meg, begging her in his best whisper to come back from Antibes.

"Do you remember that plane ride?"

"I remember that Ruth is pregnant."

"But who is the father?"

"What a terrible thing to say."

"And our train ride? Our roomette with a view?"

He began to croon: "A room with a view—and you . . ."

"All right, I'll come, if you'll only stop singing. But I'm bringing Grace with me." She hung up and turned to Grace Moore. "I'm not in love with him. Just fascinated."

Following the doctor's advice, Ruth walked two miles a day while Jed took Meg for long auto rides through the chateau country. They'd find a meadow to lay out the blanket and the wicker hamper and uncork the wine.

◆

The telephone rang as Mildred was unpacking in the same Hotel d'Iena room she'd had before. It was the whisper she knew so well.

"Meet me downstairs in fifteen minutes. Don't unpack."

"Are you crazy? I just got off the boat. I'm exhausted. Give me an hour."

Victor came around with the blue Lincoln.

◆

Ruth had given Mildred a silver cigarette case as a token of need, a plea for support. Now she was asking Jed's sister to move in and keep her company. They would seldom go out. "Her chef was superb," Mildred recalled, somewhat sardonically. And in London, Jed moved into a house in Cheyne Walk. He returned to Paris for occasional visits.

"If it's a girl, I don't care."

He stared out the drawing room window overlooking the Bois.

"I'll support her of course, but you can keep her. I'll sign papers to guarantee that. I won't abandon you."

111

"Great guy," Ruth said to Mildred. "Isn't he a great guy?"

"But if it's a boy I want custody. I've got plans. I've got great plans. I want to take him across the continent, show him everything."

"It's a goddamned infant, not even born yet," Mildred said.

"You see that Lincoln downstairs? It's nothing. What I'm going to get is an Isotta Fraschini. It's so elegant that it makes a Rolls-Royce look like a pushcart. I'm going to have that Isotta fitted out with a crib in the back instead of a seat so that I can have Jones with me wherever I go. We're going to take years. We'll live in England and he's going to have a continental education. Maybe I'll run for Parliament."

"Pardon me for even asking," Mildred said, "but would somebody mind telling me what happened to the marriage I just traveled ten thousand miles to arrange?"

"Relax, kid," Ruth said with a grin, "and help me up, will ya? Got something to show Jed."

She came back with Jones's christening dress.

"Look, I even made the buttonholes, it's going to be a *girl*."

Mildred tried to cut the tension with a joke.

"No good, Ruth. Zukor won't okay the buttonholes."

Jed roared. Adolph Zukor, the head of Paramount Pictures, had come from New York's garment industry. Zukor had been in buttons.

"That was a joke, Ruth," Jed said. "Why didn't you laugh? A sense of humor is one of the most reliable measures of intelligence. That's why you seldom run into amusing actresses."

"Why don't you go jump in your Isotta Fraschini?"

"You lovebirds will have to excuse me."

Mildred flopped onto her bed and didn't wake until morning. They were still arguing and they argued that whole day into the evening.

"I won't give it to you. Boy or girl, I'm keeping it."

"If you do that," Jed said, "if you do that, if you take my son from me . . . if it's a boy and not a girl and you don't let me keep him . . . then I don't want to see him at all. I'm never going to see him. Not in the hospital and not afterward. Not as long as I live."

❖

Before dawn on October 16, 1929, Ruth shook Mildred awake. They'd been sleeping in the same bed for the week since Jed had last been heard from.

"This is it. Push me up. I can't get up by myself. Give me a push, will ya? And don't call Jed."

They found a taxi in the dark on Boulevard Flandrin and twenty-five-year-old Mildred Harris played grandmother. In the hospital room, the damp and tiny actress was swallowed up by the bedsheets, her eyes beady with fright.

"Ow!"

"How is it?"

"It stinks. It's terrible."

Mildred held her hand at bedside, the nails clawing with each contraction. Five hours later, the nurse, Andrée Valentin, brought the newborn infant into the room. Ruth was still unconscious, and so Mildred held the child. "Jones had Jed's sardonic look from the start," she remembered. At noon she telephoned her brother.

"You have a son. A beautiful son."

"I suppose you think I'm excited. These things are always treated with such sentimentality. Spare me. Just remind Ruth that I meant what I said: unless she agrees to let me adopt him, I don't plan on ever seeing him. Or even visiting her at the hospital. Tell her that."

And he hung up.

"No," Ruth told Mildred. "I won't give him up."

Jed called to find out how the little boy was doing but he didn't relent. After four days, Ruth cried, "I can't stand it anymore. I can't stand not seeing Jed. Tell him I give up. He can have the baby."

Mildred wished she could ask Cappy what to do. He'd finally gotten his passport and was on his way. Ah, let's face it, she told herself. This is a Horowitz family matter. Cappy didn't even know that Ruth was pregnant.

Mildred telephoned Jed with the news and it seemed to her that by the time she hung up, he was at the hospital, doting over mother and child. He fell on the bed, hugging and kissing Ruth until the nurses had to urge him off with warnings that he'd be barred from the room if he continued.

"Jones will never go to school."

"What do you mean?" Ruth asked, seeming as pleased with her man-child as with her child-man. "I don't want an idiot for a kid."

"He's going to have private tutors. I won't trust his education to common minds. Four tutors, one for French, one for Latin, one for English, and one for mathematics. Each will be selected from the most qualified candidates. What's more," he added, tenderly lifting Jones and nestling him, "he is going to live in the aristocratic tradition. Jonesy, my boy. You are going to travel the world for life. And," he added, "the milk deliveries are starting immediately."

"What milk?" Ruth was aghast. Actresses do not breast-feed.

"Not your milk, darling. I've arranged for four quarts of Walker Gordon milk to be flown over every day from America."

Ruth beamed.

"Is it going to be a big wedding at Vatican City or just something informal?"

"Look," Ruth said to Mildred. "If we got married now, even if he was divorced, which he isn't, who would we fool? Everyone would know he married me just for Jones's sake."

"Whose sake is better?"

"I'm not going to have people laughing behind my back," Ruth said.

◆

Jones had to stay at the hospital. He had been born with a strangulated hernia. In his first year he would have three operations: the hernia, a tonsillectomy and an appendectomy.

Ruth went back to the apartment on Boulevard Lannes. For Jones, Jed hired the nurse Andrée Valentin away from the hospital. Then he returned to the Chambord.

There were no longer scandalous reasons for Ruth to hide in the apartment, or for Jed to maintain a separate residence. Still, he was seldom home. One day she watched and waited outside his hotel. She saw Jed's limousine arrive. She saw Victor get out and open the rear door. She saw Judith Anderson emerge from the hotel and get in. Ruth hailed a taxi and went home. Judith never knew she'd been seen until she read it years later in Ruth's book, *My Side*.

A bitter Ruth told Mildred that she wouldn't give Jones up after all. The birth certificate read, "Jones Kelly."

11
NO ISOTTA FRASCHINI
FOR JONES

JED HARRIS was on a Mediterranean cruise ship in October 1929 when the New York stock market collapsed and took down all three million dollars that Harry Content had invested for him.

He was with Cappy. They had left Ruth and Mildred behind despite Mildred's hope that a Paris holiday might be good for her marriage. No sooner had her husband arrived than Jed whisked him off. It was as if he was always ready for a toot with one of the boys when there was a marriage to be undermined.

Now, he and Cappy joined the other men crowding around the door of the ship's radio operator. They were all desperate to reach their stockbrokers in time to sell before everything was lost, but it was too late.

The radio operator had told them that he could not get through to New York. Then, frightened by their hysteria, he locked himself into the little room. They kept pounding at the door.

However stunning the loss of his fortune must have been, Harris did not reel as so many others did. He came back to New York to find that he still had an income. There were two ongoing companies of *The Front Page*. Show business was one of the few businesses that were to carry through the Depression.

But he couldn't support his father anymore. He had promised that Meyer would never have to work again and had convinced his father to give up on Waterbury and buttons. Meyer took his famous son's advice, sold the business, moved back to Newark, and entrusted all of his savings to Harry Content. Now he had to go back to work. He became a salesman at Kelly's Paper Company in Newark. He sold toilet paper.

"When I closed the office last spring," Jed told an interviewer, "I was sure that I had finished with the show business forever. I'd never regarded the theater as a profession, or even a business, but as an adventure. And the end of an adventure is like a love affair that is over; it may be resumed but it cannot really be revived."

Now he was back in the business, with a new office above the Morosco Theatre on West 45th Street. Ruth was still in Paris and Jed was living at the Madison Hotel on East 59th Street. It was at the Madison that Moss Hart had his first encounter with Harris, a story Hart relates with pained humor in his autobiographical *Act One*.

An as yet unproduced playwright, Hart had been running the YMCA community theater in Newark. It was a semiprofessional company, one of the "little theaters" that flourished at the time.

A member of this theater, Dore Schary, knew Jed's sister Sylvia and suggested that through her, Hart could get his new comedy to the awesome Jed Harris. He could and did.

After reading the play, Harris sent a wire to Hart at the Brooklyn home of his parents. The stagestruck twenty-five-year-old was instructed to be at the Madison Hotel at two o'clock that afternoon.

Hart was beside himself with excitement as he subwayed under the East River to meet the fabled producer, but after waiting in the hotel lobby until almost five o'clock he was told by the desk clerk to return the following day at noon.

That time he was kept waiting for four hours. "Mr. Harris," he was finally told, "wants to see you at ten o'clock tomorrow morning."

Hart steamed back at the appointed hour but "while the clerk went about his usual ritual of muttering into the telephone, I composed in my mind the short note I intended to leave in Mr. Harris's box when the usual message came through."

Instead, the clerk told him, "Mr. Harris says to come right up."

The door to the suite was ajar. Hart pressed the buzzer. Harris could be heard from deep within. "Come in." Hart did. He padded anxiously through the darkened living room and into the bedroom. He was summoned still further, into the bathroom. There young Hart "stopped dead." Jed Harris was standing at the washbasin, in front of the mirror. He was stark naked.

"Good morning," he said, as if they were at tea. "I'm sorry I couldn't see you until now."

Although New York's smart set had delighted in George Kaufman's "Your fly is open" story, Moss Hart was not yet a member of New York's smart set and a naked producer was news to him. "I was suffused with embarrassment," he wrote in *Act One*. "I did not know where to look or what to say."

Chatting as if there were nothing out of the ordinary, Harris said that he had read and enjoyed Hart's play. Its author was not quite able to listen, he was so dumbfounded and embarrassed. Only when Harris began dressing did Hart regain his senses and begin to focus on the spoken words.

"Jed Harris," he then realized, "is one of the finest conversationalists on the subject of the theater that I have ever listened to." Harris dissected *Once in a Lifetime*, appreciatively and critically; he talked about his forthcoming production of *Uncle Vanya;* about Broadway producers and playwrights. He so excited Hart with this "dazzling cascade of eagle-winged and mercurial words" that the young man never stopped to wonder whether it meant that Harris was going to produce his play.

They left the room as the lecture continued in the elevator, through the lobby, and into a taxi. By the time Harris leaped from the cab in front of his Morosco Theatre office, Hart was stuck with both the uncertainty about his play and the fare.

His agent felt compelled to remind him that "Jed Harris was given to expressing a deep interest in plays he had no intention of doing and took an active pleasure in torturing writers with the promise and lure of a Jed Harris production without ever actually committing himself, thereby keeping the play off the market and out of the hands of other managers." Perhaps, but likelier, Harris simply enjoyed the game of malevolence.

The agent submitted the play to another fine producer, Sam Harris, but Hart persisted in the dream of being produced by The Meteor. "I had no thought," he wrote in *Act One*, "of passing up the possibility of a Jed Harris production if Jed Harris decided to lure me, false promises or no." For "I do not think it too great a stretch of either logic or imagination to say that every aspiring playwright's prayer in those days probably went exactly along the same lines, to wit: 'Please, god, let Jed Harris do my play!'"

Sam Harris immediately agreed to produce *Once in a Lifetime*, but only on the condition that the author rewrite it in collaboration with George Kaufman. Having heard nothing from Jed, Hart agreed to that. He called Jed to advise him of the decision as a courtesy. He mentioned Sam Harris's suggestion that Kaufman collaborate on a revision. He could have had no idea of the icebound hostilities that existed between the two men.

"I think you're doing the right thing," Jed said about the collaboration. "Do you know George Kaufman? Ever met him?"

"No," I replied. "Has he read the play yet, do you know?" he inquired. "He may be reading it today," I answered. "Listen," the voice cut in. "This is George Kaufman's home telephone number. Put it down. You call him right away and tell him that Jed Harris says this is just the kind of play he ought to do. Good-bye."

Moss Hart could not reasonably have been expected to know the ways of Jed Harris's deviousness, or the lengths to which the man would go to set up a situation of humiliation, pain, and even harm. Hart innocently dialed the telephone number and asked to speak to Kaufman.

"This is he."

"My name is Moss Hart. You don't know me but Sam Harris is sending you a play of mine."

"I received it this morning. I am reading it tonight."

"Well," Hart said. "Jed Harris has read the play and he asked me to give you a message. He said to tell you that this was just the kind of play you ought to do."

Even as I spoke the words I was dimly conscious of their peculiar ring. . . . The voice of George Kaufman was glacial when it again sounded over the telephone. Each word seemed to be encrusted with icicles. "I would not be interested in anything that Jed Harris was interested in," he said and hung up. If Jed Harris intended to punish me for withdrawing the play, he had deftly accomplished his purpose in the most stinging and hurtful way. [It was an] ill-natured and wayward bit of wickedness.

Harris had mentioned, to Hart, an impending production of *Uncle Vanya*. It was a plan of casual significance. Jed Harris may have stunned the theatrical world with a series of commercial successes; he may have established the Broadway theater's character and that may have been an accomplishment of historic note. But however much one can argue the merits of *The Front Page* or *The Royal Family*, neither they nor any of the plays that he had produced were great works. They may have been defining works of the American commercial stage but they were entertainments, not high theater.

Moreover, he had merely produced them. The extent of his experience as a director was considerably less: he had taken over *Coquette* from George Abbott. He had staged *The Gaoler's Wench* for a Brooklyn tryout. His background as a director ended there.

What, then, gave him the *chutzpah* to make his Broadway debut as a director with a play by no less than Anton Chekhov?

Chekhov's plays are among the most demanding in the dramatic literature.

118

The Russian master is perhaps second only to Shakespeare in the orchestration of character drama. He does not write of heroes and villains, of juveniles and ingenues. His characters are psychologically complex; they exist in relation to each other.

Chekhov's greatness lies in his presentation of human ambiguity, confusion and aimlessness, in contrast with Harris's beloved melodrama and machine-gun tempo and farcical activity. Harris learned plot propulsion from George Abbott and George S. Kaufman. It is direct activity and always causal. For Chekhov, plot is not action but the scheme of life, leisurely and random.

It took *chutzpah*, to say the least, for Jed Harris, a Broadway showman, to make his directing debut with a play of Anton Chekhov's.

Jed's first choice had not even been *Uncle Vanya* but *The Cherry Orchard*, which is Chekhov's most subtle and delicately orchestrated work, his towering achievement. There is probably no other drama in the Western stage literature that so dares to challenge Shakespeare at the limits of artistry.

Harris wanted no one but Laurette Taylor to play Madame Ranevskaya in *The Cherry Orchard*. Miss Taylor's gifts were unquestioned. Some still consider her the greatest actress the American stage ever produced. She was, however, a drinker. When the actress slipped into Jed's office she was tense, overly made up, and too talkative. She clutched her fur collar to her chin, smiled nervously and placed a manuscript on his desk. She wasn't there to discuss *The Cherry Orchard*. She didn't know that Harris was contemplating a production of it or that for him this was an audition. She had come to discuss a play she'd written. She discussed it by reciting monologues from the script. That made up Harris's mind. He announced that he had come back from London and was emerging from retirement to do *Uncle Vanya*.

Just as with *Coquette* and Helen Hayes, once he decided on the right actor for a part, he could not settle for anyone else. He would not do *The Cherry Orchard* because Laurette Taylor, he'd apparently concluded, was beyond salvation. (He was wrong. Her greatest triumph would come years later, as Amanda Wingfield in Tennessee Williams's *The Glass Menagerie*.)

Uncle Vanya, then, was second choice for him. As he wrote, "Although . . . the lesser comedies of Chekhov are all the works of a writer of genius, it is a steep dive from the grandeur of *The Cherry Orchard* to the provincial lassitudes of *Uncle Vanya*."

He was talking as if he knew what he was talking about.

"Wherever you come to roost on these plays," he continued, "you are still on very high ground in the theater."

He commissioned a new translation from Ben Hecht's wife, Rose Caylor.

She was not a professional. It hardly boded well for the forthcoming production of *Uncle Vanya*.

◆

In Paris, Jones's hernia operation was successful. Andrée Valentin stayed with the infant during the convalescence while Ruth, Cappy, and Mildred took the boat train from Paris to Cherbourg and then Cunard's *Carmania* across. The return route was elaborately contrived to evade reporters.

Ruth found a splendid apartment in New York. She always found splendid apartments. This one was at 36 West 59th Street overlooking Central Park. Although they were now more or less together, Jed kept his place at the Madison Hotel. That bothered Ruth, and she said so, but he had the upper hand.

Strolling through Shubert Alley one day, she ran into Lillian Gish and George Jean Nathan. The actress and the critic were secretly engaged. There was no reason for the secrecy other than Miss Gish's feverish modesty.

She hadn't seen Ruth Gordon in a year. Of course nobody had. The two actresses scurried to each other, the sparrow and the hummingbird, and pecked one another's cheek. Ruth said she'd been in Paris, drinking wine, and had tasted "some stuff called Clos Vougeot and it was sen-*sa*-tional."

Nathan knew the wine. He said it was a superlative Burgundy but hard to find. "I've got a great idea," Ruth said. "I know a guy who it's his favorite wine too. He's dying to meet you, Lillian, so I tell you what. The first one that finds a bottle of Clos Vougeot, let's all have dinner together."

Ruth was a woman of many combinations, none of them foolish. She knew that it wouldn't hurt Jed to befriend a critic, but Lillian was even more important. Chekhov on Broadway needed a box office attraction and Lillian Gish was one of D. W. Griffith's most glittering movie stars.

Ruth found the bottle of wine first because she already had it. One evening not long after, they all met at her apartment. Nathan and Harris talked drama while the actresses listened respectfully, which probably was not an easy thing for Ruth Gordon to do.

"Until then," Miss Gish remembered, "I had thought George knew more about the theater than anyone I'd ever met. You'd go to a play and there was a certain scene that you liked; he could tell you five or six other plays where they had the same idea and then say how they played that scene.

"Jed was beyond that. I never heard anyone talk about the theater with the intelligence and the excitement and the interest that that man had. When I got up to get my coat to leave I said to Ruth, 'I'd work for that man for nothing if he ever had anything for me.'"

Three weeks later she received the script of *Uncle Vanya*. She probably would have gotten it even faster but Harris had to rethink the play. The role he wanted Lillian to play, a heartless flirt, was hardly one with which she would have been immediately associated. "Elena," he later wrote, "seemed to me a rather old-fashioned portrait of a 'teaser.' I decided to modify, to suggest a beautiful and desirable woman, chilled beyond hope of recovery by marriage to a withered windbag of a professor."

It was a novel interpretation, even a radical one. In most productions of *Uncle Vanya* Elena is still played as a man-eater. Gish agreed to do it immediately. She wouldn't discuss salary and there was no sense in it anyhow. Jed could hardly give her the ten thousand dollars a week she was paid by Griffith. Anything, she said, would do.

He cast the other major roles with actors he'd worked with before. Walter Connolly, his old pal from the *Applesauce* days, "would make a perfect Vanya. And [Osgood] Perkins, even without the romantic beauty and distinguished style of Stanislavsky who created the part, might make an interesting thing of Dr. Astrov."

Did he know what he was talking about?

Lillian was going to be a challenge. Her last theatrical experience had been as an adolescent, seventeen years earlier. Her voice had never been a powerful instrument. George was of no help, in fact he was antagonistic to the project. He told Lillian a bit of period stage nonsense—that it was essential for a star to have the last speech in a play. The last speech in *Uncle Vanya* was not Elena's but Sonya's. If she did the play, he warned, she might never have another job in the theater or even in the movies.

Miss Gish knew why her fiancé was so negative. Jed was planning to open *Uncle Vanya* in April, and she had promised to go to Europe with George in June. And, Nathan was an insecure man, jealous of Jed's magnetism, jealous even of Lillian's concern for her ailing mother.

Acceding to these pressures but embarrassed to tell Harris the truth, Lillian said only that she would have to leave the production after six weeks in order to take her mother to a spa in Germany. He calculated the time it would take to recover the production cost and, presuming that Lillian would be a sell-out attraction, agreed to her limited engagement.

Harris wrote:

. . . she came to rehearsal in a palpable state of fright. As she had not been on the stage since early childhood, this was not altogether unnatural. "All these people in the company are so wonderful," she said mournfully after the first session. "I really don't think I'm good enough to be on the same stage with them." I laughed. "They're not that wonderful," I said. And I told her that Helen Hayes was so nervous during the first week she rehearsed *Coquette* that she broke out in a painful rash. "And Helen,"

121

I added, "hasn't been off the stage since she learned to walk." If this was meant to reassure Miss Gish, it failed utterly. Her eyes clouded over with compassion, she murmured, "Oh that poor, poor girl."

Miss Gish recalled an early rehearsal at which Harris rose from his aisle seat and strolled to the stage. "Lillian," he said, so quietly that she had to lean over the footlights to hear him. "Just do this as if you were in a movie. Don't worry about projection. Don't worry about the size of performance. My only advice is: the woman you're playing is the pivotal figure in the play. If they believe her, everything else will be believed. And remember, she isn't merely a woman. You're playing every man's idea of a woman. Try and keep that in the back of your mind but don't worry about it. You're going to be wonderful."

As rehearsal proceeded, some were less than convinced of that. Harris let his assistant, Worthington Miner, assume more responsibilities. Some days, he didn't arrive until late in the afternoon. Osgood Perkins suspected that Jed might be having trouble with his hearing, but nobody paid much attention to that.

When the play opened at the Cort Theatre on April 15, 1930, it was triumphant. The reviews were gaudy. Jed recovered his nine-thousand-dollar investment in six weeks—almost to the day Gish left the company—and the production ran another three weeks on momentum, giving him a small profit on the risky presentation of a classic on Broadway.

These were fine rewards, but none to compare with the observations that critic Stark Young made about the production in *The New Republic*.

Stark Young was the most intellectual critic of the era. Few among those who have practiced the profession of drama criticism have been better equipped for it, or better at it, than he. And Chekhov was Stark Young's specialty. Soon after this production of *Uncle Vanya* he would publish his own translations of the playwright's works, and they would for many years remain the standard versions.

Observing the directorial debut of Jed Harris, Mr. Young wrote, "Writing criticism about a production so careful and intelligent is a pleasure and a form of cooperation with the producer. . . . The whole directing is felt out with naturalness, brains and confidence."

It was almost miraculous that Harris could have accomplished such a feat with so little preparation. His natural gift had to have been astonishing. Pity he would, in his career, do only two other classics and neither of them in a league with *Uncle Vanya*. They would be Gogol's *The Inspector General* and Ibsen's *A Doll's House*. He would never attempt Shakespeare, or even his beloved Shaw.

His return to Broadway, then, was a glittering one. He had even enhanced his image: quality, intellect and art had been added to the reputation for commercial infallibility. The dust from the Wall Street crash had cleared and The Meteor had survived.

Not so the romance of George Jean Nathan and Lillian Gish. They returned from Europe to learn that his mother was mortally ill. Lillian visited her in the hospital. On the way home she asked George whether he was Jewish. He repeated what he had told her before: that he was from a Main Line and decidedly Episcopalian Philadelphia family.

The mother Lillian had seen in the hospital had not struck her as a society Christian. She asked George's sister-in-law about it, and Marguerite roared. "If George's brother is Jewish," she said, "I might suppose he would be too."

Lillian was disgusted. She hardly cared who was Jewish. Practically everyone in Hollywood was. But she did care—or rather, did not care—about people who denied what they were. That was the end of her secret engagement to George Jean Nathan.

◆

When Jones and his nurse Andrée returned from France they were moved into a house in Greenwich, Connecticut. It was remarkable how successful Jed and Ruth had been, thus far, in keeping the scandal out of the newspapers. Jones hardly existed at all and they were free to pursue their glamorous careers. They moved from coast to coast with ease. When they were in town they could drive out to Connecticut and visit their baby whenever they wanted to.

In the year following *Uncle Vanya*, Harris produced three straight flops, but misfortune did not discourage his fancy style of living or dispel his aura. Ruth's stage season was no better. Philip Barry's *Hotel Universe* folded beneath her. They both decided to try Hollywood for a change and went out to stay awhile with Helen Hayes and Charlie MacArthur.

In the past, a number of movie studios had offered Jed large sums of money in exchange for little more than his name. He had pretended to weigh each offer, only to walk away from a contract at the final dramatic moment. This time, he told friends, he meant business.

The MacArthurs did their best to slip Jed into the Hollywood stream through industrious socializing, but whatever his career intentions, he flaunted his contempt for movies and movie makers. When he was taken to lunch at Ernst Lubitsch's home in Santa Monica, Ruth Gordon recalled, "everybody worked hard but nothing worked. A dreadful afternoon!" And Lubitsch was the one movie director whose work Harris admired. Helen Hayes swore,

"I'll never urge Jed to do anything again. He really *tried*, but he's like Garbo. They say she really can't go anywhere."

During this Hollywood stay, Harris was once again offered a producership, this time with RKO Radio Pictures. And once again he instigated a quarrel with the studio chief just as the lucrative contract was to be signed. Apparently he could not be diplomatic when fools or foolishness was involved, and self-destructiveness only made that easier.

Nothing much accomplished in California, then, Jed and Ruth came back to New York and moved in together at last; into the 59th Street apartment. Meantime they looked for a town house. They weren't planning to get married and there appears to be no explanation for this sudden willingness to live openly as a family. Perhaps Harris's fear of the illegitimate child becoming public knowledge had always been, in part, an excuse for maintaining a separate life. Now that fear had simply disappeared.

When Jed moved in with Ruth, Jones Kelly became Jones Harris.

◈

As the Double R Coffee House had been the gathering spot for theatrical aspirants, so now was Rudley's Restaurant just south of Times Square. Its generation of the stagestruck included director Preston Sturges, actor Archie Leach, a budding producer named Oscar Serlin, and a couple of would-be playwrights, Moss Hart and Edward Chodorov. It was now Chodorov's turn. The twenty-six-year-old dramatist had watched as *Once in a Lifetime* launched Hart. Now, Ed Chodorov retyped the manuscript of what he thought was his best play so far, *Wonder Boy*. He fit it carefully into a binder and brought it to his friend Eddie Carter, who was an office boy for the theatrical agent Dr. Edmund Pauker.

Pauker had an elegant reputation. His list of clients was short and prestigious, including the likes of Georges Feydeau, Ferenc Molnár, Vicki Baum. It was a league Chodorov wouldn't have minded joining.

Several days after receiving the play, Pauker asked the young playwright to stop by.

"It's not unamusing, this *Wonder Boy* of yours."

Conservatively dressed except for the handkerchief flaring from his breast pocket and plainly a cut above the gaudy horde of agents, Pauker tilted back in his chair, staring into the cigar smoke.

"Mind you," he said in his Viennese accent, "nobody's going to do it, but I'll send it around so at least they'll know you're in the field. They'll know your name. They'll understand what this Edward Chodorov is."

Chodorov still wore his checkered mackinaw, the ear-flap cap stuffed in his pocket. Pauker's words encouraged him. "Not unamusing . . . Nobody's going to do it but . . ."

The agent telephoned the next afternoon.

"Come down to the office at two o'clock. I've got something to tell you."

"Today?"

"No, in nineteen forty."

Chodorov buttoned up his mackinaw and rushed out.

"You're not going to believe this," Pauker scowled, rolling the cigar between thumb and forefinger and staring at it. Chodorov still had his ear-flaps on. "No, you're not going to believe this but Jed Harris has bought your play."

"I can't believe it."

"He must be crazy," Pauker said.

"Why is he crazy?"

"He wants to see you at three." The agent checked his pocket watch. "You've got thirty-five minutes to get over to his office."

"Jesus Christ, Doctor Pauker . . . Why didn't you tell me this on the phone? I would have worn a suit."

"Jed Harris doesn't care what you are wearing. When you get there he may not be wearing anything himself."

Recounting the experience years later, Chodorov remembered running the several blocks to Harris's office and presenting himself, gasping, at the backstage entrance of the Morosco Theatre. Soon he gripped Jed Harris's doorknob with a feeling of destiny. He paused, breathed deeply to still his nerves, and then pushed the door open. Harris was not naked. Quite the reverse. He was wearing an overcoat—a camel's hair polo coat—and even a fedora. He sat at the desk, his back to the door, and gazed through the big french windows down at 45th Street, the Booth Theatre, Shubert Alley. Chodorov waited and watched.

"Hi, kid," Harris finally said, absentmindedly. He removed the hat and tossed it onto the desk. "Siddown. Listen, I'm crazy about your play. Great title, *Wonder Boy*. Unfortunately, I can't produce it."

"Why not?"

"I can't think of the actor. There's an actor I saw in Berlin five years ago. A big, redheaded cat. I don't know the name of the play. I don't know the name of the theater I saw him in. All morning I've been calling Berlin to try and track him down. If I could get him I'd do the play."

The renowned producer stood up, still in his overcoat, and looked through the window, shaking his head.

"Can't do the play."

"Come on, Mr. Harris," the young writer pleaded, trying to rise from the sofa. Unable to find his balance he fell back down. "There must be other actors."

Harris returned to his desk and sank down disconsolately. He said that once he pictured an actor in a role, he was committed to that actor and couldn't imagine doing the play with anybody else. For *Wonder Boy*, it had to be this actor he saw in Berlin. The big red cat.

Chodorov recalled Moss Hart telling the gang at Rudley's about the long days of waiting for Harris in the Madison Hotel. The story about the naked producer had been hilarious and harrowing, but it had not prepared him for this.

Desperate, Chodorov squeaked, "Couldn't we advertise?"

The producer lifted his heavy eyebrows to unveil a glance of searing pity.

"I've gotta think," he said, rubbing his lids with the heels of his hands. "I've come up against a dead end."

Chodorov sat back on the leather sofa and stared at the famous face, now cradled between its owner's hands. "But Jesus," he finally said just to keep the subject alive, "there *has* to be another actor. How do you even know this guy can speak English?"

"I don't! That's the point!" Harris said illogically. "Goddamnit, the name of that play he was in is on the tip of my tongue."

He rose and again walked to the french windows.

"It was a lousy play but he was absolutely great. Like a big, redheaded cat." Harris stared across the street. "He just dominated the stage. . . ."

His voice trailed off, as if going into a fog with him. Suddenly, he stepped back from the window as if he'd been struck.

"Jesus Christ," he whistled, and then he shouted. "There's the son of a bitch now!" and he flung the windows open.

Chodorov leaped from the sofa and ran across the room. Harris had already stepped out onto the balcony. He was pointing as if he could shoot his finger like an arrow. There was indeed a red-haired man, standing in front of the Booth Theatre: a man wearing a theatrical, Sherlock Holmesian cape-coat with a scarf tossed over a shoulder.

"You! Hey you!" Harris shouted.

The people on the street turned to stare.

"Yes, you, goddamnit," he yelled. "You big red cat. Come around to the alley of the theater." He jabbed a finger into his own chest. "Jed Harris!" he cried. "Take the elevator to the second floor!"

The red-haired man looked from Harris to the other pedestrians as if, who, me?

"Yes, you, you dumb son of a bitch! Get on over here!"

The man started hesitantly toward the Morosco.

"Yes, yes, send him up," Harris shouted impatiently when the telephone rang, and moments later the door opened. The tall, red-haired man entered. At close range his face was as theatrical as his costume, and he seemed as bewildered as Chodorov.

"You know me, Mr. Harris?"

The accent was Russian but at least the language was English.

"What's your name?"

"Gregory Ratoff."

"Do you speak English?"

"Like you hear."

"This is Mr. Chodorov. He's written a play and I'm going to put you in the leading part. How do you like that, Mr. Ratoff?"

Harris stared at the dumbfounded actor.

"I said, how do you like that?" He said it loudly, as if volume could surmount any language barrier.

"Mr. Harris. I am sorry, I cannot do it."

"What do you mean, you cannot do it?"

"I have here contract with Shuberts I just signed," the actor said. "I go now to give to them. My wife, Eugenie Leontovich, is chorus girl with *Greenwich Village Follies* and I go with her. I get job in show."

"Let me see that contract," Harris growled. Ratoff slipped it from his breast pocket and handed it over. Chodorov, still dazed by the bizarre sequence of events, floated behind the desk to peek over Harris's shoulder. The producer read the contract section by section, turning the pages and chuckling under his breath.

"I've got to hand it to those wisenheimers," he said. Then he carefully tore the contract in half and in half again, daintily depositing the quadrants into the wastepaper basket.

"What have you been doing?" Ratoff croaked.

"Now you don't have a contract." Harris turned to Chodorov, grinned, and clapped him on the back. "We're in business," he said.

◆

Jed and Ruth moved into a town house on East 79th Street and, by her own description, she turned it into a showplace. A few pieces were Harris's, choice selections from previous stage settings. The rest was her doing: expensive china, elaborate draperies, a grand piano. When it came to gracious living, the Ruth Gordon sass gave way to positive elegance.

◆

Mildred Harris sat in the darkened Alvin Theatre and watched the rehearsal of *Wonder Boy*. Chodorov was running it until Jed arrived. Mildred turned to see her brother standing in the aisle beside her.

"You've got some great actors here," she said. The company included Sam Levene, Karl Malden, Davey Burns, and Gregory Ratoff, the big red cat.

"Isn't it wonderful?" Jed whispered. "We'll never have to worry about money again after this."

He continued down the aisle toward the stage and called a break. Chodorov trotted down the small flight of stairs that had been pushed up against the stage.

"Thank God you're here," he said.

"You're doing beautifully."

"Thanks, but I'd rather have my play directed by Harris than Chodorov."

Chodorov sat down in an orchestra seat while Jed began a run through of the first act. The young writer was much more worried than Harris seemed to be. The physical production had grown mammoth, a three-tier setting. The size of the company, thirty-eight actors, was outlandish. Actors could have doubled in many of these small parts. And there was a tremendous backstage crew required to deal with a production of such size. Chodorov was a novice playwright going through his first production, but it seemed to him that Jed had inflated *Wonder Boy* to the point of making it financially hopeless. He didn't think there was any way of making money even were they to sell out every performance. His only hope was that Harris knew what he was doing.

"Don't go very far," Jed said to him as he started up the aisle during a break. "We've got a lot of work to do tonight."

"Oh Christ, not another rewrite."

"Just a new second act."

"Are you out of your mind? I've rewritten this play two dozen times already. We've only got ten days till opening night."

"The second act is too pat. Yeah, they'll cheer. They'll yell and love it, but it's wrong. We don't want the audience so up at the end of the second act. We've got to ease them down by that curtain so we can bring them up still higher in the last act. Take it from me, kid, and give me another scene to hold back on them. Oh, and I've got more news for you. Movie rights, a hundred fifty thousand."

"Wow."

"I turned it down. Wait till we open. When *The Front Page* was in rehearsal, Millie Milestone wanted to buy it for fifty thousand. Charlie MacArthur and Ben were yelling at me to grab it but I waited. We wound up with a hundred twenty-five."

It was autumn of 1931, the pit of the Depression. The average movie sale of a Broadway play was $25,000.

Following his usual practice, Jed had rented a hotel suite for rewriting sessions. He was spending more time working with the playwright than with the actors. Perhaps directing playwrights was more interesting than directing their plays.

The suite at the Barbizon-Plaza had three rooms. Chodorov's typewriter was on the coffee table in the sitting room. Jed had gone out. The young playwright was depressed. He was convinced that his play was being over-revised as well as overproduced. Answering the door buzzer, he admitted a somber gentleman, the assistant manager of the hotel.

"Did Mr. Harris use his room last night?"

"I saw him come out of there just an hour ago. The maid was already in to make it up."

"I know."

The man opened the door to Harris's bedroom. The floor was covered with broken glass, windows were smashed, draperies ripped from their valances. Glasses had been thrown against the walls. Chodorov never learned what had happened nor understood how he could have slept through such violence.

The hotel was discreet. There was a charge on the bill for room damages and Jed paid it without challenge.

Wonder Boy opened to poor reviews. There were no more movie offers. Chodorov reeled, but, inexplicably, Harris's legend not only survived. It grew. The newspapers now called him "Wonder Boy."

Jed Harris, who produced *Broadway, Coquette, The Front Page* and other successful plays, will probably go into the talking films in the United Artists organization, it was learned last night. He plans to sever his connection with the theater after the closing of *Wonder Boy*, his production at the Alvin Theatre, next Monday night.
— *New York Times*, November 25, 1931

Chodorov knew it was Harris calling when the telephone rang in the middle of the night, just before dawn. The whisper was otherworldly as usual.

"I want you to be at the Warwick Hotel at three o'clock tomorrow afternoon."

Phone in hand, the young writer settled back into the overstuffed armchair in his parents' living room. There, in his pajamas, he chatted with Jed Harris about movie deals.

"You're going to meet Millie Milestone and Joe Schenck. Al Jolson is going to tell you a story that he wants you to write as a screenplay for him. Millie and Schenck want to finance this picture themselves. Jolson calls his story *Hallelujah, I'm a Bum* and it's right up your alley. I got you the job for seventeen fifty."

"One thousand seven hundred and fifty dollars?"

"A week; and listen to what they're offering me. Hello? Are you still there?"

"I'm here. I'm fainted but I'm here."

"I'm telling you, these movie people are such schmucks. Just for lending them my name and not having to do a goddamned thing, they're giving me three hundred thousand dollars a year. I already have the check."

"You don't have to tell me. It's none of my business."

"And that isn't all. They're going to put up a hundred percent of the financing of any play I want to do, and that's without a word of their opinion. They don't even see the scripts and I've got that in writing. The deal is, they get half the profits and the first rejection on movie rights. Even then, they have to match the highest bidder. Eddie. For Chrissake, they gave me a deal like that and *I'm broke.*"

The next day, Eddie met Lewis Milestone, Joe Schenck and Al Jolson at the Warwick Hotel. It was a heady moment for the young man. Jed explained that Jolson would outline the story. Then the glib, cocky, and showmanly star grinned, rubbed his hands, and began.

In the movie he was going to play a man who quits the crass world of business to become an idealistic hobo, living in the woods. There he gathers around him a community of similar refugees from the urban rat race. Their story is told almost entirely in mime and song.

The idea marked a bold break from the kind of work the electrifying mammy singer had been known for. "Not only is it artistic," Jolson said to Chodorov, chuckling in the famous growled baritone, "but you'll hardly have to write any words 'cause, ya see, kid, it's all sung." He paused. "Well, what do you think?"

"Be honest," Jed said.

After a pause, Chodorov began. "Mr. Jolson," he said. "That's a good story. But it isn't for you. You're famous all over the world for being a great singer, a funny man, but a real city slicker. This is for Charlie Chaplin, not Al Jolson."

The silence was paralyzing. Everyone stared at nobody.

"Excuse me," Harris finally said. "Eddie. Come on into the bedroom."

Alone in the darkened room, Jed grabbed the playwright by the tie and jerked him.

"Did you hear me tell you that I got you a deal for one thousand seven hundred and fifty dollars a week?"

"Yes, Mr. Harris."

"I'm sure that I arranged that deal and I'm practically just as sure that I told you about it." Jed was whispering so heatedly that Chodorov felt the steam. "Tell me I told you about it."

"I told you already. You told me about it. Seventeen fifty a week. I remember."

"Do you also know that you just blew that seventeen fifty a week?"

"The story isn't for Jolson."

Jed slapped him across the face.

"Now it's for Jolson." Harris let go and walked to the window. He stared out. "For Chrissakes, Eddie, I'm trying to save your life."

"You're not saving my life, not if you're asking me to work on something that's lunatic. A man who lives in a tree is not Al Jolson."

"All right, get the hell out of here. I'll try to salvage something. Be at the house for dinner tonight."

Chodorov opened the bedroom door and tiptoed though the living room. He covered his face with a saintly smile and nailed his eyes to the door. They looked at him as if they were statues, Jolson, Schenck and Milestone.

That evening, Chodorov came around to the house on 79th Street. Since Ruth was in a play, it was just the two of them for dinner, and Jed chatted breezily about his various experiences with movie people. He said nothing about the Jolson incident until coffee was served.

Then he said, "Where do you think the *Twentieth Century Limited* is right now?"

"It gets into Buffalo around nine o'clock."

"Millie, Jolson and Schenck are on it. Do me a favor and take down this wire."

The maid brought a pencil and paper.

"Just write down what I say. Send this to the three of them care of the conductor of the *Twenty Century Limited*: 'Dear Joe and Millie.' Send it to just them and fuck Jolson. 'Dear Joe and Millie. I don't think I care to accept the deal.'"

"Jed! What are you doing? How can you do that?"

Harris took an envelope from the breast pocket of his green velvet smoking jacket. He withdrew a check for three hundred thousand dollars, counter-signed by Schenck and Milestone. He tore it in half and laid it in his coffee saucer.

"You were dead right," he said. "It's ridiculous, Jolson in that story. The guy's a loud, racetrack type. He's great on the stage. The greatest. But a philosophical hobo? It's too stupid."

"But the money, Jed. You told me a dozen times you were flat busted."

"If you can turn it down, I can turn it down. Nobody who turns down three hundred thousand dollars is flat busted. I can't work for somebody else, never could, especially these Hollywood bozos."

He leaned back in his armchair at the head of the table and inhaled a cigarette as if content at last. He covered his face with his splayed fingers and told Chodorov about the time Charlie Feldman had brought him in to sign the RKO Radio deal.

"How much do they pay you?" he'd asked the studio chief. "How much," it would be, "do they pay you, Mr. Thalberg?" "How much do they pay you, Mr. Zanuck?" He would always ask the question that was calculated to outrage, and he would always ask it at the moment a contract was to be signed.

"Why do you do these things?" Chodorov asked. "You go out to Holly-wood looking for a deal. You're broke and you need the money. You get the deal and then you deliberately wreck it. Why is that?"

Harris smiled. "I'm a crass producer," he said, "but goddamnit, I can't put up with anything that's plain stupid. I tell myself I can work for an idiot until he shows me just how much of an idiot he is."

Chodorov looked at the smiling, smoking Harris.

◆

Eddie Chodorov now had no life apart from Jed Harris. He was a drinking companion on request, a dawn conversationalist on call, a play reader and rewriter on demand. Harris was his entertainer, idol, and guru, and he finally moved into the house on East 79th Street. There he labored without pay or credit on any script that Jed was interested in and there was always something. He revised *Twentieth Century* when Harris thought he'd lured back Ben Hecht and Charlie MacArthur. Hecht finally went the way of Abbott, Shumlin and Kaufman. Chodorov rewrote part of Maxwell Anderson's *Both Your Houses* before Jed lost that one too.

Sometimes Harris even took credit for Eddie's work. "If I tell Max Anderson," he said, "that you rewrote the third act of *Both Your Houses*, he won't put up with it. But if I tell him *I* wrote it, he'll accept it."

Chodorov bought it. He worked on a play that Harris did produce, *The*

Fatal Alibi, a murder mystery starring Charles Laughton. It was another flop, nothing but flops since *Uncle Vanya.* Two years. Classics failing and now even a murder mystery failing.

"Daddy?"

The two men turned as Jones pulled away from Andrée's hand and padded hesitantly in his Doctor Dentons toward the library. He stopped at the doorway, not daring to come in. He knew better. He seemed proud, Eddie remembered thinking, to have stayed up as late as eight o'clock.

Andrée apologized for being unable to control the child. The boy wanted to say good-night to his father, she explained. It happens with children.

"Good-night, Papa," Jones said in his French-accented baby English. He reached for Andrée's hand and left with her. Jed inhaled his cigarette and stubbed it out.

"That kid's no good," he said.

Chodorov turned and stared. Jones was four years old.

"Come into the living room where the big radio is," Harris said. "I don't want to miss *Amos 'n' Andy.*"

FUN AND GAMES

It is difficult to describe the elusive texture of Jed Harris's personality. There is no adequate photograph of Mr. Harris extant. Nor is there any translating him from reality into printer's copy and back into reality through the medium of words. Perhaps, like Boston, Mr. Harris is only a state of mind.
—Lucius Beebe, *New York Herald-Tribune*, October 15, 1933

HE STROLLED DOWN the *S.S. Minnetonka*'s gangplank into the semicircle of ship reporters who still considered him the newsworthiest on any passenger list. The first thing they seemed to notice—every newspaper item mentioned it—was that he'd traveled without luggage. When asked about it he replied that he'd just gone to find the best plays on the West End and the quicker he returned the better. More likely, he had done it for effect.

"I hate London," said the man who had once mused about living there and having a parliamentary career. "I see nothing there," he now said, "but a bleak, gray world. It's my dream to get the Savoy Hotel moved to New York City. Then I'd say America is the greatest country on earth."

He had returned, at least, with the American production rights for both Mordaunt Shairp's *The Green Bay Tree* and the Dorothy Massingham-Murray MacDonald drama, *The Lake*.

Noël Coward had urged *The Green Bay Tree* on him, with the recommendation that Laurence Olivier be given the lead in the New York production. When *Private Lives* had been done in New York two seasons earlier, Olivier had played the stuffy foil to Coward and Gertrude Lawrence. The London producers of *The Green Bay Tree* were unimpressed with the young actor, but Harris agreed with Coward.

As to casting the tragic heroine of *The Lake*, Harris had, some years earlier, met Katharine Hepburn among the eager actors who crowded his office. He'd seen her since, from time to time. If Mildred's looks had set the type for Anita and Ruth, Hepburn was to become the model for the second generation of women in Harris's life: horsey and decidedly Gentile.

Now a movie star, she was eager to return to the stage and Harris thought she was right for the dark and spooky *The Lake*. His opportunity to convince her of it came with an invitation for a visit to her family home in Connecticut. The family was away.

Jed asked Eddie Chodorov to keep him company on the drive. He was borrowing Lee Tracy's convertible and the overnight excursion promised to be pleasant. It was a sunny Saturday, a warm summer day, and while Harris was with Hepburn, Chodorov could poke through the local antique shops. The playwright looked forward to the trip as he waited in Jed's office.

And waited. They'd planned to leave at one o'clock. It was almost five. The bright red car, its top down, was still sitting downstairs, illegally parked in front of the Morosco Theatre.

Suddenly the door to Jed's office swung open and he popped out, heading straight for the door and down the stairs with Chodorov in pursuit. When they hit the street, Chodorov stopped short. A mounted policeman was looming over the convertible, writing out a summons.

"Let me handle this," the playwright said, walking up to the policeman and squinting into the sun. High atop the mount, the cop explained the traffic violation in painstaking detail. A lecture ensued. Eddie tried to concentrate on the officer's words while keeping an eye on Jed. The cop spoke of matinee traffic snarls and threats to life and property. Chodorov thought only of Harris, glowering on the periphery, for the producer had an edgy history with men in uniform. He was nervous and hostile with train conductors, Pullman porters, ship's officers, anyone in an authoritative position and a uniform to prove it. At minimum he refused to speak with them.

The cop again reviewed the facts of the case while Chodorov perspired. It was hardly from the heat. Trying to appear wretched and contrite, he prayed that Harris would keep away and that the officer would get on with it. He smiled and perspired and finally the cop resumed writing the summons.

Then Eddie's heart lurched. Jed had started toward them. The look in his eye was maniacal. He went straight for the cop. The officer looked down at him. Harris looked up. Then he placed two hands on the horse's flank, dug in his heels, and gave the animal a shove. The cop stared in disbelief.

Leaning into the job, Harris kept pushing until both policeman and mount were angled toward the center of 45th Street. The traffic had been slow and heavy. Now, horns erupted and shouts from impatient drivers.

Jed opened the car door and got in. "Let's get going," he said, but no sooner had he said it than the policeman reached down from on high and grasped him by the collar behind his neck. He pulled Harris upright and began to beat him about the neck and shoulders with a nightstick. Jed tried to protect himself with his arms while scrambling to keep his balance. He held his elbows up and cringed, much as he had against childhood beatings. Eddie cried out for the policeman to stop, but the man seemed possessed.

Harris, now flailing for footing on the car seat, wrenched himself around and faced both officer and horse. There was a pause in the action, a frightful calm, or so it seemed to Chodorov. Then Jed leaned out, took firm hold on the saddle, opened his mouth wide and proceeded before Chodorov's dread glaze to clamp his teeth upon the cop's right thigh, above the boot.

Ed Chodorov had been involved in escapades, stunts, and all manner of events with Jed Harris, but he had never seen the man bite a policeman. Just then a squad car edged through the traffic, its siren and flashing lights signaling a cease-fire. A police captain and sergeant sprang from the opened doors and Eddie expected the worst, for now it was Jed Harris and *three* men in uniform.

By chance, Dick Lamarr had been walking through Shubert Alley when the fracas began and he was attracted by the commotion, the siren and the lights. Lamarr was Mayor Jimmy Walker's liaison man with the Broadway theater industry. He pushed through the crowd that had gathered around the scene and of course was recognized by the police captain.

They held a whispered conference. Harris looked on, standing grimly on the front seat, his arms crossed, his collar still securely in the mounted cop's grasp. The captain turned to the policeman and told him to release the captive.

Jed slid down into the seat, ruffled but smug, with even the hint of a twinkle in his eye. The captain explained that for resisting arrest a second summons would have to be issued. Chodorov clamped Jed's shoulder to forfend any complaint about that. The crowd cleared and the mounted officer was led away by the sergeant.

Too energized by events to leave for Connecticut immediately, Chodorov and Harris were convinced by Lamarr to stop for a drink at The Tavern. The restaurant on West 48th Street was a theatrical gathering spot, better known as "Billy LaHiff's" for its owner, who greeted the three men warmly. He sat down with Ed and Jed in a corner booth while Lamarr went off to telephone the mayor's office.

Soon they were roundly laughing over the afternoon's excitement. Then there was a stir at the restaurant door.

An army of policemen entered and marched straight for the booth. At the echelon's front was the captain who had just commandeered 45th Street and, at his side, the now dismounted policeman. Behind was a swarm of policemen. Lamarr rose. The captain whispered in his ear. They turned to Harris.

"Is this the cop?"

Harris stared. With tremendous gravity, he nodded. They led the poor fellow away. Harris called the mayor's office the next day to inquire about the officer's punishment. He suggested that the fellow be dismounted. The cop was assigned to walking a beat in New Lots, a desolate stretch in Brooklyn. For months afterward, he showed up at the Harris office to beg for relief, but Jed was unrelenting.

Chodorov and Harris finally continued on to Connecticut. Upon their arrival, Harris left it to Chodorov to register in the hotel. He himself drove off to see Hepburn.

Even a half century later she didn't want to discuss anything that had to do with him. As for Harris, he was always circumspect. He did tell Chodorov, however, while crawling into bed that night, that her parents had most unexpectedly returned.

In the morning the merry song of a choir of Rotarians burst rudely upon the two sleepers. The vocalizing club members could have been in the same room. Actually, they were. The overbooked hotel had afforded Jed and Eddie only a makeshift bedroom. A hastily placed screen was all that separated them from the dining room.

Now, Chodorov lay in gleeful wait for Harris's reaction to the serenade. The producer lay on his back, his beard as spikey as a medieval mace, his eyes open, staring at the ceiling. The voices soared. He glared.

Suddenly he leaped from the sheets. With his striped pajamas flapping around his skinny frame he sent one of the screens crashing to the floor. The assembled Rotarians were stunned into silence. They gaped at the wild-eyed apparition.

"Shut up," he whispered. "Do you hear me? Shut up that goddammed singing." The silence billowed. Harris pulled the screen upright. The two of them packed, dressed, and checked out. Driving off, himself at the wheel, Harris asked how much the room had cost. Eddie said Mrs. Perkins, the proprietress, had charged sixty dollars for the improvised area.

"Oh, no!" Harris cried. "She's not going to get away with that," and over Chodorov's protestations he turned the car around and drove back to the hotel. He steamed in and returned brandishing a black crayon.

"You know that big white wall in the dining room? I wrote on it, 'Mrs. Perkins is a cunt.' But it was still worth the trip. Kate's doing *The Lake*."

◆

They continued to work together, Harris suggesting, reading, editing and above all talking the plays out while Chodorov wrote and rewrote. Now, both *The Green Bay Tree* and *The Lake* were being Americanized by the young playwright.

One afternoon, Chodorov rushed into the office. Harris had moved again, this time to a suite above the Empire Theatre.

"Get your coat! I found your boy!"

"What boy?"

"For *The Green Bay Tree*. Olivier is nothing next to this guy."

"What's his name?"

"Jesus, will you put on your goddamned coat? I've got a cab waiting."

They hurried out of the office, taking the stairs instead of waiting for the elevator. Chodorov told the hack to rush them to Carnegie Hall.

"Wait till you see. This guy is great."

They hurried up the few steps to the lobby. Chodorov produced the tickets. He'd rushed out during the intermission.

Carnegie Hall occasionally scheduled oddities on weekday afternoons when The New York Philharmonic Society was not in session. The budget-priced travelogues and vanity bookings attracted sparse audiences of the elderly and idle. Chodorov and Harris tiptoed into the darkened house. The audience was paying rapt attention to a mime-dancer-actor on stage. The music was exotic, his movements simple, the auditorium hushed.

The two men took their seats and watched the performance. After some moments, Harris leaned over and whispered.

"Is this the fella?"

Chodorov held his finger to his lips. He did not want to disturb the artistic performance. The audience, after all, was behaving as if at a shrine. He nodded his head, somberly. Despite the attentiveness and reverence of the audience, Harris continued to whisper.

"For *The Green Bay Tree*? Olivier's role?"

Eddie nodded again, searching Jed's eyes for the gratitude, the confirmation he was sure to find there. Finally, he too whispered.

"Isn't he something? Have you ever seen anything like it?"

Chodorov glanced apologetically about, excusing himself to the surround-

138

ing art lovers. Jed pushed upward in his seat and started edging toward the aisle.

"Come on out to the lobby," he said under his breath.

They slunk out as Chodorov shrugged his shoulders in apology to the people around them. In the marble outer lobby, Jed put his arm around Eddie's shoulders. He looked sincerely into the young writer's eyes.

"Eddie," he finally said. "The guy's a Chinaman."

Chodorov did not understand the relevance of that.

"We can make him up," he said in relief. "Isn't he great?"

Harris stared at him, looked around the lobby as if in search of witnesses, and then stared again, smiled, and hugged his friend.

"Yes, he's great. He's wonderful. He's brilliant. But he's a Chinaman."

Chodorov couldn't understand why Harris was making such a big thing of that.

"Can't we do something about it?" he asked with persistence. "He's just so great."

Now Jed took Chodorov by both shoulders and, pulling him up close, looked into his eyes.

"Listen, you stupid son of a bitch. This guy is a fucking Chinaman!"

Harris steamed out of Carnegie Hall, trailing wasted time. Chodorov, like a chastised schoolboy, trudged behind, then trotted along after him, down Seventh Avenue.

◆

Harris was cultivating his own legend. Just as *Coquette* and *The Royal Family* had gone into production back to back, and then *The Gaoler's Wench* and *Serena Blandish*, now *The Green Bay Tree* would open in October and then *The Lake* would begin its tryout tour, coming in to New York the day after Christmas. Olivier would star in one, Hepburn in the other, and Harris would direct both. He would also finance them himself. He raised the money by liquidating his last asset, the hundred-and-fifty-foot sloop *Señorita*. It didn't net quite enough to produce the plays properly, but he insisted on one luxury: Robert Edmond Jones would do the settings for *The Green Bay Tree*.

The celebrated designer demanded a royal price, but Harris felt that the scenery was itself a character in this play. It had to be realistic, symbolic, and atmospheric. Costs could be cut elsewhere, for instance, there would be only eighteen days of rehearsal and no out-of-town tryout. With a play so special, provincial appeal would be uncertain anyhow. *The Lake* would be another matter, likely to do well on the road because of the Hepburn name. She was to be a tremendous box office attraction throughout her career.

The abbreviated rehearsal time for *The Green Bay Tree* would have upset most directors, who feel that at least six weeks are needed to put professional polish on any production. Harris always insisted that rehearsal was not the key to performance.

"No really finished performance of any play," he said, "can be achieved through rehearsals. Only audience contact can give players the assurance that their work is properly tuned. An actor may have to re-create his entire characterization after opening night because an audience's reaction to his every reading and bit of business may be just the reverse of what the director has led him to believe it will be."

◆

Mordaunt Shairp's play, *The Green Bay Tree*, is about a struggle for control over a beautiful young man; a struggle among his dominating guardian, his nearly deranged father and his ingenuous fiancée.

The battle is waged in elegant drawing rooms and seedy parlors. It is almost always fought in subtext. Its hothouse atmosphere and unspoken sexuality anticipated the dramas of Harold Pinter that were to appear thirty years later.

As the play begins, Julian has been living with his guardian, Dulcimer, for almost fifteen years. The older man has been freed by wealth to pursue refinement in all its aspects: refinement of manner and behavior, of possessions, of education, and of artistic taste.

When Julian informs Dulcimer that he is in love with Leonora Yale, the guardian becomes so enraged that he threatens to expel and disown the young man if marriage is in fact the intention. Julian has no choice but to leave. He marries Leonora and takes her to his father's home in the seedy Camden Town district of London.

There he finds that he cannot cope with the rigors of everyday life. He has been equipped only for a life of indulgence. He will not, or cannot, live in poverty and refuses to learn how to climb out of it. After three months he tells Leonora that he must ask Dulcimer for help.

The guardian's position is intransigent. As long as Julian is with Leonora he will receive no help.

The young man buckles under the pressure. He tells his bride that he must return to Dulcimer's house, and that drives his father to action at last. The demented old preacher murders the guardian.

Now Julian is free of the effete tyranny. He is heir to the enormous fortune. He can keep Leonora with impunity.

They move into the exquisite house, but Dulcimer's death has not changed matters. In fact it has petrified them, and Julian has become the house's prisoner. For it was not the man Dulcimer who had seduced him but a per-

140

verse way of life and set of values. These continue to exist and control Julian. Now he is one of the elegant appointments in this house, along with the antiques and paintings. He is lost to Leonora and she abandons him to the house and its decadence.

Robert Edmond Jones's gold and green setting for the production of *The Green Bay Tree* was one that Jed said half the British peerage would envy. With real antiques and even solid silver picture frames on the grand piano, it projected a twisted and threatening elegance.

The designer complained about being rushed to finish it, but Harris was eager for his actors to rehearse on the set.

Company morale was low from the outset. Jed had a reputation for finding a scapegoat in every cast, usually a handsome actor. It began to seem as if Olivier had been cast in that role too.

Harris felt that even Olivier hadn't an appreciation of his own gifts. "His ambition was rather vulgar. He wanted to be another Ronald Colman. His whole life was changed when he went to the Old Vic [to do the classics]. Here was a man who had no idea what his real talent was. He wanted to be a hero in film, with a little moustache. He had one already." Still, Harris's admiration for the actor was on record.

"There is a short scene in *Green Bay Tree*," he said years later, "that [Olivier] played with Leonora after she married him. Sitting in an armchair he was stooped over, holding onto his knees. There was such tension in that holding on to his knees that you thought if he ever let go of them he'd fly apart. Tremendous power!"

At the same time, Harris continued, "Actors don't need any minds. Olivier has no mind whatever. What he does have is an immense network of nervous antennae that go out in a thousand different directions. [Although] not in terms of words, he grasps something so powerfully and can translate that. And that is what makes him such a great force in the theater."

The attitude did not endear the director to the actor, and Harris made more than one snide remark to Olivier's wife, Jill Esmond, who was playing Leonora. That was typical, seeking the space between husband and wife.

"This boy you're playing, Larry," Jed remembered saying during rehearsal. "He's a whore, after all, so when he talks to Leonora about asking Dulcimer for the money they need, he must speak as a whore does of a pimp." It was Harris's technique as a director to provide actors with such handles—specific analogies, clues to playing a character. Dozens of actors noted Harris's ability to come up with just the right example for them to grasp. This particular analogy, though, made Olivier uncomfortable, as Harris remembered with a smile.

141

A week before the play was scheduled to open, he told the assembled company, "I've rewritten the last scene." He spoke so quietly as to be almost inaudible. "As you know, in London the entire production was dominated by homosexuality. There was even swishing onstage. I'll have none of that. We've been removing all of those references. When the audience watches it here I want them to say to themselves, 'It's homosexual. Nothing is said about it but it's there. It must be there. That's the only explanation for these characters and their story.' So that's what I want. I want to create something without stating it. Does everyone understand?"

Ed Chodorov watched from the back, later to corroborate Harris's description of the rehearsal. They'd been up for thirty hours, working on the curtain scene. Now Jed handed out the new pages to the actors.

"May I have our Julian? Trump?" Trump was the valet. "Leonora?"

James Dale, who was playing Dulcimer, led the other actors from the stage.

"Now Leonora, dear. You're about to leave Julian. I've cut the last speech of yours. It's too homosexual. 'I suppose some day I shall see you walking down Piccadilly with painted cheeks.' That's the kind of heavy-handedness I want to avoid. You'll just say, 'Julian. I'm leaving. Good-bye.'

"Okay, let's try it."

Olivier had been long complaining about the Americanization and mutilation of the script without the author's consent. He said nothing now, as the actors took their places. Leo G. Carroll, who was playing Trump, left the stage.

"Julian. I'm leaving. Good-bye."

"You'll say nothing, Larry," Jed whispered. "Just watch her as she walks out. Cross stage to the fireplace and stare into the mirror above the mantelpiece. I want a hush to go out from the stage to the audience while you study your features in the mirror, so take your time about it. Now put an elbow on the mantelpiece. Okay. Line."

"Trump?!"

"Come in, Leo. Everyone must be quiet. I want the audience to have plenty of time to watch and think about what isn't being said. Larry?"

"Brandy!"

Harris held a hand up to delay Carroll's response.

"Yes, sir."

"Leo—Trump—go off for the brandy. Larry, just stand there. All right, bring the brandy in. A carafe and a small glass. Not a snifter, it'll be a shot glass. Walk straight, Trump. No telltale gestures, nothing effeminate, keep your gestures to a minimum. Larry, swallow the brandy."

"Will you have another sir?"

"When Leo asks about the refill, just raise your glass. Leo, pour it."

"That isn't the way it's done in England," Olivier said.

"It's the way it's going to be done at the Cort Theatre in five days," Jed smiled. "Now sip the brandy. Then walk very slowly cross stage. Leo, don't take your eyes off him."

The rest of the company watched from the wings, silent, absorbed in the staging process. The auditorium was dark, a clock could actually be heard ticking. The next line was Trump's.

"Would you mind, sir, if I withdrew my resignation? . . . Excuse me, Mr. Harris. You've cut the rest of my speech. I had resigned because I thought Julian was going to be living here with Leonora. How will the audience know?"

"They'll know. It's better if they figure it out than if we tell them. Leonora's just left and that's made you change your mind. They'll know why."

Returning to the script, Carroll repeated, "Would you mind, sir, if I withdrew my resignation?"

"You'd like to stay, Trump?"

Harris held his hand up like a conductor, sustaining the pause. Then he cued Carroll's entrance with a downbeat.

"Very much so."

"Yes," Olivier said, tersely. "You know our ways."

"Take out your gold cigarette case," Harris said to him. "Open it and withdraw a gold-tipped cigarette. Tap it deliberately on the case. Trump, you'll have been leaving the room. Seeing him with the cigarette, you come back downstage and light it for him. Then take your line, Leo."

"The flowers have arrived, sir . . . do you think you might like to do them?"

The stage was silent.

"Yes, Trump."

"Now, Leo," Harris said, "you exit slowly to get the flowers. Larry, you sit down in the wing chair. Smoke. Stare at your cigarette. Smoke. . . . Okay . . . curtain."

Eleven pages of script had been reduced to three and a half while Harris staged the scene to play ten minutes.

"I'll bet," he said years later, "half the audience left the theater convinced that they actually saw Larry arrange the flowers."

◆

Opening night, Harris assembled the company on stage. The audience could be heard beyond the curtain, entering the theater and taking seats.

Harris walked to Olivier in the wings. The actor was tense. Jed whispered, "Good-bye, Larry. I hope I never see you again."

It was a terrible thing to say, anytime. Before an opening night performance, it was evil. After it was said, Olivier never spoke another word to Harris, but of course he had already been nicked by Jed's knife. A nastiness had persisted throughout rehearsals. "I watched that man," the actor later said, "his every move, his expressions, everything. I knew I'd use it all."

And he did, modeling his stage and film portrayal of Shakespeare's monstrous Richard III on Harris. "I thought of the most venal person I knew," Olivier told a journalist, "and that was Jed Harris. I based my make-up and performance on him."

An upsetting opening night remark seemed the latest variation on Harris's self-destructiveness. In the days of *Broadway*, he'd taken to bed. His nastiness to the actors had been relatively subtle at the time of *Serena Blandish*. Now he sliced and cut them on stage, as if daring fate to punish him. It was like his opening a play on the thirteenth, or on the day after a holiday. It was like insulting a movie tycoon while standing at the bottom line of a desperately needed contract. It was asking for disaster—needling, goading, motivating it.

Evidently, the remark to Olivier had little adverse effect on the actor's performance. Writing in the *New York Times*, Brooks Atkinson took "the keenest enjoyment in Jed Harris's current success with his brilliant production of Mordaunt Shairp's *The Green Bay Tree*."

Jed Harris, Broadway's wonder boy, again is preening himself. No longer does he seek furtive corners to weep alone with his flops *Mr. Gilhooley* and *The Fatal Alibi*. Into his erstwhile empty lap box office plums now drop daily—windfalls from his *Green Bay Tree*, which is a sell-out at the Cort Theatre.
        —*New York World-Telegram*, October 31, 1933

◆

The Lake was a spooky play about a rich and ruthless young woman who doesn't much care for her fiancé until the day she marries him, and then he drowns. Harris's synopsis would probably have been still briefer. He was doubtless counting on an audience of romantic movie-goers eager to see Katharine Hepburn in person.

He surely couldn't have been relying on her dramatic ability to rescue this haunted tearjerker since Miss Hepburn's previous stage work had been both limited and unpraised. To protect and even carry her, he surrounded his movie star with established stage actors: Frances Starr, Colin Clive, Blanche Bates.

Business was good for the pre-Broadway tryout in Washington, even though the reviews weren't. But Harris evidently believed that New Yorkers would be less inclined than out-of-towners to buy a poor play for the sake of a movie star. He told the acting company that they were not going to open in New York, instead suggesting to Miss Hepburn that "We can tour the country with this and make a fortune. You'll sell out theaters from here to Seattle and after a year or so you'll be ready to play the part in New York."

Ever tactful.

Miss Hepburn was so determined to play New York that she offered to invest her own money in the show if all he feared was the loss of money. Harris accepted. Perhaps he'd even been manipulating her ego for just this purpose. Then he tried to avert the impending doom with pre-opening ballyhoo.

Jed Harris has issued a statement denying the rumors of hundred dollar bids being accepted by brokers for his production of *The Lake* with Katharine Hepburn that opens next Tuesday at the Martin Beck. The producer says that all of the first night seats have been disposed of for weeks.   —*New York World-Telegram*

That was of little help. Ballyhoo seldom is. Miss Hepburn could not have been more brutally savaged by the critics had she beaten her mother on stage instead of merely acting a part in a play. Writing in *The New Yorker*, Dorothy Parker used *The Lake* as an excuse for one of the most enduring of all critical barbs. "Miss Hepburn's performance," she wrote, "ran the acting gamut from 'A' to 'B.'" Even Mr. Atkinson, prone to kindness whenever a Harris production was involved, had difficulty with diplomacy. "Miss Hepburn," he wrote, "is not a full-fledged dramatic actress yet. Her rocket-like success in the talking pictures has set too high the standards by which she has to be judged in the more coherent world [*sic*] of the stage." The critic added, off-handedly, "Her voice is a rather strident instrument." Miss Hepburn's voice would become the trademark of a magnificent career.

If *The Lake* was the disaster that Harris had expected, *The Green Bay Tree* unexpectedly fared little better, running out of audience after a few months. Its planned tour was canceled. Nothing was going right.

◆

Mildred Harris had written a play. She called it *Correspondent Unknown* and she'd found the right actress for it. She claimed that if this actress could get rid of her Southern accent she'd be brilliant. The actress was Margaret Sullavan, and Jed had her come up to the office for an interview.

She was conservatively dressed, classy and Christian. Her hair was thick and curly, cut to medium length, much the same shade of brown as her serious dark eyes. They were big eyes to go with rosebud lips. Her figure was trim and athletic. An attractive woman, then, even beautiful. If Jed Harris ever fell for any woman instantly, he fell for Margaret Sullavan.

She had been married for nine months, in 1931, to Henry Fonda. They remained friends. By all accounts she had verve and a polished sexiness. Brought up in Norfolk, Virginia, she was a Southern Katharine Hepburn.

When she went home to see her parents, Harris pursued her. He commuted between Virginia and New York so frequently in the following months that the newspapers began running rumors that he was negotiating a play with some Southern playwright "and one of the Broadway games is to guess which."

His infatuation with Margaret Sullavan finally became so intense it undid his way with secrecy. Ruth Gordon learned of the affair. She was no longer willing to forgive him everything. She left the house on East 79th Street, moving out with Jones and Andrée and abandoning it to Harris and Chodorov and whomever. She found a four-story town house at 60 West 12th Street, in the fashionable quarter of Greenwich Village.

A little boy should have a garden, she believed. A little boy should have a house with stairs.

Jed Harris is searching for a new play with which to wind up his season of activities. He has dropped his plan to do Howard's *Yellow Jack* and now wants a drama to serve as a vehicle for Margaret Sullavan.

—*New York Herald-Tribune,* January 14, 1934

13

LIKE CHRIST ON THE CROSS

BESIDES HAVING a house with stairs and a garden, five-year-old Jones mostly had a nurse instead of parents. The scandal of his existence had still not appeared in print. Jed hardly bothered seeing him at all and Ruth, immediately after furnishing the Twelfth Street house in her own modest way, left for an extended stay in California. She wanted to find movie work and, presumably, lose Jed.

He had his hands full with Maggie Sullavan. He told his sister Mildred that the actress was suicidal.

"She asked me why we don't make a suicide pact. She said, 'I'm ready to kill myself out of love for you, say you feel the same way too. If we killed ourselves,'" he continued in mockery of Sullavan's Southern accent, "'at least we'd be together for ever after. It would prove how much we loved each other.'"

Mildred told him that the both of them were *meshugeneh*.

He set his own pace with the actress. He was first adoring, then demanding, possessive, jealous, abusive, and then adoring again. Finally she broke under the cycle and fled, following Ruth to California.

Many movie offers had come Maggie's way. She decided on *The Good Fairy*, to be directed by William Wyler. A few weeks after filming began, she and Wyler became engaged.

147

Harris gave chase. He flew across the country, and in 1934 that was something. He took his sister Sylvia with him.

A lithe beauty now in her twenties, Sylvia Harris was an independent young woman and not about to be her brother's acolyte. Jed arranged for her to work as Ruth's personal secretary.

They rented a house on Canyon Drive in Beverly Hills, but his sister's presence did not deter the women he attracted. One morning, Sylvia went out to the pool to do her daily laps and found a naked woman there. Jed had met a couple of newlyweds at a party the previous night. Now, it seemed, the bride had scaled the garden wall.

The young nude's explanation was familiar: she'd been unable to think of anything but Jed Harris ever since listening to him talk at the party. Sylvia tossed out a bathing suit and marched upstairs.

"Oh God, get rid of her," he mumbled.

"I don't 'get rid' of people. She's someone *you* met."

He rose and dressed in silence, trotted downstairs, and went out the front door, leaving the dirty work to Sylvia.

◆

When Margaret Sullavan's daughter was preparing a family memoir, William Wyler told her that in the midst of filming *The Good Fairy*, her mother froze on camera. Jed Harris had walked onto the set and placed himself beside the cameraman.

> "There he was, out of the blue. Stood there. Like Svengali . . . and he made her very nervous, but I think she was fascinated by him. He had kind of a hold on her . . . I think trying to get away from Jed Harris contributed to the fact that she married me."
> —Brooke Hayward, *Haywire*

Wyler and Maggie Sullavan were going to be married in Yuma, Arizona. Jed showed up at their hotel. Wyler told Brooke Hayward that her mother asked "to talk to Harris alone. I waited in the hotel lobby . . . a long time went by. . . . Down she came and said, 'Okay, let's go.' He was supposed to be a very persuasive fellow, but he didn't make it that day."

It wasn't like Jed Harris to give up in Yuma. A week later he invited Chodorov over for midnight supper. The young playwright had, like so many others, been snatched up by a studio. Sylvia was sleeping at Ruth's. It was a rainy California night, a monsoon-like night, and after vainly ringing the bell, Chodorov tried the knob. The door was unlocked.

He prowled through the empty rooms. Jed's hearing had grown uncertain, so no answer didn't mean he was out. There were cars in the driveway.

Chodorov climbed the stairs and as he stepped into the master bedroom there was a squeal and a scramble. A naked Harris popped up in bed with a grin. His partner wriggled under the blankets beside him. She refused to emerge despite his cheerful imprecations. He finally laughed, got up, wrapped himself in a blue flannel robe, and went downstairs with Eddie. He poured Hime cognac for both of them and chatted until it was almost two and the poor young lady had either to appear or to stay the night. She tiptoed down the stairs and walked past the men as if she were a part of the silence.

With her departure, Jed went to the telephone and dialed.

"I'd like to speak with Miss Sullavan."

Chodorov leaped from his chair and begged Harris to stop.

"No, not 'Mrs. Wyler.' I want to speak to *Miss Sullavan*. You wake her and tell her that Jed Harris wants to speak with her."

Chodorov grappled for the telephone but was shaken off. With a violent grin, Jed whispered into the mouthpiece, "You're a weak, untalented man married to a woman who is in love with me." He dropped the instrument into its cradle, refilled his cognac, and resumed the conversation as if nothing out of the ordinary had interrupted it. Only moments later, it seemed to Chodorov, the doorbell chimed.

When the door was opened, Wyler reached through, yanked Harris by the bathrobe lapels and dragged him out onto the soaked lawn. In the light of the lamps glowing through the living room windows, Chodorov saw the director wind up uncertainly in the slogging downpour and sock Harris. Jed fell backward, flopping into the muck. Wyler leaped on him and the two men rolled on the waterlogged lawn, Harris making no defense of himself.

Finally Wyler rose, dripping wet, got into his car, and drove off. Jed stumbled inside, toweled himself dry, refilled his cognac, and picked up the telephone. He dialed Orson Welles's number. He knew Welles's wife, Virginia, and evidently she answered. Amiably enough, as if it were noon, Jed suggested a part for her in a play he said he was producing. He thought that Virginia might be right for it and wondered whether she might come over to the house, just now, to do a reading. It was three o'clock in the morning.

Virginia Welles had been willing, Harris later assured Chodorov, but Orson, he said, felt otherwise.

Instead of driving straight home, Wyler went to the Beverly Hills police and told them he thought he'd killed a man. A month later, he and Maggie Sullavan were divorced.

◆

Jed Harris arrives here early next week from an extended Hollywood stay. The producer, who has been inactive on Broadway this season, has planned for four pro-

149

ductions next fall and winter. Among these is the dramatization of Edith Wharton's novel, *Ethan Frome*, by Owen and Donald Davis.

—*New York Herald-Tribune*, May 23, 1935

Jed had made peace with Ruth during the California stay. Their days as a couple were over though he would occasionally stop by at the Twelfth Street house and have dinner. For her part, she'd agreed to do *Ethan Frome* with him.

The popular Edith Wharton novella of 1911 may well have appealed to Harris for the way it fit in with a current stage and literary vogue for placing high tragedy in the American backwoods. It was as if, impatient for greatness, our writers thought that indigenous art could be instantly created by setting established classical forms upon an unequivocally American grid. In *Desire Under the Elms*, for instance, Eugene O'Neill had transposed the fundamental passions of Greek drama to an American farm. Soon, in such works as *Of Mice and Men* and *East of Eden*, John Steinbeck would be placing allegorical and biblical tales in rural settings.

Another American writer who sought to find Medea in the haystack was Owen Davis. Mr. Davis had achieved commercial success as the author of such melodramas as *Nellie, The Beautiful Cloak Model*. Turning to tragedy, as successful light playwrights inevitably feel they have to, Davis won the 1923 Pulitzer Prize for *Icebound*. It is the saga of a Maine family whose emotionless exteriors conceal passions of complex and perhaps incestuous varieties. The play was still another example of Greek tragedy Americanized, and so Owen Davis, as an experienced dramatist with both commercial and artistic credentials, was a natural choice by Harris for the dramatization of *Ethan Frome*.

Edith Wharton's story is set in a remote and dreary stretch of Massachusetts farmland where the title character escapes a bleak marriage by falling in love with his wife's cousin. Realizing that he will never be given a divorce, Frome tries to kill himself and the girl. The attempt misfires and they survive as cripples, to be permanently in the wife's care.

Owen Davis was not interested in dramatizing someone else's story. However, his son Donald, a budding writer, was. Harris agreed to commission the dramatization from Donald on the condition that the father co-sign the work.

Six months later, young Davis sent the script over to Harris's suite in the Waldorf Towers. His wife, the former actress Dorothy Matthews, decided to have a dinner party on the day he delivered the play, hoping that it would distract him from his nervousness. As Donald and Dorothy—he called her "Mattie"—were checking last-minute details, Jed telephoned. He suggested that Donald come right over to discuss the script. The Davises agreed that

150

the play was more important than a dinner party, and Donald left immediately.

There was no answer when the doorman at the Waldorf Towers rang up. Donald insisted that he was expected. Harris had remembered to leave his name at the desk. He was sent up.

He padded silently along the carpeted corridor and found the door to Harris's suite ajar. He rang the buzzer. There was no reply. Nor was there any response to his knocking at the door. He pushed it open. The lamps in the living room were lit, but turned down low. The place was occupied, there were cigarettes in the ashtrays. Davis remembered that detail many years later.

Uncomfortable and feeling like an intruder, he tiptoed through the plush living room toward a light that came from beyond. There, in the bedroom, was Jed Harris in red silk pajamas, "sprawled across the bed on his back, arms apart, like Christ on the cross." He was sleeping with his eyes open. "His eyeballs were rolled up under the lids so that only the whites showed."

Davis made decorous wake-up noises. He went back and rang the doorbell, he called out from the living room, opened and closed doors, flushed toilets. Finally, he shook Harris by the shoulders until the man's eyes rolled down and into focus. They stared at Davis, then locked in.

"Ruth liked it," he said.

"The hell with her! What did you think?"

Harris's eyes rotated up, beneath the lids once more. Davis shook him again, this time vainly. He stormed out of the suite. The dinner party was still going strong and he got himself drunk.

At three thirty in the morning the telephone rang.

"Donald? Oh, I'm so sorry. Please forgive me. You can't imagine what I've been through. . . . It's awful, just awful, but you've got to understand. It's my whole life. I've been through so much . . . I'm exhausted. Please. We'll meet tomorrow morning."

"It's already tomorrow morning."

"Yes, this morning. At eleven. Is that all right with you?"

So it began, again for Harris, the first time for Davis. They worked without pause that first morning, and for the playwright it was productive and exhilarating work. Rather than interrupt it, Jed ordered lunch from room service. When the waiter rolled the linen-covered cart into the room, Davis was puzzled to see lunch for only one. He watched as Harris cut the slice of roast beef precisely in half and placed one share on the salad plate. The peas were divided, the mashed potatoes. Harris smiled and extended a portion to Davis, not eating himself.

He was saving his half for dinner. His Waldorf Towers bill was in heavy arrears. He'd convinced the management, he later confided to Davis, that rather than evict a celebrated guest and accept the loss it made more sense to let him stay on until his next success made complete repayment possible. But he could charge only one meal daily.

Ethan Frome work sessions became a way of life and Davis saw little of Mattie. Evenings, the men would go to bars where Jed seemed to run into people eager to pick up his checks. Once they went to the six-day bike race at Madison Square Garden. It was not the sort of sport to develop aficionados and data addicts, yet Jed knew all the bikers, he knew their records. He and Davis would watch the race and talk about *Ethan Frome* and take breaks for dinner or drinks.

Other times the men would stop by at Ruth's. She would hand Jed a tendollar bill and he'd take Donald to dinner at a Greenwich Village restaurant.

◆

"Did you write this page, darling?"

Donald was on his way out to the day's work session.

"Sure," he said, scanning it. "Last night."

"Read it."

It was the second-act curtain scene. As Davis had originally written it, Ethan was playing a country tune on his fiddle. It was a way of articulating his feelings. In this version, though, someone else was playing the violin. It didn't make sense.

Davis reread the whole scene. It was all senseless.

He told Jed he was taking the play back; it was being rewritten to death, he said, and with a sigh Harris agreed. "I know, I know. It's all bollixed up, but I got so goddamned tired waiting for the thing."

"I still want you to produce and direct it, Jed. I just don't want you to write it. And to prove it, I'm going to sell you the option for fifteen hundred dollars."

Harris peered at him.

"I'll even lend you the money," Davis said, taking an envelope from his breast pocket. "Pay me back whenever you think of it."

◆

Those whom Harris alienated were doing just fine. George Kaufman and Moss Hart were about to win the Pulitzer Prize for *You Can't Take It With You*. Ben Hecht and Charlie MacArthur's *Twentieth Century* had been a huge success, not only on stage but as a classic movie with John Barrymore and Carole Lombard. Paul Streger had appeared in the Broadway premiere of Luigi Pirandello's *Six Characters in Search of an Author*. Herman Shumlin was established as a producer of such prestigious dramas as Vicki Baum's *Grand*

Jed Harris at nine   *(Vandamm Studio)*

Time cover of Jed Harris,
September 3, 1928

Jed's sisters, 1929. Left to right:
Florence, Mildred,
Sylvia   *(Billy Rose Theatre
Collection)*

The Green Bay Tree, 1933.
Left to right: Jill Esmond,
Leo G. Carroll,
and Laurence Olivier
(Vandamm Studio)

Jed Harris in Miami Beach
(United Press International)

Some of the women in Jed Harris's life

Ruth Gordon in *Serena Blandish*,
1929   *(Vandamm Studio)*

Judith Anderson, 1928   *(Billy Rose
Theatre Collection)*

Margaret Sullavan in *Stage Door
Canteen*, 1936   *(Vandamm Studio)*

Louise Platt, 1939   *(Billy Rose
Theatre Collection)*

Cinda Glenn, 1951   *(United Press
International)*

Geraldine Morris, 1958   Gilda Davis, 1958

Harris's umbrella scene in *Our Town*, with Martha Scott, 1938   *(Vandamm Studio)*

Jean Dalrymple
with Harris,
1944   *(Stan Lee,
Graphic House,
Inc.)*

Miss Pinchot's Suicide Follows New Play Theme

By George Kivel and Grace Robinson.

Jed Harris' new play, "Our Town," whose last act depicts a macabre fantasy of life after death, was revealed last night as the prompter behind the scene of the suicide of beautiful Rosamond Pinchot, who as a debutante fourteen years ago skyrocketed to fame in the role of the nun in "The Miracle."

In the first faint light of the rising sun, she was found dead at 7:15 yesterday, overcome by carbon monoxide fumes in the garage on the palatial estate she had rented at Old Brookville, L. I.

Calmly, deliberately she had set forth on an adventure to investigate the mysteries of death, taking the cue from the play, which she saw Saturday night during a tryout at Princeton, N. J.

The play, a creation of Thornton Wilder, makes death a beautiful thing—a realization of all the joys which humankind strives for in life. Life, in the play, is simply a strange interlude before death.

Captures Mood of Drama.

Rosamond Pinchot — child of wealth, favorite of society, onetime toast of Broadway; niece of the former Governor of Pennsylvania—captured the mood of the dra-

William Gaston
Rosamond's attorney-playwright husband.

ma. It made suicide an exciting,

The Drama Is Ended

New York Daily News, January 25, 1938   (*Copyright 1938, New York News, Inc.*)

Harris with Billy Rose on the set of *The Billy Rose Show*   (*Billy Rose Theatre Collection*)

The 1980 *Dick Cavett Show*, which was broadcast after Harris's death.
(*Courtesy of the Dick Cavett Show*)

Hotel and Lillian Hellman's *The Children's Hour.* Katharine Hepburn and Laurence Olivier were great stars, she in Hollywood and he on the international stage and screen. George Abbott had two hits in the 1935 season alone, *Jumbo* and *Three Men on a Horse*, and then became a producer himself, succeeding on his first try, *Boy Meets Girl.* Sam Behrman had rung up his greatest success yet with *Biography*, and Ina Claire had topped her career with it.

Even Anita had written a play. Her agent had contacted Jed, not about producing it but about approving it because it was transparently about him. Harris didn't much care about that play; he didn't seem to care about any plays. The only one he produced through 1934 and 1935 was *Life's Too Short*, a ridiculous comedy that Mildred's husband Cappy had written in collaboration with John Whedon. It closed in a week. Later in 1935, Anita's play, *A Touch of Brimstone*, would have a ninety-performance engagement, longer than any Jed Harris production had run in years.

It wasn't as if he'd lost his dramatic senses. Many of the current hits were dramas he'd been offered, had even optioned and worked on, such as *Twentieth Century* and *Grand Hotel*. Indeed, *Ethan Frome* would go on to success. Yet he lost them or let them go, and instead produced such suicide missions as *Life's Too Short*.

❖

"Mildred, you've got to help me."

"Whatever it is, leave me out."

Sitting in her East Hampton, New York home nearly fifty years later, she shook her head and grinned. "That brother of mine was always there when he needed me."

"She won't talk to me."

"Ruth?"

"Maggie. If I don't get her back I'm going to kill myself."

"Go ahead."

"Please. She's always wanted to meet you. She's rehearsing *Stage Door.*"

He covered his face with his hands, the picture of grief. Whenever he asked her to do something that she just couldn't do for him, she did it for him. She remembered thinking that as she sat in the darkened theater, watching Margaret Sullavan rehearse. Paul Streger had let her in. He now worked for the play's producer, Leland Hayward. Despite the enduring hatred for Jed, Paul considered Hayward "a road company Jed Harris."

At the break, a stage manager whispered in Maggie's ear. She peered into the dark and then dashed down the steps, up the aisle. Not pausing to introduce herself, she threw her arms around Mildred and burst into tears.

"What do you want with that idiot brother of mine?"

"I swore I'd never lay eyes on him again, but what can I do?"

The actress took Mildred by the shoulders and held her out for examination. Looking warmly, earnestly, deeply into Mildred's eyes she smiled. "I'm so glad to meet you at last," she said. "You're lovely."

"He wants to talk to you."

"I don't know what to do. I'm practically engaged to Leland. Where is Jed anyhow?"

"He's waiting at my place."

"Let me get my purse," and she hurried out of the theater with Mildred, waving to a cab as they hit the doors.

"Seventy-two Barrow Street. The Village."

Jed was standing at the opened door as they came up the stairs, and Maggie fell into his arms like a ballerina. They hugged all the way downstairs and out the door. Two weeks later she married Leland Hayward.

❖

At seven, Jones was a little European prince in his navy coat with brass buttons; the matching pea cap; the patent leather shoes; and his French-accented English. He held his father's hand as they climbed out of the taxi. It was April, it was *Pesach* and they were going to the Horowitz family seder.

Mildred's daughter Nina was walking toward them with her grandfather, her *zayde*. They'd just been to the park. Meyer had been explaining why the ducks, the *pachkes*, hadn't been there during the winter. They'd been in *shul*, he'd told her. "It's always warm in the *shul* and when the *pachkes* are in *shul* they behave themselves. They don't eat nuts and they use the bathroom. The *pachkes* are not so foolish as they may seem." He looked up to see Jed and Jones. "They even go to see your Uncle Jacob's shows in the theater."

"Zayde says the *pachkes* go to your shows, Uncle Jed."

"Your uncle makes shows that everybody likes, even the *pachkes* from the park, and he has special water ponds in the balcony where they can sit and watch."

Perhaps it was bankruptcy that had tamed Meyer, perhaps age.

The sight of his parents was always a sentimental shock to Boshere . . . the filial comet. . . . The Nussbaums (they had lacked the courage to alter their name to Boshere) . . . sat nodding like a pair of mechanical toys at their son's pronouncements. . . . Though their lives were filled with Jo Boshere they seemed to know nothing about him beyond the fact that he was and almost mysteriously remained, their son. . . . The . . . stubby old woman in a wrapper and faded slippers who came shuffling out of the bedroom . . . he remembered her in the days he had writhed under her scoldings. . . . That other figure entering the room, a grey man with a sheepish smile, hesitant walk—timorous—behind this [man] stood the blustering father of his youth.   —Ben Hecht, *A Jew in Love*

154

When Nina saw what was in the black cases that Jed was carrying she squealed with joy.

"Puppies!"

"Do not put your finger inside," Jones said Frenchly, "or they will nip."

"The brown one's a cocker spaniel," Jed said, "and his name is Max. The black one is Albert. He's a Scottish terrier, a Scottie."

Aunt Mildred had come to the seder alone. She and Cappy had been divorced. Aunt Sylvia was with her husband, the writer Hillel Bernstein. Aunt Florie—she'd changed her named to Harris too—looked different from everyone, like a bohemian. She was studying at the Art Students League. Uncle Saul didn't come. He hadn't changed his name yet, but he would in time. To "Horwitt."

Meyer conducted a proper seder, no short cuts. Jed assisted. As the youngest male at the table, Jones asked the Four Questions. Afterward, Nina showed him how to spritz the blue seltzer-water bottle. Memories of childhood are selective. Years later, Nina remembered Jonesy's free and elated spritzing.

After the children had been put to bed, Jed couldn't resist a final peek at his sleeping niece. He stole into the bedroom that had once been his sisters'. He touched the child's brow beneath the sweet yellow hair. Her flannel nightgown with its pink birds was buttoned to her chin. He kissed the honey cheek.

"Sssssh," she whispered, her eyes shut tight in the dark. "I'm sleeping."

He sighed. She remembered that too.

❖

Thornton Wilder had been a couple of classes ahead of Jed at Yale. They'd met there and met again on a train to Florida, but the meetings hadn't taken. The men were so different from each other. Wilder, soft and pink, was literary, an academic, thoroughly American, sexually covered. He had been born in the Midwest, had spent his childhood in China. That was a bit different from Jed's heritage of Lemburg and Newark. In short, Wilder was dairy, Harris meat.

Thornton Wilder's teaching at prep school (Lawrenceville) and college (the University of Chicago) had unexpectedly led to a great popular success with a novel, *The Bridge of San Luis Rey*. It had won him the 1927 Pulitzer Prize. When his name came up now, Harris was interested. Jed and Ruth had been discussing possible collaborations, once she closed in *Ethan Frome*. He was enthusiastic about Ibsen's *Peer Gynt*. She wasn't. The part of Peer's mother had scant appeal for her.

If it had to be Ibsen, she was more inclined to *A Doll's House*, Nora being one of the great roles. When she suggested that Wilder write a new adaptation, Jed decided that the combination of Harris, Gordon, Wilder, and Ibsen not only had real possibilities, but that it would give him the opening to ask Wilder for a new play.

Wilder would write that adaptation; he would give Jed a new play, *Our Town;* he would introduce Jed to Rosamond Pinchot; and these events were to bring Jed Harris's life to the balance point.

THE JUGGLER

"Jed Harris never bothered to lie." —Edward Chodorov

"Jed Harris never told the truth in his whole life." —Paul Streger

"Jed Harris never told a lie that didn't have a foundation. It was as if he wanted to make life more exciting, more fun." —Donald Davis

THE ONLY GOOD thing to come out of *Spring Dance* was Louise Platt. Cynicism must have led Harris to do the play in the first place. He had not produced any comedies since *The Royal Family* and frequently described them as fluff, not worth his time.

Aside from being a comedy, *Spring Dance* was an example, and a not very good one, of the society plays of Philip Barry, a playwright he particularly disliked. Barry and Harris had been classmates at Yale. Evidently Barry represented to Harris just the kind of arrogant, moneyed, Gentile mentality that had made him feel such an outsider at college. He told José Ferrer, who was appearing in *Spring Dance*, that Barry had snubbed him at Yale; that anti-Semitism was implicit in Barry's highfalutin manner.

Perhaps Harris did not know that Barry was a working-class Irish Catholic who had been just as much a Yale outsider as he. Writing these high-society

157

comedies was Barry's own way of overcoming perceived handicaps of background, much as Jacob Horowitz's becoming Jed Harris had been.

Perhaps Harris did know. Perhaps they reminded each other of each other.

Philip Barry was another golden boy who had lately lost his touch. It had been seven years since his last hit, *Holiday*, and would be another three until his next one, *The Philadelphia Story*. This play, *Spring Dance*, was just another failure of the 1936 season.

But when Louise Platt replaced Imogene Coca in its leading role during tryouts, she became the new American princess in Harris's life. In this line she succeeded Katharine Hepburn and Margaret Sullavan, but she would hardly have Jed to herself. No woman ever did. Louise Platt had to share him with the ultimate Gentile.

Rosamond Pinchot was five feet ten inches tall and her beauty was leonine, astonishing. Her parents were Amos and Gertrude Pinchot, both from prominent families. Her uncle Gifford Pinchot was governor of Pennsylvania. In addition to having an impeccable social background, "Pinchie," as she'd of course been known at Miss Chapin's School, held a master's degree in history and was an expert golfer, tennis player, and rider. She was almost a comedy of perfection.

Max Reinhardt had discovered her on an ocean liner and cast her in his 1924 production of *The Miracle*. She was acclaimed in the largely mime role but had been unable to follow up the debut. Her problem, she rationalized, was "finding men tall enough to play opposite me," but in truth she simply was not an actress. She got several minor roles in plays and movies but at twenty-five she was a has-been.

She married a society lawyer, bore him two children, and was living wealthily on Long Island when Thornton Wilder introduced her to Harris. She probably still yearned for the lost glamour of her theatrical career and Jed Harris was stage glory incarnate. The thirty-three-year-old girl left her husband and became Harris's unsalaried production assistant, lover and worshipper.

He must have been particularly magnetic at the time, attracting not only Louise Platt and Rosie Pinchot but viable projects as well. *A Doll's House* and *Our Town* were knowing choices rather than the arbitrary, impulsive, and hopeless projects that had been draining him over the previous decade. *A Doll's House* was an established classic and its star was to be the popular and capable Ruth Gordon. The production would restore the prestigious image that Harris had established with *Uncle Vanya*. As for *Our Town*, he himself said, "This is the best manuscript I ever got. If anything goes wrong with it, it will be my fault, not Wilder's."

This was more like it, the sort of plays that had made Jed Harris Jed Harris.

Moreover, as they always seem to, good things were leading to other good things. His relationship with Ruth had stabilized into something distantly but not uncozily familial. He had both Rosie and Louise in tow, as well as a flock of gifted writers: Eddie Chodorov, Donald Davis, Thornton Wilder. He was keeping all these elements in motion—the productions, the love affairs, the women from the past, the entourage of writers—as if they were plates spinning and he a juggler, running back and forth along a row of pegs, keeping the whole thing going. Just now he seemed to have all the plates spinning.

❖

He plunged into production. *A Doll's House* and *Our Town* would of course come into New York on each other's heels. Was that not his style? The Ibsen was to open two days after Christmas of 1937 and then Wilder's play would have its premiere a couple of months later.

"People [are] asking me whether it's the propitious moment to bring an Ibsen show to New York," he said to an interviewer. "Hell, why not? You know and I know and everybody who goes to the theater knows that it isn't the author that makes a given play right at a given time and place. It's the show as created by the specific cast and if that cast and its direction are characterized by conviction and rightness and enthusiasm a producer can bring his play to town in Lent, on Yom Kippur or in the first week of July . . . the success or failure are inherent in the production itself and are entirely independent of outside agencies of any sort."

Rehearsals for *A Doll's House* went smoothly. It was a company of professionals, Paul Lukas as Doctor Rank, Sam Jaffe playing Krogstad, and Dennis King as Thorwald. They were as good as any British repertory company, Jed told Ed Chodorov, "but Jesus Christ," he sighed. "It's such a creaky old play."

Presumably, that was an opinion he formed while working on the play. He would later say that nothing in *A Doll's House* supported its famous climax of Nora leaving Thorwald at the end. He'd describe that as an arbitrary turn of event devised merely for the sake of surprise.

To see in Harris's reservations about *A Doll's House* some disagreement with the idea of female independence would mistake his attitude toward women. While he was certainly abusive in his emotional relationships with them, he was never contemptuous of their intelligence. The idea of a generalized female inferiority would doubtless have seemed simply stupid to him.

His growing disrespect for Ibsen's play notwithstanding, Harris's rehearsals were stimulating. He climbed on stage to direct the play's first-act curtain scene, after Krogstad has started blackmailing Nora with the threat of exposing her as a forger to her husband Thorwald. Rosie Pinchot carried a folding chair to center stage.

"Ruth?" Harris said. "That chair. It's the sofa. There'll be a Christmas tree behind you, a small one on a table with ornaments and so on. Thorwald is in his armchair, over there at left. Reading his newspaper."

Rosie carried a second chair to the designated spot. She left, to return with a newspaper that she handed to Dennis King.

"Read the newspaper. Smoke your cigar. Nora, you sit there staring into space, but not thoughtlessly. You're focusing very intensely on the loneliness of your position. Thorwald, fold up the newspaper meticulously, then put it down on the table beside you. Yawn, then get up, take your time about it. Cross behind Ruth."

Dennis King walked slowly across the stage.

"All right now," Jed whispered. "Stop at the piano. Pick out the melody, the Grieg. . . . Take your time. Okay, line. We want the complete weight of this stodgy idiot's insensitivity."

"Dear," Thorwald said to Nora. "I'm . . . going . . . to my study. Will you . . . call me . . . when supper's ready?"

King took his exit.

"All right, Nora. Sit there. You are the loneliest woman in the world. In you we must see all the solitude that the human spirit endures. You must show it without the help of a single word or gesture. I want our audience to chill in pity. Sit in your chair and look out at us. Look . . . look . . . look. Fine, Ruth. Curtain."

❖

Jed had met Paul Osborn some years earlier, and had kept in touch with the young playwright. Osborn had submitted *The Vinegar Tree*, which Harris rejected, but without any attempt at entrapment. The producer did not pounce on every writer he ran into. Not immediately.

Now that Paul Osborn was announcing his intention to marry the actress Millicent Green, Jed grew more interested in him. That was how Paul and Millicent came to see it.

Osborn invited Harris to their engagement party, mentioning that E. E. Cummings would be among the guests. The painter and poet Edward Estlin Cummings was one of the most fashionable artistic figures of the era, and Jed was eager to meet him and prevailed upon Osborn to arrange it. Paul told the poet that Jed Harris was the theater's wonder boy, a man everyone wanted to meet. An appointment was made for eleven o'clock the following morning.

They sat silently in the anteroom of Jed's office. Many years later, Osborn would still remember turning the pages of various show-business trade publications, thinking it was one hell of a time for Jed Harris to pull a Jed Harris. At half past twelve, Cummings rose.

"Jesus Christ," he said. "I'm supposed to be a poet. What the hell am I doing waiting an hour and a half in the office of a Broadway producer?"

He left in disgust, Osborn following along, trying to make a case for Harris and eccentricity, with little success. Harris, naturally, never called to apologize, but he did show up at Paul and Millicent's engagement party and as a guest, at least, his form was fine.

It was a theater crowd and this glamorous producer had its attention as he smiled, smoked, and told his stories. By this time he consciously flexed storytelling muscles. "If I'd been an Arab," he once said, "I would have sat on a little rug with some kind of basket or pot in front of me—sat in a market and told stories and people would have thrown money into it. I know how to tell a story."

He certainly did, and at the Osborn engagement party, even so entrenched an enemy as Herman Shumlin sat on the floor and listened. The particular anecdote was about *The Green Bay Tree*. (It was one that Harris would repeat through the years. The following version is taken from an interview given some time later and, as Paul Osborn wryly noted, it was practically unchanged from the way Jed told it that night.)

"One day Noël Coward arrived on a steamer from England," Harris began with relish. "He walked down the gangplank at one fifteen, got into a taxi, and at two he was buying a ticket at the Cort Theatre for *Green Bay Tree*. I didn't know he was doing it. I didn't even know he was in town, though we're good friends.

"Late that afternoon I called my secretary to check messages and she said, 'Oh, Mr. Harris! Mr. Coward is anxious to speak to you. He's taken a suite at the Waldorf Towers. Please call him.'

"Well, he was hysterical. 'Good God,' he said, 'I've *got* to talk to you about *Green Bay*. I didn't know the theater could be like that. How did you get those performances? I've seen James Dale a hundred times, I didn't know he was that good. The man turned pale!'

"I said to him, 'God almighty, Noël, you didn't believe that Duse turned pale, why the hell should you think that James Dale did?'

"'The pallor,' he said, 'The pallor. It was there.'

161

"I said, 'Dear Noël, there is a spotlight. It puts a fierce highlight on Dale's forehead. I filled out his face with a baby spot from the balcony. Then my electrician pulls out the baby spot. That is your pallor.'"

"You fooled Noël Coward?" one of the guests asked.

"And I was ashamed of myself for it," Jed replied, still whispering and now smiling. "It was a David Belasco touch, so literal-minded. I told Noël I ought to be able to make an audience *feel* he's turning pale when *no* light is changing."

Jed then began a recollection of Bernard Shaw, but had barely started when the room's attention was distracted by another presence: E. E. Cummings's. Having let himself into the apartment, the poet was now performing an exquisitely detailed pantomime. He stood and brushed the rug with the side of his foot, as if sweeping something along. Some sort of insect. He looked so disgusted, his expression was so sour, that it must have been a cockroach.

"Get along," the poet whispered, and one head after another turned in his direction.

Harris stopped the Shaw story. He gazed narrowly at his competition.

"We don't want you here," Cummings said to the imaginary bug.

The room had fallen silent. Everyone watched as the cockroach was nudged off the living room carpet and into the foyer. Osborn felt that the people in the room were straining to avoid looking at Jed. This was between Cummings and Harris. Everyone seemed to know that.

The poet pushed the thing to the front door, which he opened. Then he kicked the creature out. He shuddered and brushed his hands clean against the sides of his trousers.

Moments later, Harris muttered an excuse and left. The poet had gotten even for having been kept waiting in Harris's office.

◆

A Doll's House opened to maddening notices, the mixed kind that made it tempting to stay open. Such a situation demands delicate objectivity and theatrical sense from a producer. He has to decide whether economic caution and crafty promotion can salvage the project, or whether he ought to accept his losses and close the play before they increase.

Show people tried to help. At the Shubert Theatre, where *Idiot's Delight* was playing, Alfred Lunt and Lynn Fontanne took their curtain calls and then urged the audience to see *A Doll's House* next door at the Morosco, but Jed posted the closing notice and another play was booked into the theater. In the *New York Herald-Tribune*, Lucius Beebe quoted a bitter Harris as saying, "There is no man in New York writing dramatic criticism today who has any creative force; they are critics only because they have jobs. When their papers fold, they are no longer critics. I've never seen so many men so ill-equipped for their jobs as the boys now reviewing for the dailies."

Such reactions are as understandable and natural as considering any praise a brilliant critical perception. Ironically, *A Doll's House* would be rescued by one of New York's critics.

Alexander Woollcott had always been a frustrated performer and print had finally proved too limiting for his exhibitionism. Given his own radio program, *The Town Crier*, on Sunday evenings, he had come into his own as the national esthete.

"Business was on the slow side after those reviews," Ruth Gordon remembered. "By Saturday night the total take for the week was eleven hundred dollars. I know some smarties who say, 'Well, you know, in those days eleven hundred dollars was really eleven hundred dollars.' Well thank God I've lived my life in show business where we know that eleven hundred dollars is never anything but eleven—hundred—dollars. So that's why Jed had decided to close us down when that Monday morning this fella shows up at the box office and he says, 'I never saw an Ibsen play but if Woollcott says it's good, give me two down front.'

"Who'd'a known Aleck, 'The Town Crier,' had spent a half hour on network radio, raving about *A Doll's House!*

"Well! We were in business, no thought of closing then. They moved us right across Shubert Alley, 'round the corner to the Broadhurst . . . and at the end of the engagement, Jed's production broke every single record for an Ibsen play on Broadway."

Harris's only regret, he later said, was that the play had been saved by a critic for whom he had so little respect.

◆

"You're being too hasty about this marriage," Jed told Paul Osborn as they strolled along Central Park West. "Millicent is a lovely girl, but you hardly know her."

"I think I know her better than most men know their fiancées."

"But does she know how to pack? When you get married you have to wipe out every consideration except, 'Can the girl pack?' People like us have to have girls who can pack."

"She can pack."

"I've been married, Paul, so I know. Domestic life is stifling."

The following day, Jed phoned Millicent and invited her to the office. She couldn't, as an actress, ignore the possibility that he wanted to offer her a part, in fact she convinced herself that was precisely why he was asking her up. But Margaret Sullavan was her best friend and so she went there with trepidation.

Arriving promptly for the ten-thirty appointment, she was called into his office six hours later. He talked about everything in the world that was not theatrical. She left convinced that all he'd wanted was to size her up as competition for control of Paul. When she signed on to tour with *Dead End*, Jed invited Osborn to sail to Europe with him. He was on his way to Zurich to pop in on Wilder, who had fled there precisely to escape Harris's collaborative efforts.

Osborn had been well at work on a new play, *Morning's at Seven*. (It would flop, only to be smashingly revived on Broadway some forty years later.) He had just broken his leg in a ridiculous accident, wrestling at a party. The cast made it uncomfortable for him to sit and write for any duration of time, and so with Millicent gone, the sail and the sea were irresistible.

The *Ile de France* plowed through the Atlantic, Jed so relentless in his criticism of Millicent that Paul telephoned her, ship to shore, just to establish his loyalty. At last, Harris left off, distracted by a beefy Southerner who had become a daily, obstreperous champagne drunk.

"You like that guy, Paul?"

"Jesus, how I hate him."

"Tell you what. You talk to him, and while you're distracting him, I'll come up from behind and hit him over the head with one of those lifeboat oars."

"Come on, I'm not going to do that."

"He won't hurt you. You're on crutches."

Disembarking at Plymouth, they waited for the boat train to London and were separated in the commotion. Jed, when Paul finally found him, was chatting cheerfully with the Southerner who had been so obnoxious aboard ship. Now he strolled back.

"You know how all this trouble started with that guy? On the boat, the very first day out, I heard him saying as I passed, 'There goes that dirty little Jew again.' It was bad enough he said that, but to say 'again' on the first day, that was infuriating. That was why I wanted to hit him with the oar.

"But then I went to my cabin and looked at myself in the mirror, unshaven and everything. I was thinking about that all the way across and so, just now, I went over to him and I said, 'You know? You're right. I looked in the mirror and I *am* a dirty little Jew.'"

◆

"I like you, *goy* or no," he had said to Thornton Wilder. Whether or not Wilder returned the affection, he certainly respected Harris and would have no other producer or director for *Our Town*. But when Jed asked for credit as a co-author of the play, Wilder threatened to withdraw it entirely. Harris had backed down. Now they were squabbling over revisions. Wilder was concerned that the audience would be confused by the play's experimentalism, particularly the time element.

"We've got a play that has no scenery," Jed told him, "and its leading character is a stage manager. There's nothing naturalistic about it, so why worry about chronology? We can have flashbacks and flash-aheads whenever we like and the audience will buy it."

Passing this along to his sister Isabel, who was friend, companion and secretary, Wilder said he was still concerned. Meanwhile, as if anticipating the misguided approach that would plague later productions of *Our Town*, Harris began rehearsals by sounding the alarm: "The key to this play," he said, "is dryness. Once it gets sentimental, the play goes out the window."

Wilder concurred. "That's right," he told the company. "The nostalgia has to go. *Sec* is the word, even acerbic. As dry and crisp as you can make it."

Jed introduced the cast members to each other. The one indispensable among them was Frank Craven, the beloved actor who was coming out of retirement to play the Stage Manager. They all sat down to read the play aloud from the script. That was a Harris tradition at first rehearsal. Otherwise, like the play itself, nothing about the production of *Our Town* was going to be traditional.

For instance, Jed had a New York opening date—February 4, 1938—but no theater. Everything was booked. Nevertheless, he mapped out a tryout route. The world premiere performance would be given on Saturday night, January 23, at the McCarter Theatre in Princeton, New Jersey. The next day they'd move and Monday night begin a two-week tune-up engagement at the Colonial Theatre in Boston. By then, with luck, some Broadway theater would have become available. He didn't worry about which theater because *Our Town*, as he took every opportunity to proclaim, was a certain classic, the greatest play that had ever come his way. He said it might very well be the best American play ever written.

He began publicizing it by going to Lucius Beebe, apparently his primary news outlet. "The risk with *Our Town*," he told the *Herald-Tribune* columnist, "is its experimentalism, but that is also its best quality. People are turning away from the photographic representation of life. The so-called realistic drama." He made no mention of *A Doll's House*. "They want to escape from everyday facts and from themselves. They want something imaginative . . . well anyway, I think so."

Then Wilder got into the interview.

The play is a close examination of the life of a New Hampshire village in which the audience may well come to feel toward the close that the whole world has been presented in microcosm. In my story, Doctor Gibbs's boy George marries Editor Webb's daughter Emily. From the opening of the first act, where the town comes to life with the milkman at dawn as the newsboy delivers the morning papers and the doctor returns from a night call, to the close of the third act, where the last train is heard leaving for Boston and the last lights of the village give way to darkness, the homely life of one New Hampshire village is presented against a wider perspective of time and social history.

◆

Rosie Pinchot was again in charge of props. It was a function isolated from the active figures in the production, the writer and director and cast. But in Isabel Wilder, Rosie had a close friend and that was a comfort.

Rosie told Isabel that she was desperately in love with Jed and that he'd promised to marry her, once she was divorced. Her family had been appalled by the prospect of divorce and apoplectic about remarriage to a theatrical Jew. She'd finally won their consent, she told Isabel, but the struggle for it had been exhausting.

At the end of the first day's script reading, Jed smiled and moved his lips. The cast looked at him and then at one another. His lips were still moving but no sound emerged. The whisper had been reduced to pure breath.

A young actor in the company, William Roerick, assumed the responsibility of telling the others what he'd concluded, through lip reading and proximity, the director had said. "Mr. Harris says it's time for a break." Harris nodded and smiled and Roerick became his official whisper translator.

Sometimes, however, the director could be perfectly audible. "Tommy Ross," he said warningly to the actor playing Editor Webb. Ross was a stage veteran, a good actor but one tempted by old stage tricks. He was doing too much business with his hands; it was an old ploy designed to divert audience attention to himself. Harris said meaningfully, "I hate an actor who knows his *business*. I don't want any of your low comedy tricks in this play. It isn't that kind of play. If you do that once more I'm going to fire you and you are the best actor in America for the part."

Roerick remembered that because he thought it was the perfect way to deal with a misbehaving actor, threatening him but flattering him at the same time. Some of the others in the *Our Town* company weren't so perfectly handled. Young Alfred Ryder, playing a bit part, became the company scapegoat and was regularly reduced to tears; one Emily had already been fired and her replacement was about to suffer the same fate. Eight days before the Princeton premiere, Evelyn Varden, who was playing Mrs. Gibbs, suggested Martha Scott for the role and Jed hired the young actress.

He was meanwhile still pressing Wilder for revisions. "You know what's missing from the play, Thornton? The moment when Emily and George first meet." Agreeing, Wilder sat down on a straight-back chair at the rear of the stage and while rehearsals continued wrote a soda fountain scene for the young lovers. At the same time, downstage, Harris was inventing what would become one of *Our Town*'s most memorable images, the funeral for young Emily: mourners standing at the cemetery, holding umbrellas. Those umbrellas would be remembered as vividly as anything Wilder wrote, and the playwright would acknowledge it.

When Martha Scott arrived, Jed welcomed her with an arm around her waist. "We're going to read this play to you, Martha," he said in a number-three whisper, one she could hear quite comfortably and be comforted by. "Just listen."

As the company recited the play, with scripts in hand even though they all knew their lines by then, Harris walked the actress through the production, from one stage area to the next. He pointed out where the moonlight would pool, how the cemetery would be laid out, Main Street, the umbrellas.

As she remembered, "He showed me the play, just how it would be. Not the script but right there on stage; and when he got up on that ladder with me, we imagined where the moon was. It was like having an alter ego, that's how well he understood what the theater means to me. I know it sounds corny but it's true. He's a spirit of some sort. He was so imbued with that play."

He called a break, asking Frank Craven to stay and play a scene with Martha.

"She's going to do it without the book."

"*What?*"

"You can do it," he said with a smile. "Don't worry about the lines. Improvise if you must, remember what you can."

It was her first day and she found that she already knew the "Mother, am I good looking?" speech. Still, it did not allay her fear about the third act, "The Black Act," she called it. That devastated her, Emily dying.

◆

Walking to rehearsal several days later, Harris ran into Brooks Atkinson. The *New York Times* critic half humorously said he'd read that Harris had been knocking drama critics. "I told him it wasn't so in his case," Harris recalled. "I said I thought he wrote beautifully but that I wished the critics knew more about the facts of theater, the real business of putting a play on. I said, 'You fellows ought to come to rehearsal once in a while,' and then I invited him over to watch the first run-through of *Our Town*. To my surprise he agreed.

"I put him up in the balcony so that none of the company would see him. Of course they would have been scared to death. But as it turned out, that first run-through was a magnificent performance. I never saw a better one.

"After it was over, I went up to see him. Tears were running down his cheeks. He said to me, 'You so and so. You ruined the opening night for me.'"

◆

The *Our Town* company arrived in Princeton, New Jersey, on the afternoon of Friday, January 22 to prepare for the Saturday-night premiere. Rehearsal was called for six o'clock that evening but when the actors got to the theater they found their director enraged. Through some mix-up, a piano recital had been booked for that evening. The McCarter Theatre would not be available for rehearsal until midnight.

When Jed finally calmed down, he told everyone to go to bed and set their alarm clocks for eleven-thirty.

They straggled in, most having tried to sleep, few having succeeded. Yet, both Jed and Rosie Pinchot seemed alert, in fact high-spirited. They were racing on Benzedrine. The drug was common enough in Hollywood, it was said, but most of these New York actors were startled by its use and gossiped backstage about it.

Work continued through the night. At eight in the morning, Tom Morgan, the company stage manager, sent out to an Italian restaurant and breakfast arrived for the company: spaghetti and coffee.

Rehearsal continued, repeating, numbing the company, draining will and valor. The extra elements of a deadline, nerves, and Benzedrine perhaps tightened Harris's strings. His treatment of Rosie grew harsh as the first public performance of *Our Town* began.

She was helping Martha Scott with the wedding scene costume change. She had designed that gown. She told Isabel Wilder that it depressed her when Jed decided to have Martha wear the wedding dress as a ghost. Now Rosie caught her bracelet in the bridal veil. Struggling to free it in the rush, she nearly ripped the veil and screamed in exasperation.

Nobody sensed how well or badly the performance was going; in what temper the audience was receiving it. But José Ferrer was in the house that night, a friend ever since Harris had directed him in *Spring Dance*. He remembered this *Our Town* world premiere as having

an understated but powerhouse impact and yet you had no idea how it was achieved. Everything seemed real, logical and inevitable without showing any theatrical machinery. It was a miracle of understatement. Thornton's achievement, so much of it, was Harris's. A playwright doesn't cast. Wilder probably knew a fraction of the actors that Harris did. Lighting is not a playwright's doing and in this production there *was* scenery: the lighting was the scenery. But the casting was what did it: Evelyn Varden, Martha Scott, Jay Fassett, Tom Ross and above all, of course, Frank Craven. Jed's casting stamp was all over that production.

Afterward, Ferrer went backstage to find "a disastrous-looking Harris standing by the pin rail, holding onto one of the cables, looking as though he was holding himself up with the rope. His eyes were bloodshot, his face ashen." To Ferrer, he seemed to be standing as if by an act of will. The actor told Harris how tremendously impressed he'd been by the performance. The producer-director smiled and nodded blankly. Ferrer didn't know that Jed had just asked Thornton Wilder whether the performance had pleased him. Wilder had said, only, "You know, you've never understood that one scene, the dead at the end."

When Rosie Pinchot tried to congratulate him with a kiss, he pushed her away. When she asked whether he was ready to go to the cast party, he said he wasn't interested in the cast party. As Isabel Wilder remembered, "Rosie still didn't know enough about the theater to realize that the director of a play can't always go running off to an opening night party; not when you're on the road and exhausted, with lots of work ahead. She was only interested in the night and the party."

Then Jed icily suggested that Rosie not come up for the Boston opening and she became visibly upset. Isabel Wilder remembered the cruelty of this public rejection. Rosie grew tearful. There were backstage rumors that she threatened to kill herself. And there were reports, none of them firsthand, that he taunted her, dared her to do it, but she drove back to New York with Jed and his sister Mildred. They talked about the performance and Jed kept mocking Thornton's complaint about his not understanding the cemetery scene. "You've spoiled my shining prose." Harris thought that was so pretentious of Wilder. "My shining prose."

Rosie was silent during the drive back. She was depressed, it seemed to Mildred, and she spoke of not being able to get up to Boston "for another four or five days." She said nothing about Jed's having asked her not to go at all.

He got out of the car with his sister when they arrived in New York. He was going to spend the night at her East 11th Street apartment. It was late, they were all exhausted, and there were perfunctory farewells. Rosie drove home to Long Island, to Old Brookville and her children, the nine-year-old William and the six-year-old James.

On Sunday, Mildred called her after Jed had left for Boston. Rosie was profoundly upset. She took a horse out for the day and late Sunday night was still wearing her tan riding coat and gray pants. She had drawn an old sweater over her blouse and had pulled on a pair of wool gloves, all of this probably to keep warm, because it was two o'clock in the morning in the dead of winter when she left the house.

Several of the servants heard her leave. They didn't realize that she'd gone to the garage, slid into the front seat of the car, "the engine of which she had started," according to the *New York Times* of January 25, 1938, "in order to asphyxiate herself.

"A length of garden hose," the account continued, "attached to the exhaust and pushed through a rear window chinked with a burlap bag carried the deadly carbon monoxide inside the auto."

Her body was discovered at 7:50, Monday morning.

Many acquaintances had commented on her friendship for Jed Harris, theatrical producer. Some even believed she was in love with him. This was emphatically denied by Sidney Hirsch, general manager of Harris productions, who insisted Miss Pinchot was merely "one of Mr. Harris's many friends."

Because Miss Pinchot had announced her intention of going to Boston for the opening, it was reported that she had a part in the show. Said Harris: "Any report that Miss Pinchot wanted to get into *Our Town* is fantastic. She attended a rehearsal in New York, along with about fifty other persons. But she hadn't asked for a part, and there wasn't a part—not even a small one—for which she could be considered."

That *New York Daily News* report was spread across three columns of the first story page of the Tuesday, January 25, 1938, issue, as the story was spread across front pages all over the country. The caption over Rosie Pinchot's picture in the *News* was, "The Drama is Ended." The overall headline read, "Miss Pinchot's Suicide Follows New Play Theme."

The contents of the notes were never divulged, it being New York State Police policy to keep such evidence confidential. One of the suicide notes had been addressed to Rosamond's father, the other "To the Authorities." But, as Martha Scott recalled, the cast of *Our Town* was told that the note to Rosie's father had included a passage from the play—Emily's farewell speech from the grave, a speech delivered in the wedding gown that Rosie Pinchot had designed.

Goodbye, world! Goodbye, Grover's Corners—Mama and Papa—Goodbye to clocks ticking—and my butternut tree!—and Mama's sunflowers—and food and coffee— and new-ironed dresses and hot baths—and sleeping and waking up! Oh, earth, you're too wonderful for anyone to realize you! Do any human beings realize life while they live it—every, every minute?

170

15

SEEING LIFE THROUGH
THE EYES OF DEATH

ROSAMOND PINCHOT'S suicide hovered over the *Our Town* company like the umbrellas that Jed had put in the cemetery scene. Everything was in that shadow, everyone was touched by it, and darkened.

Still in shock, the actors assembled for rehearsal at Boston's Colonial Theatre. They whispered in curiosity about how Jed was taking the news.

A theater in the afternoon has an unnatural darkness about it, a sense of excluded daylight. The stage light made Harris's complexion seem unnatural too, and waxen, or so it appeared to Martha Scott as he made his entrance, walking slowly down the aisle. The camel's hair coat was draped over his shoulders, its collar turned up. A cigarette was hanging from his lips. Perhaps the tilt of his gray fedora was less gangsterly than usual.

Nothing came out when he spoke, so he cleared his throat and spoke again. "Let's begin with the third act," he said, and eyes darted to eyes. The third act included Rosie's suicide speech.

The stage was cleared except for Frank Craven. Jed took an aisle seat several rows back. He slouched there, removing neither his hat nor his coat nor his hands from his pockets. After a moment's pause, Craven began. "This time," he said, "nine years have gone by, friends—summer, 1913. Gradual changes in Grover's Corners."

Scenes and speeches followed upon scenes and speeches until Tom Ross—Mr. Webb—cued Martha Scott for her graveside speech.

"Where's my girl?" he asked, achingly. "Where's my birthday girl?"

Emily's line—"I can't!"—was to be cried. Martha blurted it out and pressed on with the "good-bye, world" speech. "It goes so fast. We don't have time to look at one another!"

Despite her fears, she got through it and soon afterward, Frank was speaking the play's final words. "Most everybody's asleep in Grover's Corners," he said, and then, at last, "Good-night."

The auditorium fell silent. Breaths were held. More than one actor recalled wondering, during that stretched moment, whether Jed was feeling guilt; or remorse; or grief. Was he having them rehearse that scene to punish himself? His eyes betrayed no emotion. He said nothing. He offered no criticism, gave no notes. Finally he whispered, "All right. Let's go through the third act again."

Someone backstage muttered, "He's using it, the son of a bitch is actually using Rosie's death as a goddamned acting motivation."

Martha didn't consider it heartless. "Jed wanted them sensitive to the death of someone they knew," she said, "so that the company could see life through the eyes of death. He wanted them to appreciate life."

But when he told the company to go through the act a *third* time, she drew the line. "I can't do this anymore," she announced. "I simply cannot do it again," and he ended rehearsals for the day.

◆

Ruth Gordon came up for the Boston opening, presumably in a show of support. The Pinchot suicide had created a wave of revulsion. Even in California's movie community. Ed Chodorov had to come to Jed's defense. He had known Rosie as a student, when he was at Brown and she at Pembroke. He had admired her and liked her but, upset as he was by her tragedy, he could not blame Jed for it. "Rosie was an extremely unhappy and depressed woman," he said. "Hell, I remember an actor in a Jed Harris play jumped out of a window and killed himself and everyone said that Jed forced him to. That was the Jed Harris mystique. It didn't mean there was anything to it."

Others said Harris probably *had* forced the actor to jump out of the window.

"On opening night in Boston," Ruth Gordon remembered years later, "the Governor's wife waited until the end of Act One. She stood up. She was a big, *big* lady. She had a big hair-do and a big, *big* dress." What Ruth meant was that there was no way the audience could miss her. "She stepped into the aisle and she went right up the aisle, through the door and she hasn't been seen at *Our Town* again. The next morning the critics came out and roasted us."

It is unlikely that the Boston critics were affected by the midstream de-

172

parture of the governor's wife, or the suicide of Rosamond Pinchot. But like ports in storms, any rationalizations will serve when there are bad notices to be faced. The actor William Roerick said that one of the Boston reviews consisted of only a single paragraph. Research has failed to unearth it, but he claimed to remember the notice verbatim.

Last night, Thornton Wilder's new play, *Our Town*, opened at the Colonial Theatre. When we arrived, the curtain was up and there was no scenery on the stage. We wondered if there was going to be a play. After watching it for two hours we still wondered.

And Wilder screamed at Harris, "You've ruined my play!"

Jed fled to New York. He did not go to Mildred's apartment, nor did he stay with Ruth. Instead he went to the home of William Morris, Jr., the famous theatrical agent. He had met the Morrises some months earlier when Rosie had brought him to dinner. Whether it was the Pinchot connection that drew him there now, or simply the warmth and sympathy of the beautiful Mrs. Geraldine Morris, he showed up at the East 52nd Street brownstone and, according to Mrs. Morris, "holed up with us for two days. He was in terrible shape. For the first time in his life he was scared by something he had done to somebody."

There was a rumor that Governor Gifford Pinchot was so incensed by his niece's tragedy that he tried to arrange for a mob contract to be taken out on Harris's life. One New York producer said he had been approached by the governor's intermediary for just that purpose. In those days the worlds of show business and gangsters were connected. The producer said he talked the governor's man out of the idea. Nevertheless, for the next few weeks Harris refused to walk the streets alone.

Returning to Boston, he found the *Our Town* company in disarray. Business was terrible, morale worse. Three days into the scheduled two-week engagement, he posted the closing notice.

Then Alexander Woollcott came up from New York for the Wednesday matinee. The audience was sparse and its response apathetic, yet Woollcott assured Jed that a great success was awaiting him in New York.

With this guarantee of good New York reviews from both Woollcott and Atkinson—what luck that the *Times* man had seen a run-through—Harris decided on a daring course of action. He canvassed his friends for the additional funds necessary to move the production immediately. Chodorov was the major contributor. Doing well as a writer-producer at M-G-M, he wired $15,000 from California. Donald Davis and Marc Connelly contributed smaller investments.

"I've had some people from New York come up to take a look," Jed told the *Our Town* company, "and they all feel the same way: 'This play is too good for Boston. Take it straight in to Broadway.'"

The actors cheered.

"So that's just what we're going to do. We've got just a one-week interim booking at Henry Miller's Theatre, but if we keep our confidence we'll do well enough to get another house. I'm counting on it. We've got guaranteed raves already from Woollcott and Atkinson. Too bad they don't know anything about the theater but I'll take the raves anyhow."

He didn't even bother finishing out the week in Boston.

New York preparations began with a warning by Vincent Jacoby of the stagehands union that he had heard all about *Our Town*, the show without scenery, the show whose actors moved the props. Jacoby told Harris, "You're not going to get away with that in New York. You're going to have to hire the same number of stagehands as any other show, even a ten-act operetta, and we're going to move the props. You're just running a conspiracy against the stagehands and you aren't going to get away with it."

However simply Harris tried to describe the innovations of Wilder's play, Jacoby would not budge from his position. Finally, the producer said he was willing to pay the stagehands but was damned if they were going to touch a single prop on stage during the performance. Thirty minutes before the opening-night curtain was due to rise, the issue remained unresolved.

Jed assembled the company on stage. There was a fire axe in his hand. "Don't you worry about Vincent Jacoby and his idiot stagehands. If any one of those bums even gets near a prop, he's going to get it with this." And axe in hand, he positioned himself in the wings.

There were other problems. The actress playing Mrs. Gibbs—Evelyn Varden—was running a fever; Tom Bodkin, the company stage manager, had broken his shoulder just that afternoon; six angry stagehands were sitting around a table in the basement, playing cards because Jed refused to let them within sight of the set. They glared at Martha Scott as she hurried past them in her stage cross-under, halfway through the performance.

Then, somehow getting past Jed's stage-door guard, Jacoby appeared in the wings. He demanded that Harris let his men work. Jed stared a murderer's stare and turned back to the performance on stage.

Still waiting for an answer, Jacoby stalked toward the stage. Harris, as if seeing the union man with eyes in the back of his head, reached out for the fire axe that was resting against the wall. Jacoby edged past a descending flight of stairs. His men were below.

Harris didn't need the axe. One good shove did the trick. Jacoby tumbled down the stairs, not seriously hurt and ultimately to be calmed by his men there. Nobody was available to calm Harris and he tried to send Martha Scott on stage two speeches before her next cue.

For all this, the opening-night performance proceeded smoothly. Craven came to his final lines. The auditorium was hushed. "Good-night," he said, and the curtain fell.

There was no audience reaction. The cast took its positions behind the curtain to take bows. They glanced anxiously at one another as they lined up. Could the audience ignore them entirely? Would they have to take their bows into the silence?

The curtain soared upward. Only then did the moment break and the audience's emotion flow over. The theater erupted into cheers and piercing whistles; a standing ovation.

◆

Martha Scott thought she was the last cast member to change and leave for the opening-night party. Jed was giving it himself, champagne and caviar, served on stage. She didn't want to get there yet. This had been her Broadway debut. She wanted to savor it. Her roommates had come backstage to visit; to kiss and flatter. At last they were all off, clattering down the twisting metal steps, chattering and giddy with the night's excitement.

As they came to the first level, Martha saw a light in Craven's dressing room. She paused to tell him how grand he'd been, but looking in, she saw not Mr. Craven but Jed, alone in the room, stretched out on the settee. He was wearing his camel's hair coat, the collar turned up. The gray fedora was pulled down over his face. Did he, she wondered, even sleep in that costume?

She poked her head through the door.

"Jed?"

He looked up.

"What did you think?"

He squinted at her.

"I don't know about the play. But kid," he whispered with a wink, "you did all right."

The play did all right too. Brooks Atkinson called it "One of the finest achievements of the current stage. . . . With about the best script of his career, Mr. Harris has risen nobly to the occasion."

The next week, they moved to the Morosco Theatre where *Our Town* ran for over a year and won the 1938 Pulitzer Prize for Drama. It was to become a staple of the American stage, of course.

I was only the midwife. All I did was serve a fine poetic talent to the best of my ability. The credit belongs to Mr. Wilder. It is a tribute to him. He has produced the greatest piece of pure stagecraft in the history of the American theatre. . . . Without scenery, without props, he creates a world in which you can find your own image, your own youth, your own memories.

You ask me about my ambition. It's to make the theater an exciting, wonderful adventure and to enrich the lives of people who go to see the shows I produce.

I'd also like to have one show in town which brought me in enough money to make up for the $6,000 deficit which the Boston engagement of *Our Town* piled up. Boston? Boston is my favorite backward city.   —*New York Post*, May 15, 1938

The success of *Our Town*—its commercial success, its artistic success— should have given his career new momentum. Instead, the best scripts stopped coming his way. People were beginning to shrink from him. In June of 1938, high on *Our Town*, he had announced that he would present five plays in five months, beginning in August. Only one month later, in the *New York Herald-Tribune*, he despaired of the theater's future.

Seven years ago no fewer than 140 legitimate shows played on Broadway. This year there were just 44. Next year there will be 24, after that 14 and after that none at all. . . . The business of staging theatrical entertainments besets a producer with the overwhelming demands of no fewer than 14 trade unions. . . . I personally find this very tiresome.

The swivel of Jed Harris's life can be seen in this change of attitude: producing in June, inertia in July. It fell hard upon the tragic events surrounding the production of *Our Town*. Instead of Wilder's play bringing his career to a crest of greatness, which in all reasonable circumstances should have happened, it was washing him out to sea.

◆

Energy must go somewhere. Harris's went into pursuing Louise Platt, who had gone to Hollywood after the failure of *Spring Dance*.

The dormant love affair escalated to hysteria. Pledging the best forever, he would settle down with her, as he had with Ruth Gordon. He'd throw her out, as he had Rosamond Pinchot, only to seek desperately to regain her, as with Margaret Sullavan.

They flamed back and forth across the country, Louise hiding with her parents in California, plunging into his arms when he chased her down, streaking back east when she could no longer endure his rages.

Then the cycle began anew: dawn telephone calls, Louise's shrieks of despair, Jed's threats of suicide, tearful reconciliations.

Louise's career had been well launched. She had been a promising stage actress and a busy one in the movies. Now her professional life was being trampled in the emotional melee.

His professional life lapsed into inertia. Louise said, "When dealing with production, he was at his sanest," but he had no productions to deal with. He wouldn't have any for the next five years.

The Broadway theater was also in retreat, for there was truth in Harris's remarks about labor complications. Though the New York stage would regularly survive predictions of its demise, unionization was already crowding its free action and that was but one troublesome factor. The stage that Harris had machine-gunned into life was finally entering the industrial age. Its entrepreneurs, these Belasco and Ziegfeld highwaymen, were marked for extinction.

For business-oriented minds were being attracted by the growing value of hit shows. Records, movies, and television would make the theater a multi-million-dollar industry. One day, Broadway would be dominated by businessman-directors, theater owners, movie studios and entertainment industry conglomerates. No more would it be the artlessly tough theater of New York; no more to reflect the brainstorm, however inspired or ridiculous, of a lone, stagestruck showman. Little time was left for the independent producers, those desperadoes of the midway.

Harris had already given up on the idea of personally financing his shows. He would soon have difficulty finding individual investors capable of financing productions. As for groups of investors, he reared at the prospect of searching for them and could not conceive of submitting a script for their approval. That he would never have.

◆

Stagecoach was the name of the movie that Louise agreed to do. She could survive without Jed Harris. Perhaps this demonstration of self-sufficiency was what impelled him to propose marriage. A man nearing forty, he went to meet her parents.

Louise's father was a Navy doctor stationed in San Diego. She had been a "Navy junior," brought up from base to base. Her parents were impressed with their daughter's fiancé, even if he was fifteen years her senior. He must have seemed a real catch, this famous Broadway producer. Lucky Louise.

With the family blessings bestowed, the couple flew to Mexico City for a romantic wedding. By the time they got there, Jed's angers had been refired. Even the Spanish-spoken ceremony depressed the bride. Her memory of it was of being lost in a foreign world and not knowing what she was doing there.

177

On the trip back to California, Jed told her how sorry he was that he had married her.

And so they set up house. Louise had looked forward to domestic life. Jed would have no part of it. She once tried to surprise him with a home-cooked meal. He loved Chinese food. She spent the day preparing it.

He scowled, uncovering one dish and then another.

"Did you make all of this crap yourself?"

"No dear," she replied, smiling. "Isn't it amazing what you can get out of cans?"

Only then did he devour every noodle.

"When we did Philip Barry's *Spring Dance*," Louise recalled, "he was even-tempered and brilliant, really brilliant. He could control his temper, he could deal with people. But when things began to dry up and more people turned against him and fewer scripts came his way, that was when his quest for power over people became frightening."

She was still struggling, forty-odd years later, to articulate her sense of his Machiavellianism. She had been petrified of him and in her late sixties still was. "His anger with people and his anxiousness to control their lives was something you just didn't see in anyone else."

As the cold and dark gel of professional rejection began to set around him, Harris's manipulative side—the "hideous side," Louise called it—became dominant. He was occasionally violent with her but more often he would direct his physical abuse at objects, hurling ashtrays or kicking out windows. Such rage was of course terrifying, but more cruel, in a way, was the sadism to which Harris applied his intelligence.

Harris once made the mistake of demonstrating his sadistic arsenal for Louise's father. Doctor Platt had been dismissing his wife's complaints about their son-in-law. Men owed each other a certain allegiance. But when Jed ripped into Louise one evening in her parents' presence, Platt rose from the living room chair.

"I'm going to punch you in the nose, mister."

Jed promptly collapsed on the rug. He lay on his back with arms outspread and stared at the ceiling. Then he smiled up at his father-in-law, a man no more than a dozen years older than he.

Dr. Platt glowered above him. Harris remained supine. Louise and her mother goggled at one husband on the floor and the other with fists cocked to fight.

"Get up, goddamnit. Get up and fight like a man."

Harris kept smiling and looking eye to eye.

"Why should I get up, my good fellow, if you are only going to knock me down as soon as I do?"

Louise's father seethed as he clenched and unclenched his fists. The women stood beside him, staring at the adult on the rug. Then Dr. Platt began to laugh and, in a moment, Louise joined in. Jed watched them. He watched Mrs. Platt. She alone was grim. Then he laughed too. He laughed the loudest of all.

◆

The door revolved without relief. Whenever Jed's cruelty would finally drive Louise away, he would seek desperately to regain her. He once asked Ed Chodorov to use influence at M-G-M on her behalf. The result was her best role yet, co-starring with Melvyn Douglas in *Tell No Tales*. It was, Chodorov felt, "one of the most unusual and original movies our unit made at Metro." But able as Harris was to promote Louise's movie career, he could not bring himself to capitalize on the chances that came his own way.

Jed Harris, the Broadway producer who joined RKO last September, will leave the studio without having made any pictures, it was learned today.
—*New York Times*, March 30, 1942

He sold the film rights to *Our Town* despite Wilder's protestations that the play was too theatrical for the movies. The price was $25,000, a negligible sum. It made a poor film.

◆

Louise had told Millicent and Paul Osborn that she felt "destined to have Jed's child." On April 27, 1941 she did. He was not with her at the time. They were already divorced. He was in New York writing articles for the new liberal tabloid, *PM*.

A GAME FOR DAY-DREAMING AMERICANS

Imagine that England has fallen. First, panic and then appeasement sweep over America. . . . Hitler now offers the world a thousand years of peace and prosperity. Naturally there is nothing more in the world he desires than friendship and trade with the USA. But he cannot reasonably be asked to deal with the war-mongering, Jewish-backed government of Franklin D. Roosevelt . . . he calls upon the *real* leaders of the USA to assume the responsibilities of government. . . . Riots and shootings take place all over the country. . . . The cabinet resigns. . . . In short order, the president and vice-president are impeached. . . . The way is now clear for the new executives to take over the government. No provision of the Constitution has been violated.

Who among these American leaders do you consider the most acceptable to the Axis?

Harris then listed Henry Ford, Charles Lindbergh, Joseph P. Kennedy, and a number of senators, all known isolationists.

Louise had decided to name her daughter "Abbie." When the certifying nurse asked whether that stood for "Abigail," the mother was still in an anesthetic fog. Her mute gaze was read as affirmation and the birth certificate was mistakenly issued in the name of "Abigail Harris."

Upon learning that he was a father for the second time, Jed hurried to California and stormed the hospital, demanding that Louise come back to him. When she refused, he threatened to abduct the baby. He became so enthusiastic in his expressions of paternal devotion that the hospital staff threw him out and barred him from visiting his newborn child.

Convalescing in her parents' home, Louise refused his telephone calls. As he had raged and begged for Jones, now he did for Abigail. As he had flown Walker Gordon milk to Paris, now, he told Donald Davis, he bought a cow. The animal would be maintained at a nearby dairy farm. Wartime or no, Jed Harris's daughter was going to have fresh milk.

"Only Jed Harris would have done a thing like that," Donald Davis said.

Hearing the story, Louise laughed derisively. "He told that to Donald? There was no cow. He was never interested in his daughter."

◆

When war was declared, fatherhood, middle age, and a degenerative hearing problem spared Jed Harris the army and the army Jed Harris. It is a stunning thought, Harris in the military service.

The uniforms alone.

At forty-one, Donald Davis talked his way into the Navy. He believed that joining up was not a matter of patriotism or even commitment to a cause; rather, he felt, "to miss out on the war was to miss a unique experience, a national and fraternal experience." Jed told Davis he considered the attitude sentimental and senseless. He wrote more political articles. Some had a satiric touch worthy of Orwell.

In this war . . . all the glamour is on our side. . . . Hirohito and Hitler, Laval and Mussolini are not only murderous fiends and crackpots, but are obviously as ugly as the devil. To see these jerks on the screen is to know at a glance that they are villains. And that's a fine thing. It gives you an enemy you can see and despise . . . and, incidentally, it's a fine thing, too, for the people behind the scenes . . . you don't even know them.

But it is these folk who own the show. . . . They do not rant . . . they are nice people, pleasantly rich and powerful. . . . They may have friends in companies like Standard Oil of New Jersey, or Dutch Shell in England, or General Motors in Detroit. . . . They may be decent Englishmen interested in, say, rubber in Malay, or shipping or airplane companies. . . . One may say they have a capacity for loyal friendship that is truly global, and this compels them to enter into gentlemen's agreements with other nice men in Italy, Romania, Chile and Vichy France.

Like all people who hate bloodshed, they can only deplore this war, although they admit that by destroying so much of Russia it will help kill Bolshevism all over the world.

However they still remain optimistic. They know that when it is all over, the world will need enormous quantities of oil, timber, rubber, steel, cement, copper, tin . . . and they know who will control all these commodities.

—*PM*, October 6, 1942

It was now four years since *Our Town*. Four years under the covers. He began at last to make gestures toward producing. He commissioned a new translation of Euripides' *Medea*.

Judith Anderson was with a USO troupe in California, doing Robinson Jeffers's *Tower Beyond Tragedy*, an adaptation of *The Oresteia*. The draftees from nearby Fort Ord made an attentive audience in the ravishing setting of an outdoor theater high above the Pacific. Jed telephoned Meg and crooned: "A room with a view—and you . . ."

She winced at the singing, sighed with the romance. Then, engagement concluded, she flew to see him in New York.

Upon reading his new version of *Medea*, she pronounced it "mediocre, darling. The only man to do it—the only man capable of writing a faithful and poetic new version of *Medea*—is my friend Robinson Jeffers."

"Fine," Jed said, picking up the telephone and handing it to her. "Ask him to do it."

She insisted on privacy. He went out for a cup of coffee. She placed the call.

"I'm going to ask you a question, Robin, and I want you to say 'no' to it. Jed Harris wants you to write a new adaptation of *Medea*—for Broadway. I think we can convince him to do *Tower Beyond Tragedy*. It is a great, great work, darling."

"I'd rather do *Medea*."

She tried to change his mind, but he was challenged by the new project and could not be swayed.

Jed insisted on going to see Jeffers immediately. He was filled with ideas for the new version. Along the stunning drive from the San Francisco airport to the poet's home in Carmel, Judith warned him about dealing with the poet.

"This isn't one of your Broadway characters, Jed."

"Yes, I know."

"He is a very gentle human being. You must be tender with him."

"Oh, Christ."

"I mean it. Forget about that New York Jed Harris."

"Yes, yes, yes," he said impatiently.

No sooner had they arrived at Jeffers's home than Harris excused himself, saying he had "a few things to do." He drove off, returning with arms full of wine, cheeses, and a special gift for Jeffers.

A necktie.

"It was simply the most wonderful and original gift," Miss Anderson recalled with a chuckle. "You have to remember that this was California and Robin and Jed. Nobody wore ties in California, certainly never Robin, and it was Jed's play on the tritest of gifts, a *necktie* for God's sake."

She laughed in recollection of laughter years earlier, hers and Jeffers's and Harris's. "It was just the dearest thing to do," she said, wiping her eyes.

Jeffers was so disarmed that Judith abandoned hope of convincing him to press Harris toward *Tower Beyond Tragedy*. Jed, meanwhile, spilled over with suggestions about *Medea*. Of these the most striking seemed to cast no less than Laurette Taylor as The Chorus.

He looked up and whispered, "Do you think that's a good idea?"

"She is a glorious actress," Meg said, and Jeffers beamed. Whether Taylor would be interested in playing Chorus to Anderson's Medea was another matter.

Then Jed went on about the production, the scenery, the lighting, the music, the performance itself. After each suggestion, he would look up again and whisper, "Do you understand what I mean?"

They did. Judith could see it all in her mind. And so everyone moved into the house while Jeffers wrote.

"Jed's ideas were magical," she remembered. "They flowed without stop."

When most of the job was done, he brought up the subject of royalties and credit. He felt that he had earned a half share in everything and that he should be listed as a co-author. Jeffers was astonished, Anderson embarrassed. She took Jeffers aside.

"Get in touch with your agent. Have him protect you fast."

The more Jed talked about money and credit, the less enthusiasm Jeffers and Miss Anderson felt, until the project collapsed entirely. Asked to leave, Jed went back to New York. Jeffers finished the adaptation. Robert Whitehead produced it on Broadway and Judith Anderson starred. It was the triumph of her career.

Harris had almost willfully torpedoed an opportunity he had created himself, an idea charged with originality and promise. At least that was how it seemed to Judith Anderson.

"*Medea* wouldn't have happened without him," she said, "and we incorporated every single one of his ideas into that script."

❖

Medea had almost gotten him out of bed. Inertia had been prodded. Now another play interested him. The script had been written by a pair of actresses, Eugenie Leontovich and Elena Miramova. Leontovich had last crossed Jed's path when her husband, Gregory Ratoff—"the big red cat"—had done *Wonder Boy*. This new play, *Dark Eyes*, struck Harris as possible, though it did need rewriting. For him, everything needed rewriting.

He took it to California while negotiating yet another movie deal; a consultancy with Twentieth Century–Fox. There, he sought out the respected screenwriter Nunnally Johnson to revise *Dark Eyes*. It was not difficult to set up a meeting: he was still Jed Harris.

Dorris Johnson greeted him at the door. She was a lovely woman in her twenties, a fresh-faced and curly-haired starlet with sweater-girl prettiness. Her husband came up behind her and the men shook hands.

Nunnally Johnson was a tall and athletically built man, as straightforward and uncomplicated as his crew-cut hair. Success had made him strong, his career and talent were healthy, and he had no patience for the neurotic, which made it surprising that he took so immediately to Jed. The answer was in the brains. Nunnally Johnson enjoyed intelligence and intelligent people.

Within weeks, Harris was virtually living with them, but unlike all the other writers, Nunnally would not be dominated, nor Dorris estranged. She in fact welcomed Jed's distracting her husband because she was having a difficult first pregnancy and preferred that Nunnally have company less irritable than she.

Harris certainly tried to elbow in on the Johnsons. He engaged Dorris in intimate conversations about her pregnancy; if it was a boy, what would he become and how would he be educated and what would he be named? Jed decided on "Christy," in honor of the great baseball pitcher, Christy Mathewson. And if a girl, he informed the Johnsons, then "Christie," after Eugene O'Neill's *Anna Christie*.

He was going to be this child's godfather. He proclaimed that too. Dorris reminded Nunnally that they had already promised the honor to their old friend, Sinclair Lewis. She reminded him that in 1938 "Red" Lewis had been in love with Rosamond Pinchot. Red had told Nunnally that he considered Harris to be Rosie's murderer. Still, Nunnally hardly cared who the godfather would be.

"For God's sake," Dorris cried, "just tell Jed you're sorry but we already decided."

She put her hand to her mouth to still the snap in her voice. She was not ordinarily short with Nunnally.

"You know," she finally said to Jed, "Red Lewis is going to be the godfather. I already asked him."

"Nonsense. I'm going to be the godfather," Harris said, closing the subject. The Johnsons made their excuses to Lewis.

Jed brought a sapling as a present for Christie's birth. "I've arranged for a gardener to come and plant it," he said, making himself comfortable in one of the living room's overstuffed armchairs. He gazed out on the pool and the back garden and pointed. "Right there."

When the gardener arrived, Jed drew a gaily wrapped box from his jacket pocket. He undid the ribbon and unfolded the paper. Lifting the lid and the cotton batting, he withdrew a gold link bracelet. He unclasped it, walked out to the garden with Dorris, and put it around the young tree. The bracelet was inscribed, "Christie's Tree."

"When she grows up," he said, "this tree will be fully grown too, and she'll know it's hers. You'll have to add links to the bracelet from time to time as the tree grows, but that's no problem. There are extra links in the box. And she'll be able to swing from her tree; she'll have a tie with nature, a tree for a relative. She'll understand what growth is; and age."

◆

Mrs. Platt telephoned Ed Chodorov at M-G-M.

"Jed found out where Louise is. He's trying to break up her engagement. This is her chance to have a normal life with that poor baby. Will you talk some sense into that girl?"

Louise was living with Abigail in Guilford, Connecticut. She had met a quiet young businessman and they were going to get married. Chodorov telephoned.

"Why don't you live your life? You know you can't live it with Jed. Nobody can live a normal life with him."

There are moments in vampire movies when we realize with a shudder that the lovely young maiden in the flowing white gown is already a victim, already a vampire herself. It was such a moment for Chodorov as Louise's voice came back at him: "Don't say that, Eddie. He needs me. Jed needs me."

She broke the engagement. Jed came and stayed with her in Guilford. As a condition of the reconciliation he agreed to see a psychiatrist. The director Joshua Logan, who was a friend from Louise's days with the Princeton University Players, recommended Dr. Merrill Moore of the Harvard Medical

School faculty. Moore had successfully pulled Logan out of a nervous breakdown. As a result, other theater people had flocked to Boston. *Life* magazine ran a feature story about this fashionable psychiatrist, among whose patients were Lynn Fontanne, Alfred Lunt, and Eugene O'Neill.

Moore considered himself a poet. He had published several sonnets. His psychiatric specialty was creative people. Logan's wife, Nedda Harrington, said acidly, "The psychiatrists thought he was a wonderful poet and the poets thought he was a wonderful psychiatrist."

Louise didn't consider Jed a good candidate for psychiatric treatment because he did not honestly want to change. Nevertheless she was unyielding in her ultimatum, and he traveled to Boston for several sessions. Moore subsequently told her that Jed was "a cyclical genius. There are times when he is utterly brilliant, certainly when discussing drama. Emotionally, however, he is like a child in any situation that frustrates him—any denial of a basic request. If you say 'no,' he screams. But," Moore concluded, "he is not mad and certainly not institutionalizable."

Going west again, divorced yet still a family, Jed and Louise and Abigail moved into a big house on San Vincente Boulevard in Los Angeles. Dorris Johnson became Louise's best friend "because we had so much in common. Each of us was an actress who had married an older man very well established in show business. In each case the husband had been married before and was generally more experienced and worldly than we."

Her husband, Nunnally, enjoyed a large circle of male friends and one evening he gave a dinner party for Red Lewis. Among the guests were John Steinbeck and Carl Sandburg. The party was strictly a male affair.

Drinks were being served when the door chimed. Dorris gulped to see Jed in the foyer. She didn't know how he could have heard about the dinner. He would sometimes drop in unannounced, but this particular occasion made coincidence unlikely. He had to have been aware that it was a party for Sinclair Lewis, who had not spoken to him for five years.

Jed embraced Dorris, kissing her on the cheek and telling her that she looked marvelous. He rubbed his hands in social anticipation as he smiled and leaned toward the hum of conversation. She suggested he get himself a drink. She didn't apologize for not having invited him. He knew why he hadn't been asked.

He strolled into the living room, went to the bar, and asked for a Scotch. Dorris watched apprehensively. When Lewis spied Harris, he turned his back. To Dorris's horror, Jed took the drink from the bartender and walked directly toward Lewis.

"Hello, Red. How are you doing?"

He said it as if they were old pals. The celebrated novelist responded reflexively.

"I'm okay, Jed. How are you doing?"

Whatever his own manners, Harris knew how to capitalize on others'. There was nothing for Lewis to do but be cordial. Only then did Dorris enter the room. It was not going to be a battlefield after all.

In fact Jed took Lewis by the elbow and guided him to a sofa. They sat beside each other and as Harris began to talk, his magic wafted across the room. Soon the party was gathered around them.

Red Lewis ultimately became the life of that party. Harris made him so, setting him up and directing the show. Dorris reckoned the room had its share of good talkers. Steinbeck, for instance, had been a frequent guest and on previous occasions had held forth eloquently on Soviet art and politics. Carl Sandburg played the poet, with his cowlick of straw hair and his theatrically baggy suit; people seemed to feel privileged just listening to him, though Dorris found him "pontifical and a bit much." Nunnally, she thought, had great moments as a talker, especially on the subject of Hollywood and writing.

But if this evening was one of the most vibrant she had ever hosted, she credited it to Red Lewis and Jed Harris, sitting there on the sofa. "They talked personalities, they talked politics, they treated subjects and ideas as if sauces to cook with, to mix and blend and spice and then ladle out for the group to taste and enjoy.

"Red," she recalled, "would bring in this subject, Jed the other. Their exchanges would be dazzling. They would settle into an area and suddenly one would break out to hook onto a tangent. Or a wonderful anecdote. Or play a scene. And then Red launched out on his own. It was a wonderful evening. Brilliant.

"Red was never funnier or more charming."

❖

When Jed had first introduced Dorris and Nunnally Johnson to his wife, or rather his ex-wife, and child, the reunited family seemed to be clinging together. "Louise adored Jed," Dorris remembered. "She was almost worshipful." And he was an attentive husband, a doting father.

But at home in Cutchogue, Long Island, forty years later, Louise clutched her second husband's hand as if still in need of protection. "That was another life," she said, "and I would prefer to live as if it had never occurred at all."

For as soon as Jed had won Louise and Abigail back, he no longer seemed to care about them. Instead, he put his wife in bone-rattling fear for her safety and even the child's. He never struck Abigail, but his furies made danger a regular presence. Even after the little girl had grown up to be a strong and sensible young woman, she would still quiver at the remembered crash of smashed objects and the caroms of rage.

He would leave, be gone for days, only to reappear without explanation, to taunt Louise as if just for target practice. His abuse was arbitrary and merciless. If she fled he would plead remorse and vow repentance. Finally she lost the energy to flee. She withdrew from all outside life; she refused to accept Dorris Johnson's calls. And then she decided that if she could not leave the house she would have the house leave her.

She announced a yard sale. Everything was to be sold. An auctioneer would deal with the more valuable items.

"It was as if the house symbolized the nightmare," Dorris said, "and she had to cauterize the experience. Throwing the stuff away wasn't exorcism enough. The tastelessness and embarrassment of the sale was necessary to cleanse the wound."

On the day of the sale, Dorris came to the house on San Vincente. She had come, she told herself, to buy back a silver cruet set that she and Nunnally had given to Jed and Louise as a house present. She didn't like the idea of strangers buying it. But on reflection, many years later, she decided that she had really come because of concern for Louise's emotional state.

The place was crowded with people, the front lawn, the back garden. They were milling in the living room, looking under sofa cushions and poking through drawers; pushing up the stairs and into the bedrooms.

Dorris found herself face to face with Louise.

"I want that silver cruet set we gave you."

Louise stared senselessly at her. Then a look of grief-stricken terror flashed across her face.

"No! Take it! Take it!" she screamed, and pushing toward the dining room, she snatched the cruet set from the table and thrust it into her friend's hands. To Dorris, it wasn't the silver and crystal that Louise was screaming about. It was the friendship with the Johnsons, the life with Jed.

"It was as if she was crying out, 'Take it and take yourself and get out!' She wanted everything related to Jed Harris cut from her life."

It wouldn't be that easy.

187

ONE MAN SHOW

Jed Harris was an extraordinary presence with an authentic flair for the theater. He talked brilliantly and turned on, whenever he considered it worthwhile, a considerable charm that was impossible to resist. He had made a large fortune, but beyond a shining Packard car the evidence of it lay only in his conversation, and then only occasionally. His was one of the most interesting, self-devouring egos I had ever met and I found him enchanting company. Now and then he suggested to me that strangely ruthless insect, "the praying mantis." I couldn't help wondering how long it would be before Jed's ego, prompted by sheer passion, ate up every scrap of him.

— Noël Coward

EVER SINCE THE Chicago days, which may have been the only joyful ones that Jed Harris ever had, he'd loved cabarets. *Broadway*, the show that made him, had been a theatricalization of cabarets. His personal style was taken from that show. Now his life was beginning to resemble a cabaret act.

He wore a costume: the fedora, the camel's hair coat on his shoulders, its collar upturned. He performed in a whisper as the unshaven, naked raconteur. Mysterious, elusive, devious.

The act might have been called "The Director." Harris was playing out his own legend, directing lives now. He had long since been setting people up for real-life dramatic scenes: urging Moss Hart to telephone a livid George Kaufman, or letting Donald Davis tiptoe through the suite at the Waldorf Towers to come upon an eyeless Harris.

Now Jed had found that by starting a rumor, placing a strategic phone call, or telling the particular truth or lie he could provoke circumstances to create character reaction, plot development, conflict, irony, tension, suspense and anxiousness, leading to action and denouement.

In a little while he wouldn't need scripts or theaters or actors at all.

◆

In the winter of 1942, Harris came back to New York with Nunnally Johnson to put *Dark Eyes* into rehearsal. He worked as if he hadn't been away from the stage at all, though it had been almost five years since *Our Town*.

Del Hughes, his new stage manager, was impressed by the way the play was deliberately withheld from premature staging. The actors were seated around a table, repeatedly reading the script aloud. Hughes was unaware that this was the longstanding Harris approach. "When the company was finally put on its feet," the stage manager recalled, "everything went together in a flash. This way of handling the actors worked beautifully."

It did not work beautifully for Nunnally Johnson, whose temperament was a movie-making, easygoing, California one. Theatre people thrive on the tensions of a Broadway tryout. Johnson didn't, and Harris let him go home while *Dark Eyes* was on the road. It was good for their friendship, and gave Harris freedom to rewrite the play since he had no trouble charming its original authors, Eugenie Leontovich and Elena Miramova. The play became the first hit of 1943. The Jed Harris touch was by no means lost.

The man was even able to complete such deals as he'd scorned in the past. It had once seemed as if any successful relationship, whether domestic or business, somehow signified for him a compromise of his integrity; as if he considered alienation the price of superiority. But now he brought *Dark Eyes* to peaceful fruition while at the same time concluding a most attractive arrangement with Twentieth Century–Fox Pictures.

If the phrase "well adjusted" has any meaning, Jed Harris seemed to have reached that plateau for once in his life. This brutally logical man, so ferocious in his gifts, was suddenly in stride with the productive world.

His deal with Twentieth Century–Fox provided that the studio would subsidize a theatrical producing office in New York. It would pay the rent, the cost of a staff, and handsome salaries (five thousand dollars a week each) to Harris and his partner, Harry Goetz. Related to an influential Hollywood family, Goetz was insurance for both Harris and the studio. If Spyros Skouras, the head of the studio, liked any play that Harris and Goetz wished to do, Fox would finance the production and in return acquire movie rights. Harris would also scout other shows for movie potential. (He saw *Oklahoma!* out of town and rejected it as hopeless.) Even were nothing produced or found, the office would be supported for two years.

Dark Eyes was the only play to come out of it, although Harris apparently found a way to divert the studio's money toward his purchase of a town house—a brownstone on East 82nd Street between Park and Lexington avenues. In that house he began work on another play, *One Man Show*, by trying to divide its married authors, Ruth and Augustus Goetz (no relation to his partner).

Her resentment of him notwithstanding, Mrs. Goetz conceded long afterward that Harris had put a stunning house together, decorating it with exquisite understatement. Each piece of furniture seemed chosen and placed after the most painful deliberation. Yet, she said, the place did not seem bare but, rather, elegantly austere.

Harris spent a great deal of time in that house, much of it in the canopied four poster bed on the second floor. Occasional appearances at the office were made at his traditional business hour of four in the afternoon. At such times the secretary would greet him with a pile of scripts. Her name was Shirley Berick and she was a hardworking young woman of medium height, appearance, and manner. Conservative eyeglasses and hair styling made her seem prematurely matronly.

Shirley Berick considered herself a bookkeeper and office manager rather than a mere secretary. She didn't realize that Harris always delegated administrative responsibilities to his secretaries; that he invited their mothering. When he asked her to accompany him on a business trip, she first took a train to Boston for a secret meeting with his psychiatrist; she didn't trust the telephone. She had to know whether it was safe for her to be alone with Jed Harris.

"Dr. Merrill Moore patted me on the arm," Shirley Berick remembered years later, "and assured me that it was perfectly safe to travel with Mr. Harris. He said, 'Jed has such respect for you he won't touch you.' And it was true. Mr. Harris treated me with the greatest respect. He always called me Miss B."

From the suite of offices at One East 57th Street, he would then begin his evening forays. He might be having drinks with one of the girlfriends he had held on to through the years, Geraldine Morris or Jean Dalrymple or the Smith girl. Dinner was invariably reserved for whichever writer he was currently romancing. Just now it was Augustus (Gus) Goetz. By midnight, however, he would be jogging down the flight of stairs to his favorite underground watering hole. The love of cabaret rhythms and his identification with that life had led him to America's premier nightclub.

The Copacabana on East 60th Street off Fifth Avenue was the nightly headquarters for the crowd that lunched at the Gaiety Delicatessen in Times Square, spent afternoons at Aqueduct Race Track, and then had high tea—cheesecake and coffee—at Lindy's Restaurant on Broadway. It was a fast crowd, gangsters and other flashes, at the "Copa," as the nightclub was called by everyone.

Late one night in the Copa lounge, chatting with the promoter Mike Todd, Harris was introduced to a muscular young fellow with the hewn features of an American Indian. Frederic Wakeman was a tall, dark, tremendously handsome Kansan and an advertising executive turned writer. His first novel, *Shore Leave*, had just appeared on the best-seller lists.

Wakeman had held on to his job as an account executive at Foote, Cone and Belding because it was well-paid fun. He handled the agency's musical radio programs, *The Kay Kyser College of Musical Knowledge*, *The Tommy Dorsey Show*, *Your Hit Parade*. At least one night a week the job brought him to the Copa, where he would scout new talent, coddle the performers he handled, or simply entertain sponsors.

The next morning, Jed telephoned Wakeman at the agency. He'd been up the night reading *Shore Leave*, he said, and was certain it would make a marvelous play. Could Freddie stop by the office to talk about it?

At that first meeting, Jed talked his way through a curtain-to-curtain dramatization of Wakeman's novel. The author hurried home to tell his wife about the astonishing development: work sessions with Jed Harris himself were to begin immediately.

Margaret Wakeman joined them for dinner that night, but on few others as Harris pried his way into her husband's life. His path was by now well worn: intense sessions that involved profound conversations and little work; nightly dinners; pub crawling and then dawn telephone calls urging immediate work sessions. Ruth Goetz once said to Margaret Wakeman that Jed "became a kind of lover to my husband. Not a homosexual lover, but just the same a lover. If you had to go through what I had to go through with Harris . . ." But Margaret Wakeman interrupted. "I did go through it," she said.

Freddie Wakeman couldn't grasp that until later. "I was too caught up in this new friendship with a famous and charismatic man," he said, "and too caught up with my own success as a novelist. Whenever Jed invited me to dinner, if my wife insisted on coming along why he would say, of course, she was perfectly welcome. But she was leery of him from the start."

Wakeman soon realized that the intense relationship was Jed's main purpose and that the dramatization of *Shore Leave* merely the excuse for it. The high point of work had come at the first meeting. Moreover, Wakeman ultimately found (as had all the writers before him but how could he know?) that with each Harris-supervised revision, the play became more diffuse instead of more sharply focused. When he finally asked whether he could bring the script to another producer, Harris seemed relieved. Wakeman was eager to begin a new novel about the advertising business. He agreed to let a professional rewrite the play. It was ultimately produced as *Kiss Them for Me*, by Frederic Wakeman and Luther Davis, and had a respectable run of 125 performances.

◆

Jed and Wakeman were having dinner one evening when a young man of sixteen or so suddenly appeared at their table. They looked up as he stood and stared at Harris.

"I just thought I'd say hello, Dad."

Jones was living with his mother and her new husband, the screenwriter Garson Kanin.

"You have got to stop bothering me," Harris said to the boy before turning away to resume the conversation.

Jones froze, stared for a moment, then fled.

Restaurants seemed to generally make Harris feverish and prone to violent outbursts. Dining on sliced veal one evening in a French restaurant on West 46th Street, he decided that the cream sauce had been burned. Rising, he yanked the tablecloth, sending the veal and everything else crashing to the floor.

Another time, dissatisfied with the wetness of his breakfast eggs, he complained to the room service waiter at the elegant Hotel Prince de Galles in Paris. Before the poor man could respond, Harris picked up a jar of mustard and hurled it. The waiter ducked. The mustard splattered against the wallpaper.

Some of Harris's friends attributed these explosions to an emotional soreness about food and hunger. Others connected the violence to the waiters, likening the behavior to Harris's problems with cab drivers, policemen, and anyone in a position of authority. Whatever the explanation, dining with Jed Harris was a chancy business.

Yet Frederic Wakeman recalled at least one perfectly pleasant restaurant meal with Harris and it led to a memorable evening with the jazz musician Duke Ellington.

They had been dining on Chinese food. Jed was crazy about Chinese food. Satisfied, finally, and passing the napkin across his lips, he pushed back the chair and said, "Let's go."

He rose and strode from the restaurant, leaving the writer to abandon his own dinner, pay the check, and hurry out in pursuit. Jed was already breezing down the street toward Broadway.

"Look who's at the Cotton Club," he said with delight, pointing to the nightclub that had recently been transplanted from Harlem to Times Square. "They've got Duke Ellington. Let's go see him."

The band members in their pink dinner jackets were seated behind the sequined music racks. At front, Ellington and his baby grand piano were sheathed in white, his formal clothes reflected in the instrument's mirrored underlid. Introducing each song, he meticulously modulated the level of irony in his voice.

When the musicians took a break, Harris sent a note backstage, and minutes later Ellington joined them. Over coffee and cognac, Harris engaged the musician on the subject of the jazz business. What, he wanted to know, were the musical, social, and money differences between a Negro jazz orchestra like Ellington's and a white dance band like Tommy Dorsey's? He asked about jazz clubs across the country and what they were like; what kinds of audiences they attracted. He asked about traveling and the band bus and where the musicians slept and how much they were paid. He wanted to know how colored people were treated in the small towns of the Midwest and what it had been like for a Negro to perform in the original Cotton Club, playing to white society slummers in Harlem.

Ellington responded to each of these questions with a thoughtful answer as Wakeman watched him light one cigarette with the last.

Harris finally leaned back in his chair. "I think there's a musical comedy in this life of the jazz musician," he said. "It's a world that's alien to most people and that makes it theatrical. And of course it's musical. Isn't it amazing that no Broadway show has ever had jazz music except *Porgy and Bess?*"

Ellington frowned at the reference. Much as he admired Gershwin, the opera offended him. He found its treatment of Negroes condescending and had publicly said so. That, Harris pointed out, was all the more reason for doing this show. It would be an accurate reflection of Negro life. "It would be a jazz musical about *your* life," he said to Ellington, "and of course you and the orchestra would be in it."

Ellington said he thought the idea was wonderful and Wakeman enthusiastically agreed. Harris proceeded to lay out the show as if he were unfolding a blueprint. "He made it sound real and alive," Wakeman later recalled, "but it was like my *Shore Leave*. He spent all his excitement in one night. His energy and fun were depleted after that, with nothing left for actually doing the show. But wasn't it amazing how he came up with that musical comedy between walking down the street, going in to hear the band, and talking to Duke Ellington?"

◆

Work on *One Man Show* had been productive despite Jed's attempts to insinuate himself between its authors, Ruth and Augustus Goetz. Ruth was a strong personality. Harris concentrated on Gus. He would sit for hours and listen to the big genial fellow reminisce about boyhood days in Buffalo.

"This is opening up a new world for me," Jed said to Gus, one day, in reaction to an inconsequential anecdote. Ruth could hardly contain her snicker.

Jed turned to her. "You look beautiful. There are a lot of times when you don't look beautiful, but tonight you look beautiful. Where did you get that dress?"

"I made it."

"*You* made that dress? Turn around."

She modeled the dress for the two men.

"Quite a shape on her," Harris said sarcastically. "Hasn't she?"

In a fury, Ruth sat down, excluded, insulted, and defensive. Harris persisted in appreciating her dressmaking talent. His implication was clear, she recalled. "What he was saying was, 'You're good for dressmaking but a playwright you aren't.'"

Such games failed to divide the Goetzes. Ruth was crazy about her husband who, despite his German name, "was the most beautiful Irishman I ever laid my eyes on." At thirty-one she was fourteen years younger than he, but she was brainy and sharp-tongued. Jed Harris would not get the best of her. Every night she would tell Gus how Jed had criticized his work to her. Then he would describe how Jed had slighted her work. They would lie in bed and chuckle over the Harris tactics.

Still they were pleased that he was producing and directing their play, and *One Man Show* was a particularly sensitive drama. Based on Ruth's relationship with her father, it dealt with an art gallery dealer and his psychologically incestuous relationship with his daughter. The suppressed, heated, unconventional passions surely reminded Harris of *The Green Bay Tree*. Ruth Goetz was certain of that, in fact she felt it was one reason why he was so well suited to the play, and he was tremendously enthusiastic about it.

He was so sure about *One Man Show* that he allowed Twentieth Century–

Fox only a token investment. The greater part of the financing he personally assumed by selling the house he (or they) had just bought. He got $40,000 for it.

The agent Irving Lazar, himself to become something of a legend, was also allowed a small investment. As he would recall, "I was as sure of that play as you can be sure of anything in the theater, but I began worrying when I saw Jed sitting in the last row during rehearsal. He seemed either uninterested in what the actors were saying or unable to hear it. They were stumbling over their lines and he didn't seem to know it. Opening night was a nightmare. In the middle of the play, one of the actors lost his teeth."

Years later Lazar remained bemused by the experience. "Jed's directing genius was real, make no mistake about that, and *One Man Show* was one of the best scripts I ever read. I still wonder why it failed."

Some felt that the title was misleading. Ruth Goetz blamed the brief, one-and-a-half-month run on miscasting. Fred Wakeman, however, thought that *One Man Show* failed because Jed wanted it to, and Harris's lawyer at the time, William Fitelson, agreed. For the morning after the show had opened, with the negative reviews still burning their way through the newspapers, Jed showed up at Fitelson's office. He was looking unusually spruce in a crisp new gray flannel suit. Fitelson remembered Harris's appearance with particular vividness because, for a change, Jed sported a close shave.

"Too bad about last night," the lawyer said sympathetically.

"Last night?" Jed asked, absentmindedly. Then, as if suddenly recalling the production, he snapped his fingers. "It was as if to say, 'Oh well, another day, another dollar,'" Fitelson recalled, "and I chilled. It was weirder than a bold front. Jed didn't know where his next dollar was coming from and that play had not been flop material. The thought crossed my mind, 'He wanted it to flop.'"

◆

Harris responded to the failure by pursuing Louise, his former wife. They had a series of California reconciliations, each ending with his return to New York in less than a week. In the summer of 1945, however, he brought Louise and four-year-old Abigail back with him. They took a summer place in the Seaview community of Fire Island and there this divorced family settled in among such personable friends as Fred and Margaret Wakeman; Wolcott Gibbs, the drama critic of *The New Yorker;* the respectable brothel madam, Polly Adler; Fanny Brice, Ira Gershwin, and Jed's sister Mildred.

She was now Mildred Wilcox, married to Philip Wilcox, a successful businessman. Nina lived with them and she had a five-year-old half brother, Daniel.

According to Mildred, that Fire Island summer of 1945 was a good one, with cookouts and cocktail parties and beach picnics and V-J Day and only a few all-night arguments between Jed and Louise. There was even a memorable summer storm. It struck while Jed was visiting at Mildred's place. The rain was torrential and it pounded the thin skin of the vacation house. After a few hours the place was flooded. The foundation was insubstantial. Inside, the water was ankle deep.

Mildred and Nina, who was then fourteen, found two buckets and tried to bail the house out. Jed watched. He appeared to be profoundly concerned about the emergency. He concentrated on what Nina and her mother were doing. But he made no attempt to help.

"Then," Nina remembered, "as if in a paroxysm of guilt, he got, of all things, a *broom*. He stood there with it, offering it, holding it out, as a nurse would a scalpel. He just stood there and held it in his extended hand.

"He didn't even sweep."

Sometimes, when the beach routine turned monotonous, Jed and Freddie would spend a few days in town. Wakeman would stay with Judy Holliday, with whom he'd fallen in love when she'd been in his play. Harris saw Cinda Glenn.

Cinda and Jed had met after he'd seen her act. She was an acrobatic dancer, but hardly the usual sort. She wouldn't have been the first American to play the Folies Bergère had she been a mere contortionist. Cinda Glenn was a *sexy* acrobatic dancer, sexy and funny.

As Harris and Wakeman watched from the bar of Versailles, an East Side supper club, she began her closing number. She was spectacular looking, with endless legs and fiery red hair.

She turned her back to the audience and wrapped her arms around herself so that it appeared as if she were being embraced. The "hands" tried to caress her. Noting them over her shoulder, she closed her eyes with disdain. Then, with feline flirtatiousness, she nipped the hand on her shoulder. The other groped for her breast. The audience cheered and so did Jed. He told Fred that he had to meet her, and as they all three sat at the little table he gave her his advice about the act.

So, that was how it had begun and now Cinda was telling Wakeman what Harris saw in her.

"Jed doesn't like Jewish girls. Ruth Gordon, Rosamond Pinchot, Louise Platt, Margaret Sullavan, me. A great list of *shiksas*. Ruth Goetz noticed it too, but being Jewish she'd naturally notice. I'm a hundred percent *shiksa*, so it means more coming from me."

Moreover, Cinda thought she knew why Jed didn't like Jewish girls.

"It's because he doesn't like being Jewish. I know he tells a lot of Jewish jokes, but jokes are either just jokes or they can hide all kinds of feelings."

Harris in fact did have Jewish girlfriends. Geraldine Morris, now divorced from William Morris, was one of them. Geraldine thought that "Jed missed Jewish women all his life," but others agreed with Cinda. "He despised himself for being Jewish," the Smith girl said.

The way Harris himself saw it, although he made constant references to his Jewishness and seemed fond of it, "I don't like being around Jewish people. Among peacocks a peacock isn't a peacock; only another lousy squawking bird with outsize feathers."

Cinda Glenn had an apartment on Madison Avenue near 78th Street. Like many actresses, she considered beauty her only asset and had little faith that she could hold a man once it was lost. Although wealthy lovers often kept her in luxurious circumstances, she anticipated a solitary end. That was why she held on to this little place. Its security provided her with a certain dignity. For instance, when Jed hurled a ketchup bottle at a waiter in Grand Central Station's Oyster Bar, she could leave and have a place to go to. Harris might appear at midnight on the sidewalk, pounding on the door downstairs and bellowing for forgiveness, but she didn't have to let him in. She invariably did.

More than the *shiksa* business fascinated Cinda about Margaret Sullavan. "Jed," she theorized to Wakeman, "was the love of Maggie's life. She couldn't get him out of her mind and she still can't."

"How do you know?"

"I know women. It's what's keeping her neurotic. And something else. She was pregnant when she married Leland Hayward."

Paul Streger had said that too, but at eighty his memory had been shaky.

"Jed tried to kill that baby," Cinda continued. "He kicked Maggie Sullavan in the belly and threw her down a flight of stairs."

Along with a number of other rumors of sadism, the story of the baby and the kick had trailed Harris like cowbells.

"That's a terrible thing to say about anybody," Wakeman said.

"He tried to kill that baby," Cinda said, "because Maggie wouldn't have an abortion and marry him. Doesn't that sound like Jed to you?"

◆

The extent and precise nature of Jed Harris's hearing problems cannot be definitely assessed. He did at times seem to be selective in these difficulties: some thought that he pretended not to hear when it was convenient.

At the same time, however, there had been a measurable deterioration in his hearing ability, and partial deafness did run in the Horowitz family. It has been suggested that Harris's career problems either began or were at least intensified when his faulty hearing became critical. However, nobody has ever suggested that the key to the mystery of Jed Harris lay simply in his hardness of hearing.

When he learned that a Dr. Julius Lempert had developed a "fenestration" surgical procedure to correct partial deafness such as his, he decided to undergo it. Several days after the operation had been successfully performed, the chief nurse at the Lempert Institute telephoned Harris's secretary, Shirley Berick.

"Take this man out of here," she pleaded. "We can't keep this maniac."

"Isn't he supposed to stay for a few weeks?"

"Get him out!"

Harris was supposed to have complete rest. There was to be no exertion, no movement, not even train travel, and under no circumstances was he to fly.

Homeless, now that the house on 82nd Street had been sold, Jed and Louise decided that he would convalesce in her old Connecticut place. He dutifully let her do the careful driving and they settled down in Guilford for a few days. When they had a fight and she fled to California, Jed took a plane in pursuit and was partially deaf for the rest of his life.

◈

The Wakemans lived at 1035 Fifth Avenue, facing Central Park at 85th Street. Jed sometimes stopped by to play with the children, impersonating animals and supervising impromptu shows.

On one occasion, the maid told him that Mrs. Wakeman was in the park with seven-year-old Fred Jr. and four-year-old Susan. Harris found Margaret in the playground, sitting on a bench. She was watching the youngsters play.

He sat down beside her without saying hello and no words were exchanged for the moment. Then Jed whispered, "Do you know something I've been thinking about?"

"What's that?"

"Suppose that not me but a man—a stranger, a good-looking man, not me—sat down on this bench and started to look at you. And when he'd finally made you acutely aware of his presence, his staring, he said, 'I've been looking at you and your children in this park for some weeks now. And I've fallen in love with you.'"

Jed looked at her deeply.

"'I know you must be happily married,' this man said to you. 'You must have a nice husband. But I'm prepared—I only want to spend one night with you—and I'm prepared to give you, for that one night of love, twenty thousand dollars.'

"Now don't laugh, Margaret. That could happen. That's possible. Suppose he offered you twenty thousand dollars and he was not unattractive. Quite the contrary. He was young and all of that. And there was the money. And not a soul would know. Just you and this stranger."

As Margaret Wakeman described the experience to her husband, she was still mesmerized by the manner and mood of the moment Jed had created.

"I stared at him, I just stared. I was truly in delight with Jed at that moment. His black eyes were full and round. They looked directly into mine. It was just magical."

"But what did you tell him?" Freddie asked. "What did you say about the man in the story?"

She laughed. "I told him I'd ask you. It was enough. I finally understood what you meant about his being wondrous. I was also glad to break the spell, there in the playground."

"And Jed?"

"Oh, he let his head rear back as he roared with laughter. 'Wonderful!' he said, and I think he meant it. He seemed to love the story and the mood and the blackout line."

This kind of magic, the Harris charm, seemed to come and go like light and shadow that passed across his spirit. Children often coincided with the light, occasionally even his own children. He was strolling along Broadway, hand in hand with Abigail on her fourth birthday. He paused to ask the child what she would be if she could be anything she wanted.

"A bunny rabbit, Daddy."

Wakeman watched father and daughter be serious with one another.

"So would I," Jed said. "So let's be rabbits."

He curled his hands together and, with knees bent and ankles locked, began to hop along the street. Mimicking his manner, little Abigail hopped beside him. They proceeded along Broadway and it seemed to Wakeman, as he strolled alongside, that Harris was unselfconscious about it. He concentrated on Abigail and his own hopping and if anyone was amused to see the famous producer being a bunny rabbit on Broadway, the producer didn't see them.

◆

When the agreement with Twentieth Century–Fox was not renewed, the 57th Street office was closed and Harry Goetz returned to California. Harris offered Shirley Berick a raise if she would stay with him but it meant little, as he hadn't paid her in weeks. His sister Mildred helped find him an office at 39 Park Avenue, in a building owned by her husband Philip. Of course, Miss B. went along with him.

There he was sent Ruth and Augustus Goetz's new play, *Washington Square*. It was a dramatization of the Henry James novel. Jed had wanted to do something of James's ever since seeing John Balderston's *Berkeley Square* twenty years earlier. He was enthusiastic about the Goetz dramatization although, as with every play, he thought it needed work. The authors disagreed and they were leery of working with him again anyhow.

Ruth, particularly, was ambivalent about submitting the script to him. While she did not share the feeling that he had subconsciously wanted *One Man Show* to fail, the experience had been a difficult one. His interference with her marriage had been off-putting; she'd wearied of the subtexts and insinuations in every conversational exchange. Yet she respected his mind and talent.

She and Gus made their decision when Jed insisted on casting Wendy Hiller in the leading role. Miss Hiller was in great demand. She had been acclaimed in the movie version of *Pygmalion* and worked steadily on the London stage. Harris had met and romanced her while directing the troubled London production of *Our Town*. Now he was informed she couldn't be available for *Washington Square* until the fall at least.

He was willing to wait. The Goetzes were not. When Oscar Serlin offered to produce *Washington Square* immediately, they went into rehearsal in the spring of 1947 and opened disastrously in New Haven.

"You should have let me do it," Jed told Ruth at the intermission that night.

"You're right," she replied, and she felt that even more intensely a week later at the Boston tryout. The audience streamed out jeering at the play.

"I read the Boston notices," Jed was saying on the telephone to the Goetzes. "What are you going to do?"

"Serlin is giving up on it," Gus said.

"Have Ruth call him and see if I can buy the set. It's better for him to sell it cheap than to burn it. I know a way of fixing the play. If I can buy the set and costumes for ten thousand dollars, we'll replace some of the actors, go right back into rehearsal and do it."

Like the suggestion, years earlier, that Moss Hart call George Kaufman, this one, too, was contrived to backfire—in the case at hand of Ruth Goetz. For the insult was implicit: Harris could save what Serlin had blown.

"I'd rather burn the set than let Harris get to it," the producer predictably snarled at Ruth, "and the costumes too. It's a rotten play anyhow and tell him not to bother calling me because I won't even speak to him."

This little staging of life succeeded doubly for Harris. It shook the strong-willed Ruth Goetz and won him the delay needed if he was to get Wendy Hiller. He was more certain than ever of her importance to the production after having watched a twenty-one-year-old ingenue play the role in the failed production of *Washington Square*. The thirty-five-year-old Hiller would be more appropriate as a young spinster.

The only gamble was that she hadn't even been sent a script, or apprised of the fact that the play had just been panned to closing in Boston.

The Goetzes spent the summer of 1947 rewriting their script while Jed sought a backer. It was no easy assignment, finding someone to risk $35,000 on a play that had just failed. The man he went after was Fred Finklehoffe, a playwright (*Brother Rat*) who had become a successful movie writer-producer (*The Egg and I, Meet Me in St. Louis*).

Finklehoffe was a peppy man of five feet three inches, with sandy hair and a pronounced limp. He was a natty dresser who favored bow ties and small fedoras and was an obsessive gambler. Supposedly, Finklehoffe had once turned down a lucrative Hollywood offer on the grounds that having just figured out a foolproof roulette system he would never have to work again. Perhaps it was the gambler in him that agreed to be the sole backer of the Goetzes' play.

The first thing Finklehoffe did was put Jed's hotel room on the production budget. Jones moved into that room with his father. He was now an independently wealthy seventeen-year-old, the beneficiary of a trust fund that Jed and Ruth had set up years earlier.

Harris berated Jones for abandoning Ruth and Garson Kanin after they had done so much to bring him up. He berated Jones for school performance, for sleeping late, for being a "party girl" interested only in good times.

Geraldine Morris came up to the hotel room one evening, to meet Jed before a dinner date. She recognized Jones from the Friends School, where her son was a couple of grades ahead of him. He was sitting and playing gin rummy with his father, "and playing it humorlessly," she recalled. "They played as if they were killing time. It was so peculiar, so unfriendly. A *grim* game of gin rummy."

◆

Fred Wakeman's new novel, *The Hucksters*, was an even greater success than *Shore Leave*. Its popularity led to a handsome movie sale and convinced Wakeman that he could make a living on his fiction. That wasn't the only reason he quit the advertising job, or separated from Margaret, or broke off entirely with Jed, or moved to Mexico. His affair with Judy Holliday had already destroyed his marriage and he had to get away from Jed because his new novel was *about* Jed.

He rented a house in Cuernavaca. He let Cinda Glenn move in as a friend. She had also decided to break with Harris. The careening of their love affair may have been the usual for him, but the arguments, the fights and pursuits, the suspicion and abuse, the threats of suicide, had given her a case of eczema. She believed that if she didn't get away she would go crazy.

Neither Cinda nor Wakeman would ever be able to come back comfortably. They would always be afraid of Jed Harris.

Evidently he was too engrossed in *Washington Square* to fret over the departed Wakeman and he didn't know where Cinda had disappeared to. No matter. He convinced Finklehoffe that a trip to London would be worth the expense if it resulted in the signing of Wendy Hiller, and the producer agreed. Jed wasn't finding it difficult, working for another producer, but of course Finklehoffe was giving Harris more than a director's usual authority. And in justification of that authority, Harris returned from London with a signed contract.

◆

Henry James's *Washington Square* is the story of a wealthy young woman who has accepted repression as a way of life, and lovelessness as her lot. She even concludes that an emotionally arid existence might be useful. She decides to forgo love and be "a maiden aunt to the younger portion of society."

The ironies and self-deceptions implicit in James's story are too subtle and literary for the stage. The Goetzes made the tale more dramatic. It is still set in the New York town house of Dr. Sloper, whose daughter Catherine realizes that her mother's death has hopelessly embittered her father.

Dr. Sloper subconsciously blames Catherine for the loss and constantly reminds her that she will never match her mother's beauty or wit. When she falls in love with the penniless Morris Townsend, Dr. Sloper pronounces him a fortune hunter and takes Catherine off to Europe to forget him.

She does not. Her aunt, Mrs. Penniman, sympathizes but at the same time has a stake in Catherine's submissiveness since it is the daughter rather than the aunt who rightfully should be running this household.

When Dr. Sloper threatens to disinherit Catherine, Morris's loss of interest convinces her that he was indeed interested only in her fortune. So the climax is set as Morris returns after Dr. Sloper's death, again seeking Catherine's hand.

In the James novel, she now refuses him, but when the Goetzes dramatized it, their producer Oscar Serlin insisted on a happy ending. In the final scene, then, Catherine first rejected her suitor and sent him away. About to shut down the house and commit herself to a life of solitude, she saw him through the window. "Morris!" she cried. "Come back, come back," and the final curtain fell.

It was "this piece of dreck," as Ruth Goetz put it, that the audience mocked while leaving the theater in Boston. "Come back, Morris, come back," they cackled, trudging up the aisle. "We tacked it onto the play," Mrs. Goetz said, "because Serlin demanded it." But now with Jed doing the play, Gus told him, 'I have the new ending.'

"'Good God,' Jed said, 'you're not going to rewrite it again!'"

"'No,' Gus said. 'But this is how it's going to be restaged: the aunt is going to leave; there will be a knock at the door; it's Morris, and then—'

"'Boy!' Jed cried, when Gus finished. 'Is that the way we are going to do it! We sure are!'"

Harris, on the other hand, wrote a book called *Watchman, What of the Night?* about his experiences with the play and in it he took exclusive credit for the new ending. Likely, the revision was collaborative. And the fate of the new production was riding on it as Wendy Hiller walked onto the Biltmore Theatre's stage to join a company that included Basil Rathbone, Patricia Collinge, and Peter Cookson. The premiere was scheduled for September 29, 1947, with no tryout tour and only three previews. Failure only months earlier made the show unattractive. Its opening would be virtually "cold."

It was clear from the outset that this was no ordinary Jed Harris production. As it seemed to both Ruth Goetz and Peter Cookson, he was in an almost palpable sweat. They each felt that everything was on the line for him; that he would never do another show if this one failed.

"We all knew he was on the skids," Cookson recalled. "His career was on the skids, his life was on the skids. The man was dead broke. He told us so himself. He couldn't even pay his own rent."

That, then, was Harris's gamble. He was taking a corpse that had been left for the maggots and was attempting to miraculously resurrect it. Only so flamboyant an achievement could restore his legend.

As usual, rehearsals began with the company around a table, reading the script. Jed had already said in an interview that "The reason Henry James himself never made a go of the theater, I think, was that he dealt in moral values that only seldom are found in the internal economy of the stage. It is for this rather abstract reason that greater concentration of effort is needed to make a good show of a James story."

Perhaps he thought this perception of James would be best served by a certain stillness in staging, for when he finally put the company on its feet he said, "When I tell you to move an inch, I don't mean two inches. I mean an inch."

Such freezes were the first sign of a cancerous element in his directing. Picture-making, like melodrama, was now old-fashioned.

Nerves grew tauter. "The cast was becoming edgy too," Cookson remembered, "but Jed seemed to know exactly what he wanted and most actors want their director to be like that. On the other hand, his cruelty was now a developed instrument and when he could get away with it this was a terrible cruelty."

One day, after rehearsal, Cookson repaired to a bar next door to the theater. Harris was already there, perched on a stool. "Come on over and sit with me," he said warmly, "and I'll buy you a brandy."

Cookson accepted the invitation warily. "I was terrified of him and of his energy, his animal power, his available cruelty." (Cookson spoke that way.) "Jed was sitting in his shirtsleeves, that hot day, rubbing his hairy chest; embracing his own elbows. He was a china bull, and so we sat and then he asked me about my girlfriend at the time, Patricia Neal. He said, 'She's going to be a big movie star, you know. Can't be much of a future with a girl like that.'

"I looked up at Jed, he was so cunning about these digs. 'Maybe so,' I said, 'but we're having a good time enjoying each other.' He smiled at me, 'Fine,' he said, rising to leave and paying our checks. 'Oh, by the way Peter,' he said over his shoulder as he headed for the door. 'Give my best to your wife,' and he was gone."

But Harris could be intimidated when somebody struck back, and Ruth Goetz did, a week before opening night. Jed had started coming to rehearsal late, as he had with *One Man Show*.

"I'm going home," he said during a lunch break. "I don't feel like doing any more today. The stage manager can take them through."

Ruth grimly responded, "Jed, if you do on this play what you did on *One Man Show*, we are through forever."

"What are you talking about? I saved this play for you. Who would have given you another shot after flopping in Boston?"

"I don't give a fuck about that. I want you to go over to that theater and I want you to finish getting that second act done."

Gus was stunned. Ruth could see that. Jed was stunned. She was stunned herself. But he went back to rehearsal.

Sometimes Harris's annoyance was justified. In the last act, Peter Cookson had a scene with Wendy Hiller in which she was seated as he addressed her in profile to the audience. "When Peter got to the line, 'And I was out in California,'" one of the actors recalled, "he 'opened up.' That's an actor's trick to take the audience's attention, turning the body a full 180 degrees to make a clean sweep of the house. He turned and pointed in the opposite direction."

Jed came running down the aisle crying, "Peter! Peter! What's this opening up to the house?"

"Oh," Cookson said, startled by the interruption. "I wasn't opening up, really. I was just pointing to California."

"Peter, we are on the north side of 47th Street in Manhattan. California is *that* way, but if at this point in the play anybody knows where California is, we're in trouble. I can't give you any psychological reason why to do this but don't take your eyes off her. It's just theatrically more effective if you play it all to the girl."

Cookson had memories more painful than that. "I'd heard he always found a scapegoat in the company. Well, I was the lucky one this time. One day he came right up to me and whispered, 'You know, Peter, I've only fired three actors in my life. You don't want to be the fourth, do you? I don't want to frighten you but you just have to realize that that might be a possibility.' My agent," Cookson added, "told me not to worry because I had a run-of-the-play contract. Jed didn't have the money to pay two actors for one part. He just wanted to upset me, maybe even for the sake of my performance, who knows? For as cruel as he could be, you couldn't help admiring him because he was so much *what he was.*"

Whether or not Harris was singling out Cookson for punishment, his nervousness infected all the actors. As it was, Basil Rathbone was frightened to begin with. He was eager to erase his Hollywood image as Sherlock Holmes but he hadn't been on a stage in many years and movie acting, of course, is done in short takes. Rathbone was petrified about learning his lines.

Shirley Berick, watching rehearsal from a front-row seat, heard Jed whisper to Rathbone not to worry, not even to *try* to memorize his lines. "I want you to know the sense of them before you commit the actual words to memory."

The actor's fears were not noticeably allayed.

"You have to feel," Harris continued, "that Catherine is your daughter and that you resent her because she is not attractive or gracious like her mother— the mother you were so in love with."

Rathbone smiled, only to panic anew. "I won't be ready! There isn't a chance of it!"

Harris soothed him. "If you aren't ready at that time, I give you my word of honor I'll postpone."

The next day it was Patricia Collinge, playing Catherine's aunt, who collapsed in sobs. "I can't do it, Jed. I can't do it. I can't."

He took her aside, stretched an arm around her shoulder, and walked her toward the wings, then back to center stage. William Roerick, also in the company, overheard him whispering to her, "Now Pat dear, you know and I know that when you get finished with this jilting scene you only have seventy-five seconds to make your costume change, but when you come back and the curtain goes up on your final scene, all of your relationships have to have changed. When your brother was alive you were the duenna of the house; the servants were servants and just so much dirt. You held the purse strings. But now that your niece holds the purse strings you are nothing but a poor relation, so when we see you talking to the maid that you've always been rather superior to, she's now only your equal."

It was such practical advice as this that endeared him to actors and made him seem a director who understood their problems, a father-actor, which is what actors want their directors to be. His own thoughts on being judged as the director of this play were jotted down several years later, in a letter to his business manager, Herman Shapiro. He'd asked Shapiro to contribute a section about his directing the play in the account of the production, *Watchman, What of the Night?* Harris wrote to Shapiro:

> First the outsider must remember how the play seems when first read. Was what developed on stage exactly as he visualized it when he first read it or was it different? Did I improve on what I read or did I degrade what I read? How was I with the company? How did I stand up under the heat? Was I patient or impatient?
>
> It is not enough to say I was wonderful. You must say how I was wonderful, if I was wonderful. That is necessary to a portrait of me as a professional man of the theater.

As the final scene began on opening night, Ruth Goetz saw Jed stumble drunkenly from the lobby into the back of the theater. The auditorium was hushed, the stage lights dimmed on the drawing room, entranceway, and stairs of the Sloper house.

The doorbell rings. As Catherine, Wendy Hiller stoically orders the maid to bolt the door. It is done. After a pause there is a tapping at the door. Then knocking. On Catherine's orders it is disregarded by the maid, Maria. After bidding her good night, Catherine turns the lights down. The knocking persists. She walks to the hallway, picks up a lamp at the foot of the stairs.

The knocking grows louder and more urgent. Catherine ascends the stairs, her back straight. Morris can be heard faintly from outside, calling out to her. She mounts the stairs slowly but unhesitatingly. She climbs them grimly, purposefully, steadily. Then she is gone.

For a moment the stage is empty as the knocking and the cries grow louder. They echo up the stairs, across the stage and out through the auditorium. They continue unanswered as the curtain falls.

There was a moment's intake of breath, as if all the air in the Biltmore Theatre were being sucked in and held by the audience. Then it was let out. The applause swelled.

As always, the response of an opening night audience was an unreliable gauge. Hits and flops alike receive first night ovations. Harris stood at the back of the house, appearing tense as he watched the actors in the glow of their curtain calls and listened to the cheers. Then he overheard, or thought he overheard a critic badmouthing the play to a colleague as they hurried up the aisle toward their deadlines. That was his only explanation for what he did.

As Ruth Goetz looked on in horror, he whipped out a furled copy of *Variety* that he had in his jacket pocket and hit the critic over the head with it. The second critic, attempting to intercede, received the same treatment. In a frenzy, Harris thrashed the two of them about the necks and shoulders until they escaped.

MAD SCENE

By HIS OWN ACCOUNT, Harris stayed up until the morning newspapers were available and then he walked over to Times Square to pick up the *Times* and the *Herald-Tribune*. He superstitiously carried the folded newspapers back to his hotel room before reading them. Whether the news was to be joyous or grievous, it required privacy.

The news was grievous. Brooks Atkinson in the *Times* seemed to set a record for rejection. "The authors have had a good deal of difficulty making a play out of undramatic material," he wrote. "To make a stupid woman the heroine of an interesting drama is the basic infirmity. The story cannot be dramatized."

Atkinson's record was promptly broken by Howard Barnes of the *Herald-Tribune*, a man disinclined, evidently, to leaven disapproval with wit or compassion when straightforward abuse was available. "It is a soporific show," Barnes wrote, "as limp as a rag doll."

And neither Barnes nor Atkinson had been swatted by Harris the previous night. The reports from those critics were still to come.

In *Watchman, What of the Night?*, Harris wrote, "They [the actors] had all trusted me. I wondered if I could ever face them again, or anybody else."

And then something very pleasant occurred to me. And the more I thought about it, the more relieved I felt. I had seen a way out . . . an actor friend of mine had given me a whole bottle full of sleeping tablets. I poured a glass of water and began to take the pills two at a time.

It would not have been the first suicide motivated by a flop. To those who work on a play, the production becomes its own world, and even after a long run there is a sense of death at the closing. A quick end can be devastating. Harris's depression over these particular reviews, appearing as they did in the most important newspapers, must have been exceptional. Had not his trashing of two critics on the opening night betrayed just how much was on the line for him?

I must have swallowed a dozen of the pills when suddenly I was shaken with a fit of coughing. And then everything began to come up.

There is no way of knowing whether or not this account is true, but it is unlikely to be, for the following reasons.

Harris was a frequent, almost compulsive liar and he never lied more frequently, or compulsively, than when the subject was his past.

He was not the suicidal type. If he was he would have committed suicide already.

He was so melodramatic that friends felt no act he ever committed, however emotional or enraged, was unselfconscious. He would always stand back and watch his own routines. One cannot watch the finale of a successful suicide.

Finally, suicide was a constant and therefore idle threat of his.

No, it is not likely that Jed Harris swallowed all those sleeping pills. His true aches were submerged deeply beneath the melodramatic cloak. He was more interested in a prolonged sort of self-destruction, one whose agonies could be savored. For ever since the thirties, he had been producing doomed plays, passing good ones by, rewriting promising ones into the ground, and, in such cases as *One Man Show*, perhaps even trying to sabotage himself when something worthwhile managed *not* to slip through his fingers. He had long since refined his technique for making enemies, and all of this may have been developed for the sake of a deliberate sort of self-elimination; intensifying the death motive to test limits of endurance; committing suicide indefinitely by perpetually failing at it.

Or writing about it.

I took off my clothes and turned on the shower and got into fresh pajamas. I left a call for a quarter of eight in the morning, put out my light and went to sleep.

Ruth and Augustus Goetz and the show's press agent, Bill Doll, trooped into Harris's hotel room. With resigned energy, Doll telephoned his office to inquire about the afternoon newspaper reviews.

They were wonderful. Thrashing the two critics had made no difference.

Neither, unfortunately, were these raves likely to. The *Times* and the *Tribune* carried too much weight with the ticket-buying public to be offset by the afternoon newspapers except on rare occasions. In the faint hope that this might be one such occasion, Doll next called the Biltmore Theatre's box office to find out if there was any business.

He hung up the telephone and smiled. "There's a line curled all the way through the lobby. It's halfway down 47th Street."

They all four ran from the hotel and took a taxi to the theater. It was true. There *was* a line. *Washington Square* may have been a flop but *The Heiress*, as it had been retitled to disguise the flop connection, was a smash hit.

Jed burst through the line and into the theater lobby "looking like a tramp," according to the actor Peter Cookson, who had come over to enjoy the success. "He wore a ragged coat, his beard was heavy and he pushed into the box office where Freddie Finklehoffe was already crowding the treasurer. Jed couldn't stand still in there. He kept writing down figures and shouting gleefully, 'I'm going to make a fortune! This is going to make me a millionaire!'"

Almost. Finklehoffe had generously given him a producer's share and Harris would get part of the $250,000 movie sale too. The enterprise would buy him the yacht of his life, the *Grande Dame*, with enough left over to take a big apartment facing, of course, on Washington Square.

Louise lived nearby with Abigail. The family had separated again, this time forever. Louise wouldn't even talk to Jed on the telephone, although she sometimes allowed him to see his daughter. A feature story about Harris in *The Saturday Evening Post* described the seven-year-old Abigail as:

A beautiful child whose seraphic face is framed with long golden hair. Harris adores her. He invents long and intriguing games that he plays with her. He often calls for her at The Bank Street School, a progressive play school which she attends. . . . One morning in Washington Square he was lugging a large suitcase and trying to flag a cab. Asked where he was bound he said ecstatically, "I am going to collect Abby at her mother's. Then [we] are going to go to the Half Moon Hotel in Coney Island, and we are going to live there for three days. I am going to show her all the gaudy sights of Coney Island. We'll ride The Whip and see The Wax Museum. Isn't it wonderful?"

Louise frequently brought the child to Washington Square Park. She would sit on a bench below Jed's windows and let Abigail play in his sight. Donald Davis saw them there. Living in California but in New York on business, he had called Jed and stopped by for lunch. Louise was pleasant when he greeted her in the park. She did not mention Jed and neither did Davis, as best he remembered. Then he went upstairs where something happened that he definitely remembered. He and Harris had a disagreement over the meaning of a word. Jed went to check its definition in the big dictionary that was kept in the bedroom.

"He walked across the living room," Davis recalled, "and swung the door open. Wide open. There was no question in my mind, then or now, that he had calculated this from the start. He'd made sure there was a disagreement about a word so that he could open that door wide enough for me to see who was in there. She looked up. It was Margaret Sullavan. She was married to Leland Hayward at the time.

"I stayed for another hour and a half. We talked and she waited."

Jed took the opportunity to repay the fifteen-hundred-dollar loan that Donald had extended him ten years earlier, ostensibly to buy the option on *Ethan Frome*. He had money now, but the success of *The Heiress* could not save the man if he did not want to be saved. "I was sick of the theater," Harris wrote, "and hoped that this would be my last production. And it could very well [have been] my last if only it made enough money."

When Wendy Hiller refused to renew her contract for a second season, business waned. Harris, all of his pleas exhausted, scribbled on her dressing room mirror, "There is nothing so ungrateful as an English whore." Miss Hiller announced that from then until her departure, she would not go on if Jed Harris was in the theater.

"There have been some wonderful moments during the last twenty years," he told an interviewer. "Working with Edna Ferber and George Kaufman, working with Ben Hecht and Charlie MacArthur and Helen Hayes. But now," he concluded, "I want to go away, to England or France or possibly Palestine."

He was beginning to talk as if his life were over.

◆

Fred Wakeman's new novel, *The Saxon Charm*, was published that year, 1947. Its disguise was nonexistent. Matt Saxon is an egomaniacal Broadway producer who befriends a successful novelist, offers to present his first play, and then bewitches him. In the course of revisions the script is nearly ruined, along with the writer's marriage.

Of the women in Matt Saxon's life, one, a combination of Louise Platt and Rosamond Pinchot, is browbeaten into suicide while the other, based on Cinda Glenn, is almost driven mad by his tantrums.

As with the other works about him, Harris reacted to the book with equanimity. *The Saxon Charm*, however, proved the most successful of them and was sold to the movies. Jed was rankled enough by that development to tell his attorney to sue for libel. The lawyer pointed out that a handsome and popular leading man, Robert Montgomery, would be playing the Harris character while the merely pretty John Payne was to be Wakeman. Also, he said, a libel suit would only help promote the movie.

Harris relented, settling for an interview with the *Hollywood Reporter* columnist, Radie Harris:

> I can't tell you what I think about *The Saxon Charm*, because I never got beyond the first few chapters. I found it such dull going, I couldn't finish it. Wakeman dedicated *The Hucksters* to me. That, I imagine, was in appreciation of the friendship I gave him when he needed it, and of all the knowledge of the theater I poured into him during the labor pains of his first play. If *The Saxon Charm* is supposed to be further expression of his gratitude, I'd like to see what he writes about his father. This should be his next book. He dedicated *The Saxon Charm* to his father.

◆

At nineteen, Jones Harris returned from a summer in Europe with Ruth and Garson Kanin. He moved in with his father for a few weeks before going back to Brandeis University, but couldn't endure the abuse.

That year, 1948, was a year of family change. Meyer Horowitz died, but if a father's death had special emotional significance for Harris, it didn't show. Relatives remembered his grief as appropriate and friends noticed nothing unusual in his reaction.

He did seem suddenly inspired to resume family ties. None except Mildred had been hearing from him. Now Jed invited his mother to move into the Washington Square apartment with him. She did.

For a while it was an enclave, there in Greenwich Village. For although Sylvia and her husband lived uptown, Mildred was on University Place and Florie on Ninth Street, both within walking distance. The closeness, however, was brief. One day Harris lost his temper with his mother and stopped talking to her. Esther Horowitz had to move out. She went into a home for the elderly. He wouldn't speak to her while she was there, either.

◆

Jean Dalrymple had adored Jed ever since he asked her to release James Cagney from the London company of *Broadway*. He'd held on to her with regular telephone calls and occasional visits. After receiving Harris's approval—at least that was the way he read it—Jean had married General Philip DeWitt Ginder. But she would always be taken with Jed and his talent. When he asked her to co-produce Jean-Paul Sartre's *Red Gloves* there was hardly room for refusal. They promptly sailed for France, the venture from the start a combination of business and romance.

Harris insisted that Charles Boyer play the lead role and that was one of the reasons they were going to Paris. The movie star had not been on a stage in fifteen years and had never played in English. He had already turned down the part with a certain amount of conviction: "This is not a play I want to do, I don't like it, it's not my kind of play. I just won't do it." Harris apparently did not consider that a definite "no." He was convinced that Paris would serve as a positive setting for renewed appeals. It would also provide the chance to meet with Sartre and discuss the adaptation, which Jed meant to write himself.

He arranged for dinner at Monsignor, with violins and champagne. The Boyers were there, and the stage producer Gabriel Pascal. As was traditional, they all went from the restaurant to Les Halles marketplace for midnight onion soup. Then, delivering everyone home, Jed had the chauffeur stop and buy out every flower stall along the way. By dawn, when he finally brought Jeanie back to the Hotel George V, the limousine was choked with blossoms. She could not recall a more romantic evening in her life.

A similar charm succeeded with Boyer. In an astonishing reversal, the actor agreed to do *Red Gloves*, to his subsequent regret. "That was one play that Jed made a mess of," Jean had to admit. "Sartre was very much against his adaptation and frankly [Jed] made a lot of stupid changes. He treated it as if it were a melodrama by Ben Hecht and Charlie MacArthur, a *Broadway* kind of play. It didn't help for Sartre to give interviews all over the place saying how much he hated Jed's version. All the critics knew about that. The truth was that he hadn't written a very good play in the first place but Jed only made it worse. So naturally, I went ahead and co-produced another one with him right afterward."

That was Herman Wouk's *The Traitor*, an atomic age drama about scientific espionage. This time Jean suggested that she be a silent partner so that Jed might have exclusive billing. "He needed help," she said. "He needed psychological help, he needed career help.

"At forty-nine he was a man who had been Jed Harris."

The success of that season was not *The Traitor*, but Arthur Miller's *Death of a Salesman*. "A stupid play," Harris said, "I can't understand anyone's admiration for it. There is no drama in an ass like Willy Loman. A tragic figure is a failed hero and he must have the greatness of a hero. To me, high drama is Shakespeare. The heroes and villains are kings. There is no drama in a bush being overswept in a storm, but if a giant oak tree is brought down by a bolt of lightning you have a tragedy."

He was right in principle, wrong in the instance. *Death of a Salesman* is one of the twentieth century's great plays. It is fair to speculate, however, that in speaking of tragic figures and failed heroes, Harris may well have had himself in mind. He was a melodramatic personality. He probably did see his life as high drama, himself as a failed hero.

◆

Some months after *The Traitor* flopped, the telephone rang at dawn in the home of Michael Abbott. The slight, bushy-haired, twenty-two-year-old actor had played a bit part in the Wouk play while doubling as assistant stage manager.

"Mike? Jed Harris. I will be at TWA Flight Six leaving Idlewild Airport for Los Angeles at nine-fifty this morning. Going out there for six months. If you want to come along and work with me on all my various projects, I would love to have you. Don't waste your time discussing this with your Jewish middle-class parents. They have no imagination. I expect to see you at the airport."

Then, as Abbott's groggy parents stood in their nightclothes and stared at him with worried curiosity, the telephone went dead in the young man's hand.

Harris bought four first-class tickets for the two of them so that they could stretch their feet out. Once on board he handed Michael five scripts and said, "Read them. We'll talk about them later. I am going to sleep."

They were met by a blue and white Cadillac and taken to Lee Tracy's ranch in Rivas Canyon. Tracy had invested heavily in Beverly Hills real estate and as a result, he and his wife could afford to spend most of the year cruising the world on their yacht. So Jed had the run of "this very California place," as Abbott described it. "It was all Ponderosa style with Navajo blankets and Western decor and a Chinese houseman named Sing. The first thing Jed said when we got there was that I'd drive the two of us to dinner in Santa Monica. 'Mr. Harris,' I said, 'I don't drive.'

"It was dead silence for three beats and then he said ominously, 'You don't drive? What am I doing wasting my time with you? Sure, from middle-class Jewish parents, I should have known. Who would expect you to drive?'"

The subject was resumed at breakfast the following morning.

"Now I have to be very serious with you. I am appalled that you can't drive. This is 1949, who doesn't drive? It's simple, Mike. I have no use for you, no *need* for you. But before I send you back to your middle-class Jewish parents, I give you one last chance. I am taking the Cadillac. I am going to Palm Springs. I will be back one week from Friday. I expect you to have a driver's license or else *back to New York*." And he left the New York youth in the middle of a ranch "twenty miles from nowhere with a Chinese houseman who barely spoke English and a houseful of longhorn decor."

Abbott found a driving school in the classified telephone directory and arranged for lessons, all day, every day, for seven consecutive days. At week's end he had the license.

214

Harris walked through the front door "looking suntanned and thoroughly Palm Springs," according to Abbott, who was sitting in an armchair reading. Jed said nothing. He just stood there and extended his hand, palm up. Masking his glee with effort, Abbott rose and with one motion took out the license and slapped it into Harris's hand.

With theatrical solemnity, Jed said, "Now let's see how good a driver you are." Abbott got in behind the wheel of the big Cadillac. Alongside, Harris crossed his legs, lit a cigarette, folded his arms, squinted, and said, "Let's go!"

"And," according to Abbott, "we sure did. 'Make a left turn here,' 'Pass that idiot,' 'Step on the gas,' 'Blow your horn,' all the way down Santa Monica Boulevard to downtown Los Angeles. Then he told me to park and get out and we walked across the street, right into a car dealer. He bought me a brand-new green coupe. He said, 'This is little Michael's Ford.'"

The excuse for the California trip had been a consultancy with one of the studios, "but basically," Abbott recalled, "all Jed did was a lot of fucking around for six months while he pushed Tom Reed to finish the screenplay so he could sell it." Reed was a Hollywood writer and the screenplay was Jed's notion, the story of how Jeanie Dalrymple had met and married her general in postwar Berlin.

Harris sold the screenplay too, *Night People*, for $80,000 (and ultimately Nunnally Johnson made the movie). Michael was not impressed, in fact he was depressed because much as he idolized Harris he sensed that "Jed hustled movie scripts when he became afraid he'd lost his stage touch. He would provoke fights to get out of projects before they got far enough to happen. Or else he would almost deliberately let a good play get away from him. One of the plays we brought out with us was *Command Decision*. It ended up making a lot of money on Broadway and was then sold to the movies, but Jed didn't do it."

California cheer began to ebb. The Chinese houseman quit when Harris threw a plate of scrambled eggs at him. As abruptly as Michael had been asked to go west, Harris told him they were returning. There had been an offer from the songwriter-turned-showman, Billy Rose: the producership of a television series.

The series that Billy Rose offered Harris was to be a weekly anthology of original teleplays. These scripts would supposedly be based on anecdotes that had originally appeared in Rose's newspaper column, "Pitching Horseshoes." That was the collaborative inspiration of Rose and the talent agency packaging the show, the Music Corporation of America.

They'd sold the American Broadcasting Company on the idea and under

215

the sponsorship of the Hudson Motor Car Company, the program was to be televised on Tuesday evenings at nine. Jed was going to be the producer-director and the network's publicity department was already promoting him as "Mr. Theatre."

But while it was hoped that the Harris prestige and taste would rub off on the show, Rose and the people at the agency agreed that an experienced television director would be necessary for actual studio work. Daniel Petrie was brought in from Chicago.

Dan Petrie had been a minor Broadway actor before leaving the theater to pursue directing ambitions. He capitalized on the infancy of the television medium, where he was just as inexperienced as anyone else. Directing local shows in Chicago, he earned reputation enough to win the *Billy Rose Show* assignment. Rose told him that he "certainly understood" Petrie's irritation with Jed Harris's billing but said, "You'll do the actual directing," and Petrie was so eager for a New York assignment that he accepted. He was in awe of Harris anyhow.

As Petrie recalled, his first meeting with Jed was at the MCA offices on Madison Avenue near 58th Street. Harris strolled into the office where Petrie and the MCA agent were waiting and sat down on the sofa. "He arrived precisely on time, despite his reputation for lateness, looking very fashionable in a camel's hair polo coat and fedora." Ignoring the agent, Harris turned and looked straight at Petrie, taking the young man's arm.

"Kid," he said. "You have theater sense. Brooks Atkinson, no matter how long he works as a critic, will never have theater sense. My syphilitic old uncle in Brooklyn, he's got theater sense. You either have it or you don't."

Then he rose and Petrie felt there was no choice but to rise as well. They ignored the agent, "he just didn't seem to exist," Petrie remembered. Harris towed him from the room and they sailed past the antiques and paintings and leather furniture of the pretentious offices. Years later, Petrie shook his head in wonderment at the recollection of Harris heading straight toward one of the elevator doors. "As if it were the Red Sea, it opened just as he arrived."

After a descent in silence, Jed rushed out of the elevator, walked briskly through the small marble lobby, out across the sidewalk and directly into Madison Avenue traffic. "I was flabbergasted," Petrie remembered. "I stood and gaped as he plunged in front of all those cars. Without pausing he grabbed the door handle of a passing taxi and although the driver must have seen him and braked to a stop, to me it looked as if Jed had stopped this car with the force of his grip on the door handle."

It was a routine of Harris's. He'd done it with other people.

He gave the driver his destination and then turned to the neat and shy young man beside him. "When I did *Our Town*," he said, taking Petrie's topcoat and draping it around the young man's shoulders, "I called the stage-hands union." He turned Petrie's collar up. "I told them that I would supply games," he said, unbuttoning the shirt collar and loosening the tie knot. "Checkers, chess, cards, they would all be in the basement of the theater for the stagehands. And I told that union if I ever saw any one of those stage-hands up on the main floor of the theater, I would take his head and bash it against the wall . . ."

Harris ran a hand through Petrie's carefully combed hair, raking it. "And then," he continued, "I took Frank Craven and I made him up like you are now." Harris sat back in the taxi and stared warmly at Petrie. He smiled. "Relax, kid. We'll work together beautifully."

Jed rummaged through his past to select a staff for the television show. He brought in the actor William Roerick, who'd been in both *Our Town* and *The Heiress*, and made him a personal aide. Michael Abbott went on the payroll as the show's casting director. Jed hired Judith Anderson, Lee Tracy, and Walter Hampden to star in individual shows. He had Edward Chodorov write most of the scripts.

But insofar as producing *The Billy Rose Show* was concerned, there was only so much that he cared to do and nothing he chose to learn. He told a news-paper interviewer that he never watched television, didn't even own a set. "All those technical details about dissolves and other camera incidentals, they're all rather childish," he said.

Of the six rehearsal days allowed each telecast, he would show up on only the first and treat the program as if it were one of his plays. The cast would be seated around a table in the rehearsal hall and he would have them read and reread the script aloud.

Petrie felt that this method was blind to the realities of live television. Left with only a five-day rehearsal period, he would then begin the basic blocking of scenes and plotting of camera angles. "Mind you," he later said, "when Jed worked with the actors, however briefly, I was awed. I was nowhere in his league. His feeling for the theatrical moment was intuitive and impec-cable. It's just that live television didn't leave room for that kind of thing."

If one of Harris's old friends was appearing on the show, he would stick around. Roerick, working as Harris's general assistant, came over to pick him up for the first day's rehearsal with Judith Anderson. Harris put on a shirt and buttoned it only to fumble with the cuff-link.

"God damn," he bellowed, tearing off the shirt and tossing it into a corner of the room. He chose another and this time, as if the shirt controlled the

217

functioning of the cuff link, the maneuver was completed flawlessly. Knotting his tie and putting on his jacket, he left the room with Roerick; they went downstairs and got into a taxi. Only then did Harris say, "You know what all this temper is about, don't you? I'm terrified at the thought of directing Judith."

"And she," Roerick later said, "was equally terrified by the thought of being directed by Jed. But the show went off beautifully."

Relations between Harris and Billy Rose were predictably disastrous. After a few weeks the men weren't speaking. Rose made Michael Abbott his go-between. Doing a script that was set on a beach, Jed demanded that real sand be used on the set. He had mounds of it hauled in and poured on the studio floor. It got into the cameras and the cables and the dollies, and when Rose was informed of the damages he shrieked for Michael.

Rose's office was above the Ziegfeld Theatre, which he owned. He had a Rembrandt painting displayed on an easel, a Picasso hanging on the wall, a window from which he could look down on the stage below, a disc system for recording telephone calls, and a mammoth semicircular desk in the top drawer of which he kept a revolver.

When Abbott arrived, Rose pushed the weapon across the desk top and said, menacingly, "I keep this because in show business you never know what's going to happen."

He had once said to Paul Osborn, "There's only one man in the world that I'm afraid of and that's Jed Harris. It isn't physical fright. I just can't cope with him. He buffaloes me every time." That was why he needed Michael to carry his messages, and so he flashed the gun at Abbott, not Harris.

Now, with the young man scraping and shuffling uncomfortably, Rose plunged into a diatribe about Harris and the sand and the studio. "You tell that fucking maniac," he growled, rising to a full stature of barely more than five feet, "that first of all this will be the last job he's ever going to get in television. I'll see to it that nobody hires him."

When, with a certain rephrasing, Michael relayed Rose's displeasure, Harris's reaction was whispered evenly. "You tell that tailor," he said, "that fucking midget, that he hasn't talent enough for even *television*."

Going back and forth with such messages earned Michael a Tiffany tie clasp from Rose; a clasp engraved with the initials, "ITM." Rose told Abbott they stood for "In The Middle."

As Abbott recalled, "The series itself did fine. It did fine for thirteen weeks until, for a Christmas show, we put on an O. Henry story about two con men posing as Santa Clauses. ABC didn't like Santa being defamed that way and they wouldn't take O. Henry for an excuse, so we were canceled."

That Christmas Eve, Harris called Roerick in for advice about choosing a present.

"I've got these two drawings by Kokoschka," he said to the tall, erudite, good-looking actor, "and I can't make up my mind which one to give my lawyer."

"Is he the kind of person who would care more about the picture or the artist's importance?"

"I think he'd be impressed with getting a Kokoschka."

"Well then, I think the big one would hold up in a large room. It's smashing. But personally, I think the small one has the greater quality."

Harris held his hand to his chin and pursed his lips as he examined the two drawings. Then he abruptly said, "I'll give him the big one. Would you wrap them both up, Bill, and drop them off on your way to Louise's with the other stuff?"

"What other stuff?"

"Presents for Abigail," Jed said absently.

After leaving the larger picture at the lawyer's home, Roerick opened the envelope for the destination of the second Kokoschka. "Merry Christmas, Bill," the card read, "with all my love, Jed."

As for Abigail's presents, the child was overwhelmed. Louise, less so. "He was marvelous with Christmas gifts," she said, "but he didn't worry about whether she had food or clothes."

With the television series canceled, Harris had his own food and clothes to worry about. Having made easy money selling the movie script *Night People*, he found another compliant screenwriter with whom to piece together not even a screenplay but merely a treatment. He sent it out to Ed Chodorov at M-G-M.

"It was no good at all," Chodorov remembered. "Every studio turned it down. Finally I decided to talk to Dore Schary myself. He was the studio chief at Metro and he went all the way back to Newark with Jed.

"'Listen,' he said to me. 'I'll buy it. I'll give him fifty thousand dollars for it. Now tell Jed not to ask for any more, because if it's over fifty I have to get an okay from New York and the minute I have to ask New York we've got trouble, because I've got to send them the treatment and everything. I can pay up to fifty thousand on my own.'"

Chodorov relayed the good news.

"I want fifty-five thousand dollars," Harris replied.

"For Christ's sake, will you stop it for once?"

"That's the deal," and the telephone was hung up.

Chodorov called Schary. "Okay," he said. "Jed'll take the fifty."

However, Harris would not help himself. Michael Abbott had come across a play that interested him. It was an army comedy set, of all places, in a Nazi prisoner of war camp, and its title was *Stalag 17*. Abbott was a member of the Lamb's Club and he decided to use the organization's studio theater for a workshop production of the script. He convinced Jed to direct it as "a friend of the court."

The single performance, given on March 11, 1951, was so rousing a success that Abbott suggested they co-produce the play on Broadway. Harris said it had already been done where it deserved to be done.

José Ferrer had been in the audience for that single performance. Now a hugely successful actor-director-producer, he did *Stalag 17*, first as a stage play and then a movie. It was a tremendous success, culminating the list of hits that Harris had let pass by.

Even a professional director can mistakenly visualize a production from a script, but to see in performance a play that works as smoothly as *Stalag 17*, and then reject it, is either perverse, a sign of shattered self-confidence, or headlong suicidism.

◆

Del Hughes had gone from stage managing for Harris to a similar job with Kermit Bloomgarden, a young producer who was earning a reputation for doing important plays. Hughes was on West 45th Street when Bloomgarden hailed him from beneath the marquee of the Morosco Theatre.

Hughes crossed over and said hello to the producer and the tall, skinny, bespectacled young man with him. It was the playwright Arthur Miller. Hughes had stage managed his *Death of a Salesman*.

Tennessee Williams and Arthur Miller were then the reigning kings of the American stage. Williams's *The Rose Tattoo* was a success of the current season. The New York theater now impatiently awaited Miller's next work.

At the same level of prestige was Elia Kazan, who had directed Williams's *A Streetcar Named Desire* and Miller's *Death of a Salesman*. Kazan, however, had grievously damaged his personal reputation by testifying as a friendly witness before the House Un-American Activities Committee. Miller had refused to cooperate in the hunt for Communists in show business. It was hardly surprising that he now refused to work with Kazan. A theatrical plum, then, was available.

"We're thinking of hiring Jed Harris to direct Arthur's new play," Bloomgarden said to Hughes. "You worked for him. What do you think of the idea?"

Hughes remembered pausing to consider the consequences of his reply.

"Harris," he finally said, "is bad news. He is tremendously gifted but the conflict he creates just isn't worth it."

When Harris learned that he was being considered for the Miller play he implored Jim Proctor, his latest writer-acolyte, to help him impress the playwright. Proctor knew Miller and he was aware of Harris's plight. Jed had done nothing in the theater since *The Traitor*, three years earlier.

This absence could in part be attributed to a crippling insecurity about his own talent as a director, but there was also a concrete reason for Harris's inactivity. The economics of the theater had changed. Production costs had soared past the $50,000 mark. Limited partnerships were the only approach to financing. Investors shared the cost.

Harris had not yet produced a show that way. Having sold his last possession, the beloved *Grande Dame*, he had no personal assets. He could not find a businessman willing to risk such a large amount on a show. He remained adamant in his refusal to seek out investors, still too proud to submit his choice of play for someone else's approval.

Cut off, then, from producing, his only recourse, if he was to stay in the theater, was to hire himself out as a director for other producers. But where was the producer he hadn't offended?

Jim Proctor agreed to sail across Long Island Sound with Jed, from Shelter Island to the Connecticut shore. They would entertain and perhaps impress Miller, who lived in Roxbury, a short drive from the water.

Harris still had prestige enough to borrow a yacht on approval. The yacht he borrowed was his old *Grande Dame*.

At dinner aboard the boat, Harris romanced Miller with all-night conversation and anecdote, political opinion and philosophical inquiry. The playwright brought the conversation back to his play, *The Familiar Spirits*, which Harris had not yet been shown. Proctor, however, had told him that its subject was witchcraft trials in the Salem, Massachusetts of 1692 and that its theme was the Communist witch-hunts of 1951 America.

"Harris had done his research for that evening," Miller recalled, "and was familiar with the play's setting and era. And I was aware of a tremendous visceral force emanating from him. Because my play was so emotional, in story as well as theme, I thought that this energy of his would help a production."

In a letter to prospective backers, Kermit Bloomgarden described Jed Harris as "America's most distinguished director." They were being asked to invest in the new Miller play, script unseen. Bloomgarden had no trouble raising the money.

221

For Harris, it was a shining chance.

Work began, predictably, with Harris telling Miller that the play needed revision. "He couldn't read a newspaper advertisement," the playwright said, "without telling you it needed a rewrite." The script went through three drafts as it was reduced from an enormous original to manageable size. According to Del Hughes, the playwright who had so serenely polished *Death of a Salesman* was now becoming tense and irritable. Miller was not a dependent personality likely to fall for the Harris charm, and he laughed off the inevitable suggestion of co-authorship and shared royalties. Privately, though, he was infuriated by the proposition. "The only reason Arthur didn't fire Jed," Jim Proctor recalled, "was because they had worked so long on the script; past the point of no return."

Miller and Harris drove to Boston to watch Arthur Kennedy act. Kennedy had been in *Death of a Salesman* and Miller admired his work. Harris disagreed but was willing to consider the man.

With Miller at the wheel, they pulled away from a toll booth on the Merritt Parkway. Suddenly Harris shouted, "Stop the car!"

"What's the matter?"

"The toll. I've got the money right here."

"I've already paid the toll," Miller said, driving on.

"But you forgot the tip!" Harris cried, waving a dollar bill. "We have to go back and give him a tip!"

Miller laughed out loud. Then he realized that Harris wasn't joking.

Jed gave in on Arthur Kennedy but one problem smoothed only seemed to raise another. Now it was the settings. Boris Aronson was the production designer and his original conception had been "perfectly lyrical," according to Miller. "The idea I had in mind was a physicalization of infinite space so that the play wouldn't be happening now or in 1692 but was instead going on forever. Boris's original set emphasized that idea by dividing the stage between two funnel-like openings that led the audience into a tunnel."

Harris rejected the idea. He insisted on traditional, naturalistic settings. "They looked like paintings," Miller said glumly. "Jed kept talking about the image of a Dutch master. It was as if he could see no further than a pilgrim play."

Rehearsals of the drama, now called *The Crucible*, began of course with the company around a table, reading the script. The author was off to the side. Among the cast, in addition to Arthur Kennedy, were Walter Hampden, E. G. Marshall, Cloris Leachman, and Beatrice Straight. Miss Straight had met Harris when she succeeded Wendy Hiller in *The Heiress*. That production also introduced her to the man she would marry, actor Peter Cookson.

"Jed's discussions and character insights were exciting and bold," Miss Straight would later remember, "but company resentment was already building because he'd begun feeling out the cast. Who could he dominate? Walter Hampden. Who would he have to tolerate? E. G. Marshall. Who could he abuse? Cloris Leachman. And grapple with? Arthur Kennedy. 'Johnny' Kennedy was Jed's personal scapegoat for *The Crucible*."

Harris complained to Miller that "Kennedy doesn't have class. He's just an Irishman from Worcester." Humoring him, Miller replied that the character Kennedy was playing "is just a peasant himself," but that didn't keep Harris from needling the actor, and his moods grew blacker. One wintry day he didn't show up for rehearsal at all.

"Jed? Is that you?"

Miller had telephoned him at home.

"I am dying."

"Of what?"

"I'm *dying*, Arthur. You'd better take over."

Miller could hear "ghastly teeth chattering." Giving the company an early lunch, he ran over to Harris's current home, a small apartment at 43 East 73rd Street. Naturally, the door was ajar. Jed always left the door ajar when setting one of these scenes. The playwright let himself in. Harris was bundled up in a bathrobe beneath blankets pulled under his chin. As he lay there shaking, he croaked that the doctor had just left. Asked what the diagnosis had been, he just shook his head.

"What do you want to do? Go to the hospital?"

"No, no. You'd better go back and take rehearsal."

"But Jed. If you're this bad—if you've got something seriously wrong . . ."

"Never mind about that," Harris whispered hoarsely. "What's wrong with me is my business. Thanks for coming."

Miller returned to the theater and told the company to resume where they'd left off. A short while later Harris came in. He sat down in the rear with his overcoat on, a muffler wrapped around his throat. In an hour he was directing again.

"I think he was terrified," Miller said on reflection. "I think he was afraid that he didn't know what to do with my play. He seemed so uncertain all the time."

Inevitably, Bloomgarden and Miller asked Harris how he would feel about stepping aside for another director. It was the first time in his career that such a thing had been suggested, and it must have been a terrible moment for all of them. Miller recalled Harris's response as being even tempered and whispered with a cool smile. Replacement, he said, would be acceptable as long as he was paid his full fee and royalties. If those conditions were met, he said matter-of-factly, a new director would be perfectly acceptable to him.

Was he fighting back by making replacement economically impossible for the producer? Or was this egoist now so bereft of ego that any humiliation had merely a price tag?

Bloomgarden was willing to consider the proposition. Miller, however, felt guilty about publicly insulting a man of Harris's reputation, especially a man in such a state. Too, in a play for sympathy, Harris had said that he could no longer work in Hollywood because of blacklisting. This was a shabby lie, designed to play on Miller's political convictions. Harris was not given to causes; he was too Hamlet-like in his reasoning for conviction and commitment. He in fact once *refused* to support an advertisement condemning the blacklist on the grounds that it was futile to appeal to the rational side of the American people.

So he stayed on and tensions heightened. There were tantrums at rehearsal. "He was a dangerous child with a bomb in his hand," Miller said. "Here was a marvelous group of actors, dying to work, and this mad director screaming at them." Yet, Miller held on to his hopes "because it is in the nature of theater people to be forever optimistic despite signs of disaster everywhere."

He shuddered at such directing choices as having all the dialogue read straight out to the audience instead of being addressed by one character to another. Harris also had positions chalked on the stage floor with the actors instructed not to move from those marks.

It was *The Heiress* and picture-making all over again.

"This was not the same man," Jim Proctor said, "that I'd once hidden in a balcony to watch direct *The Green Bay Tree*. There was a quality of desperation in his work now. It was frenetic. He was trying too hard. The values emerging were overly melodramatic, making it into a neat play with a beginning, a middle, and an end instead of this rocklike, tremendously original thing that Miller had started out with. That was a tumultuous and vigorous work. I think that Jed was making a tremendous effort to have the whole business under control and acceptable as a commercial play."

Making the same observation of frenzy, Ed Chodorov came to the opposite conclusion. "I think he was doing everything he could to destroy the play and make it flop."

By the time the company traveled to Wilmington for the first tryout and world premiere, Harris had "quit on the play," according to Beatrice Straight.

"Mr. Miller had already started rehearsing Arthur Kennedy and me privately, although Johnny [Kennedy] wanted out. And Walter Hampden still didn't know his lines."

Finally, the distraught and nearly hysterical Harris barred Bloomgarden from the theater. He told the producer, "I am a latter-day Duke of York, the Prince of Wales. You, my dear man, are a mere accountant."

On the opening night in Wilmington, Miller watched the performance between onslaughts of nerves. He regularly retired to the bar that adjoined the theater, consoled there by his literary agent, Kay Brown. As the play's final scene was begun, he could watch no longer. He and Miss Brown sat in a booth, silently sipping their drinks.

The applause erupted. Miss Brown rose. She walked toward the theater entrance. Miller stayed behind. As she entered the auditorium she heard the audience crying out for the author. She turned to look for Miller as the ovation and the demand persisted. Then, shocked and bewildered, she watched Jed Harris stroll from the wings to center stage. He smiled and bowed in the stage light, a marionette. The applause continued as he peered into the glare and the darkness beyond it and bowed again, awkward and self-conscious as nonperformers tend to be on stage. Then he hurried off stage and into the wings.

Miss Brown turned angrily as Miller came up behind her. He'd been told of the audience's call for him and started down the aisle, toward the stage. Harris came hurrying up the aisle toward him.

"Jed was grasping the lapel of his sport jacket," Miller remembered, "and holding a button in his fist."

"*They* pulled me on stage," Harris burst out defensively, showing the button as if it were proof. "The actors did."

"Good God," Kay Brown said later. "What was he doing, taking Arthur's bows? He had to have been mad."

❖

The Wilmington reviews were good but Miller and Bloomgarden knew there were problems. Harris had gotten Jones a job as a production assistant, Beatrice Straight recalled. "The only thing the boy would do was warn us if Jed was going to attend one of our performances. That was unlikely.

"One time Jones said that Jed had watched the show but had to leave his notes with him because he had an appointment. Jones read them to us. We were disgusted. These weren't the notes of Jed Harris, not even a demented Jed Harris. Jones had been asked to cover for his father. E. G. Marshall wrote Jed a note. 'Dear bullshit artist. Thank you for your wonderful criti-

225

cism of the play. It's been a tremendous help in spite of the fact that you weren't there.'"

The New York opening night was January 22, 1953, at the Martin Beck Theatre. Miller was depressed. "The actors," he said, "were dried up from the tryout ordeal. They couldn't maintain a level of life, and of course the play opened in the teeth of the McCarthy gale. As soon as the audience realized that's what it was about, they froze—and the critics likewise."

Not one newspaper critic noted any relationship between *The Crucible* and the anti-Communism then fevering America.

In the *New York Times*, Brooks Atkinson tried to be kind to his old favorite. "No doubt the overwrought direction by Jed Harris is deliberate," he wrote, "for a specific dramatic reason." But Atkinson did not specify the reason and he concluded, "Although the performance is brilliantly organized and paced, it becomes a little tiresome before the play is over."

The other reviews were no better, and the play faltered through a disappointing run. Five months into it, Miller decided to restage the production himself. He reinstated a scene that had been deleted and had the heavy scenery removed, leaving the drama to be played against simple black curtains and the basic props. He didn't bother asking Harris's permission.

The critics did not come back to see whether the restaging had made any difference even though the work of an important playwright was involved. It was only a play they had not liked to begin with.

The Crucible has since been acknowledged as a masterpiece of twentieth-century drama and one of the few international classics to be produced by the American stage. It fulfills the essential requirement of high theater, being both substantial and dramatic. Yet it was ill-received.

Miller's theory—"in the teeth of the McCarthy gale the audience froze and the critics likewise"—is a playwright's rationalization. Audiences and critics do not refuse to enjoy themselves because of a political climate unless they are in fear of a fascist state. However heated was the anti-Communism of the period, America in 1953 was not a fascist state.

Harris's production was surely the reason why the play's excellence was overlooked. Professional drama critics should be able to separate a play from its production but some cannot when mired in the sludge of a tedious presentation. Fortunately, history corrected this error.

The experience was a tragic one for Jed Harris. He had the opportunity he needed desperately, a last chance to make a healthy accommodation with life and work. He was handed a great play while standing at the brink of oblivion. He could have made a new start as a director for other producers, proving that his talent was worth the trouble of his personality. Yet he could not, or did not, choose to grasp the ledge that fortune held out in the form of *The Crucible*.

Arthur Miller's last words on the subject of Jed Harris were, "People thought he was brilliant. I certainly thought he was charming. But if you put it on a record and played it back, why—there was nothing *there*."

PREGNANT WITH FAILURE

IN HIS GOSSIP COLUMN for February 1, 1953, Robert Sylvester reported in the *New York Daily News* that "Jed Harris has a new gimmick this year. He wears his glasses hooked behind his ears but with the lenses resting on his balding head."

It was the last trend that Harris was going to set. His accomplishments, once glittering, artistic, even historic, were concluding in the trivia of fashion. His active engagement with life, trusting to and exercising talent, *producing*, had been unraveling ever since Rosamond Pinchot's tragedy. Now he'd developed a hustler's concentration on survival and he stooped to consummate such deals as he had once scorned.

He even developed a fancy kind of panhandling. He would cultivate friendships with wealthy men who were impressed with his fame and glamour. They would eagerly become his personal angels, not merely picking up dinner checks or buying airplane tickets but advancing him sizable amounts of cash. Sometimes they would receive, in exchange, an interest in nonexistent projects.

Among these angels were Jay Darwin in San Francisco, one of the country's leading labor lawyers, and Samuel Haas of Cleveland. Haas was Harris's most recent sponsor but the little fellow had been smitten with Cinda Glenn and after tracking her down in Mexico with Wakeman he moved her into a big house in Montego Bay.

Now Jed hoped that he had found a new angel in Jacques Traubee. A mutual friend had arranged for them to meet over dinner. As Traubee remembered it, Harris began the conversation with candor, as if hoping to disarm.

"I understand that you are an extremely wealthy man."

"I understand that you are an extremely wealthy producer."

"That is correct."

"In that case," Traubee said soberly, "you ought to know that I am flat busted."

He burst out laughing. Harris stared at him blankly. Finally, he said, and just as soberly, "So am I." They both laughed, through dinner and then until dawn, from one bar to the next. It was the start of Harris's last, best, and perhaps only true friendship.

Jacques Traubee de Miramar sometimes admitted to the name of Jack Traub. A Russian immigrant, he had learned to survive at an early age and now lived, by his own description, from one score to the next. Although the flash of his style suggested show business inclinations, his game was real estate, the deals ultimately to involve such properties as the Castaways Hotel in Daytona Beach, Florida; apartment houses in the Bronx; the Mickey Mantle Holiday Inn in Joplin, Missouri. Between such empires, he scrambled for basic shelter. His courtly manner, his continental accent, his worldliness and sophistication were as convincing as the reddish toupee perched upon his head. Even when in the money, Jacques Traubee managed to engage butlers who served drinks with their flies open.

In short, he was entirely adorable.

"Though I was dead broke," Traubee later reminisced, "I wasn't as broke as Jed was." In fact Harris was so broke that he was being threatened with eviction for nonpayment of rent on the 73rd Street apartment, and that was a matter of more than the usual importance. Ever since *The Crucible*, he had been spending virtually all of his time in bed. He would lie among the rumpled blankets, the mess of books and newspapers and half-empty coffee cups, never bothering to dress. He would read anything, it seemed to Traubee, except a script, and would only go out in order to buy a newspaper or pay the rare call on Jean Dalrymple.

Traubee thought "Jed was finally convinced that he could not do it again, could not succeed again, could not match his fabulous youth. So now he tried to hide in bed. Every venture scared him, as if he was pregnant with failure."

Traubee took care of the rent that month and saved Harris from the street, but "my whole idea at that time," he said, "was to get him *on* the street; to put clothes on him and get him out of bed."

229

Jean Dalrymple made sure that the apartment was cleaned, sending over her housekeeper, Mrs. Carey, to do the place every Thursday. Rather than hire a baby-sitter, Mrs. Carey brought along her daughter Alice. The nine-year-old would wander through the place, ogling the theater artifacts. Years later, she would remember the sketches of scenery for *Uncle Vanya;* the commemorative ceramic ashtray from the *Our Town* opening night; the ratty bathrobe with the Abercrombie and Fitch label; the mirror that was smashed when Mr. Harris threw the ashtray at Jones.

It had been over an alarm clock.

Having been graduated from Brandeis, Jones had not yet gotten a job, other than the brief assignment with *The Crucible*. His family background made him choosy about what he did. His mother was not only a celebrated actress but had also become a successful writer of screenplays and dramas. The world that she and Garson Kanin traveled was international and glamorous, and Jones had traveled that world with them. He knew everyone they knew.

But glamorous couldn't compare with legendary, and even when Jed Harris was down he was a legend. In fact Jones talked as if his father were a bigger star than his mother. His ambitions were affected by these connections. As he said to more than one friend, an ordinary job was inappropriate to the son of Ruth Gordon and Jed Harris.

Jones, or "Jonesy" as he was by then known, moved in with his father and, like his father, spent a great deal of time in bed. Harris would lecture his son about getting up and looking for work, but he was hardly setting an example.

One noon he roused Jones, furious over an enormous bill that had just arrived from Western Union. It didn't matter that Mrs. Carey was there, cleaning the place, or that little Alice stood and watched and listened, to remember it many years later.

Sloshing through the torrent of abuse, Jones said that the telegram bill had been run up so that he could look for work. Every night, he explained, he called Western Union and arranged for a wire to be delivered the next morning. In that way he would be awakened so that he could get an early start looking for a job.

Jed stared at Jones until little Alice Carey thought that his face would pop.

"You're an idiot!" he finally roared. "Plus, you go right back to sleep after those telegrams are delivered. Can't you get yourself a fucking two-dollar alarm clock? A goddamned Big Ben?"

"Big Ben is in London," Jones sarcastically replied.

That was when Jed picked up the ashtray.

"A fucking Baby Ben!" he roared, hurling it. He never was a good ball player. The ashtray missed Jones by a few feet, shattering the mirror.

When Harris told Jacques Traubee about Jones's Western Union wake-up service, Traubee said, "The apple never falls far from the tree," whereupon Harris picked up another ashtray and hurled it at *him*.

❖

I have at last learned to understand something of the blind forces that are all but strangling me. With this knowledge has come *some* measure of self control and *some* capacity to see, understand and even love others. My behavior is still far from perfect. I still have some problems to overcome, not so much in understanding but in the only field that counts: action. This is going to be a slow process and at times a most painful one.

The letter was addressed to Gilda Davis. Jed had met her a few years earlier when he'd sailed the *Grande Dame* down to Miami Beach. Gilda had been living there with her husband, the lyricist Benny Davis. He was thirty years older than she and had grown rich writing such hits as "Margie" and "Baby Face."

Benny Davis was by all accounts a decent fellow, very taken with his pretty blond wife, and she loved him. The only trouble with Benny, according to Gilda, was that he played too much gin rummy. It made her feel neglected. He would sit at some hotel poolside or other, playing cards with such show business pals as Chico Marx or Tony Martin while his young wife yearned to go out dancing.

Jed offered to take her to a nightclub when Benny introduced them. Davis was aware of the Harris reputation as a ladies' man. He asked Gilda to stay with him. She glanced around the pool.

"Not if you're going to play cards all night."

"Benny," Jed interjected. "Are you really going to play cards and leave your wife with me?"

Davis reacted, as Harris surely had reckoned he would, by sending the couple off to prove that he could trust his wife.

Jed soon sailed away on the big, beautiful boat that was no longer his (an item of information that he failed to impart to Gilda at the time). But he was smitten with her and over the years conducted a long-distance courtship.

"Jed called me 'Chasha,'" Gilda Davis recalled. "That was my Jewish name. He told me that I was the first Jewish girl in his life and he said he only wanted to make a home for me and have a normal marriage. I should have worried when he said he looked forward to my home-cooked meals. I never cooked for anyone in my life."

Harris's was a fearful ardor, of quick vows and hurts. His four-year correspondence with Gilda, written in a neat but minuscule hand, mostly on foolscap and in pencil, is a study in the banality to which romance reduces even the toughest minds.

Dear Mrs. Davis: About our mutual friend, please tell her for me that she cannot go on saying that she loves people but she has no confidence in them, as if love were an unfortunate disease.

Darling sweetheart, I ought *not* to tell you what to do about us because if it were just a question of my telling you what to do and you did what I said then you would be acting on *my* convictions, not your own.

Dearest: Just as I sat down to write the mailman came with your letter. It is one letter I shall keep forever because it proves once and for all that you are married to me and living in sin with somebody else.

> How I
> Wish I
> Thought you did!
> Could you
> Would you
> Love this kid?

Dearest Chasha: Writer honestly believes he will make a very good husband.
                                                    Marital Dreamboat

Gilda Cooper was, by her own description, a naive girl from New Jersey when she married Benny Davis, but she grew up quickly and became knowledgeable about the reassurances of a bank account. Jed was exciting and funny and romantic and attentive, but if he was ever going to lure her into divorce and remarriage he was going to have to prove that he was capable of providing for her. A tall order indeed.

Dearest Chasha: I wish you could love me less but a little more steadily. It needn't be for long as I am wearing out fast.

By 1955 he finally convinced Gilda to move out of Benny Davis's house on Pinetree Drive. She came to New York, but not to live with him. "After all," she said, "I was still a married woman."

She took a suite at the Alrae on East 64th Street, an expensive hotel, and naturally, Jed was expected to pay for it. Gilda insisted that her attorney substantiate Harris's financial claims and formalize his promises about insurance policies. Meanwhile, Traubee was telling him, "You're dead broke and you're promising this lady the moon. She's not a kid. She's bound to find out."

She did, and when she did she went right back to Miami Beach, Pinetree

Drive and Benny Davis, spurring Jed to action at last or, as Traubee put it, "to make his last score."

A play had come his way, a military farce called *Operation Mad Ball*, written by Arthur (Archie) Carter. Harris told the playwright that "Broadway has had it, dear boy; the theater's buried, but your play would make a hell of a movie."

Carter replied that he'd never written a screenplay. Harris generously offered to collaborate. They went to Clearwater, Florida, to work because winter was warm there; because there were elaborate marinas and Archie Carter loved boats almost as much as Jed did; and because Clearwater was within skipping distance of Miami Beach and Gilda.

Working full time with Jed Harris was a stunning experience for Carter. Of all the writers sucked into the emotional maw, only Fred Wakeman was so swallowed. Carter abandoned his family in Providence, Rhode Island to live, work, eat, and once even fight with Harris. Jed threw the first and only punch. Archie was an advanced weight lifter.

When Jed showed *Operation Mad Ball* to Gilda as proof of his financial substance, she replied that an actual sale to a movie studio might be more substantial. He promised that he would go to New York, sell the script, return triumphantly to the stage, and then take her for his own. But he did not go to New York. He invited himself to his sister Sylvia's vacation home in North Canaan, Connecticut, near the Massachusetts border.

Sylvia Harris had married Hillel Bernstein, a *New Yorker* writer. She was a successful advertising woman. The two careers enabled the couple to live well. Harris, left alone in the house when they drove back to New York for the week, promptly moved into Hillel's study.

Bernstein was usually a reserved and unflappable man, but when he discovered the intrusion he exploded. "As a writer," Sylvia said, "my husband naturally saw the room where he worked as an extension of himself. Jed kept saying he was writing a book, but his aspirations to writing were the pretensions of a dabbler as far as Hillel was concerned. The symbolism of the move into the study was obvious. It could not be tolerated and I stood by Hillel in that."

When she removed Jed's papers from the study, he stormed out of the house. Peter Cookson and Beatrice Straight had a place nearby. He dropped in on them.

"I'm staying with my sister down the line," Jed said when he materialized at the door of the two actors' handsome home. Asked in, he first spent a half-hour in serious and intimate conversation with their two young sons. That always seemed to impress people. Then he told the Cooksons why he had come. He was interested, he said, in obtaining a loan of $50,000. He could offer as collateral the original copy of a movie script he had written. It was called *Operation Mad Ball* and was certain to be a great success. Consequently, he said, the manuscript would become a collector's item.

"We were not that wealthy," Miss Straight said about the incident, although she was an heiress to a considerable fortune. "Of course, that wasn't the point. His proposition was ludicrous and quite mad. He seemed so confused."

It is fair to speculate that in Harris's mind, however harebrained this proposal, he was contriving not merely to profit but to raise money for a stage production; still trying to produce the old way. Alone.

He insisted on staying the night so that he could read the script to them. In the wintry morning, Miss Straight drove him back to his sister's house. She had to drop him off at the roadside, the driveway not yet having been plowed. She sat at the wheel and watched him slog through the snow toward the door. He slipped and fell and lay there for a moment, silent in the deep drift. Then he rose, limped to the house, and disappeared inside. Beatrice could see Sylvia watching from the window.

◆

Jean Dalrymple, ever faithful, asked Jed to direct her production *Child of Fortune*. It was a dramatization by Guy Bolton of the Henry James novel *Wings of the Dove*. Harris, ever faithful, convinced Bolton to take the rights away from Jeanie and let him produce the play himself.

Standing outside the theater with Jacques Traubee and Archie Carter at the start of rehearsals, Harris said, "I have such power over myself—not self-control but actual power—that I could, if I wanted to, *will* myself to death at this moment. I could order my heart to stop. And it would obey."

On that note, work started. Gilda came up from Florida to watch, but there was nothing to see because as soon as rehearsals began, Jed stopped coming. Archie kept him informed about what the stage manager was doing and how the run-throughs went. Then Jed would give notes to the cast at the end of the day. He fooled no one.

Yet, even while disaster-bound with the play, he maneuvered to sell the movie script. Carter joined him for lunch at the Carlyle Hotel with John Johnstone, the eastern story editor for Columbia Pictures. Johnstone said that Harry Cohn, the tyrannical head of Columbia, had expressed an interest in *Operation Mad Ball*. "But," as Carter remembered the lunch, "every time that Johnstone brought up the subject, Jed would change it to something else. He would ask, 'Where did you say you were from? Minnesota?' Anything to change the subject."

Fifteen minutes into the lunch, Harris rose and extended a hand that the surprised Johnstone reflexively shook. Jed stood there and whispered, "Mr. Johnstone! Mr. Johnstone!"

"Yes?"

"I have a message for Harry Cohn that I want you to deliver, but you must listen carefully and deliver it personally and verbatim. Any deviation from my phraseology would lead to misunderstanding and misinterpretation and you know about Mr. Cohn's temper."

"Shall I write it down?"

"That won't be necessary. You seem a man of reliable memory. I would like you to tell Cohn that I wouldn't sell him *Operation Mad Ball* if he were the last producer on earth. Good-bye, Mr. Johnstone."

Stunned as much as Johnstone by the performance, Carter stumbled along as Jed strode to the exit. But it was simply a ruse. Within the week, Cohn bought the screenplay. He made Harris the producer on the movie and gave him a twenty-five percent interest in it.

Carter was thrilled by the sale, but ultimately he saw a darker significance in the way Harris had orchestrated it. "Jed," he said, "had stopped being the great Jed Harris and had become a con artist." And Carter watched Harris finagle much smaller deals. "He would do anything to make a buck. He'd lie, he'd misappropriate, he had lost all self-respect. It was a moral thing, a *character* thing. He had lost the integrity that had sustained his judgment. His judgment was no longer determined by artistic values but by self-serving motives."

One trait had not changed, however. Just as the deal was to be consummated, Harris told Carter that he'd changed his mind and was going to try and sell the screenplay to Twentieth Century–Fox instead. Carter telephoned his attorney. "Do me a favor and give Jed this message. He knows that I mean it. You tell him that if he doesn't go through with this deal, I give him my word of honor that I will never sell this property as long as I live. I will take it and scrap it."

Only then did Harris go ahead and make his last score.

◆

Betsy von Furstenburg was hired to replace an actress whom Harris had browbeaten out of *Child of Fortune*. The first gossip Miss von Furstenburg heard when she joined the company in Washington was that "Jed Harris has forgotten how to direct. He isn't directing us at all."

Although that seemed inconceivable to her ("People had told me he was the greatest director in the history of the American theater"), she was appalled to find it true. "He directed *Child of Fortune* as though it were an Egyptian frieze. Everyone was lined up across downstage in profile. That was the extent of his direction."

His work on the script was little better. He had brought Archie Carter along to rewrite for Guy Bolton. After reading one of the revisions, he threw it to the floor, snarling, "This is a piece of shit!" Then he retrieved the script in hope that "perhaps a line or two is salvageable." He scanned the pages, changed one word, inverted a sentence, and then fell back in his seat with a sigh of satisfaction.

"Ah," he said to Carter. "That's just fine now."

There were problems *not* of his making too. Others around the show agreed that Edmund Purdom, the leading man, was unsatisfactory. Harris suggested that rehearsals be suspended until a replacement was found, but that was the nub of it. He could only *suggest*. He was no longer the one man show. *Child of Fortune* had been financed through a group of investors, the first Jed Harris production to be done that way. He had gotten a co-producer to seek out those investors. Now, Harris had to ask the man whether he could postpone production and replace Purdom, for that would require additional funds.

The permission was denied.

Dearest Chasha: *Child of Fortune* opens at the Booth the end of September. I love and trust you but I do not share with you. I just give you outright everything I have. But you are leaving me, aren't you?

> If I
> Thought I
> Had a chance
> I would
> Dance and dance
> And dance
>
> Not like Bolger
> Or Nijinsky
> More like Trotsky
> A real Kossatsky
>
> Your late husband,
> M. Pasternak.

Child of Fortune was a disaster. Jed Harris would never again have to seek anyone's approval. Broadway, which he had played so great a role in developing, had changed and done him in. The theater he personified no longer existed, and his theatrical career had ended.

So had the affair with Gilda Davis, in a movie theater of all places. The man in front of them was eating a candy bar and doing a noisy job of it. As Gilda remembered it, "Jed asked him to stop making so much noise. No. He didn't ask him. He *told* him, and he *kept* telling him."

When the man turned around, Harris started kicking at the back of the seat. He kicked so hard and was so vicious that he frightened Gilda.

"I knew right then, I made up my mind," she said, "that I had to break it off with him right away. He was a violent man. I knew it from that. I knew that one day he would hit *me*. I couldn't have that so that was the end of it."

The double rejection, the play and Gilda, shot Jed all the way to California. He bought a house in the Hollywood Hills with the *Operation Mad Ball* advance money and he pursued a dancer he had met in Las Vegas. She was half of a nightclub act, her name was Beatrice—"Bebe"—Allen and she looked quite a bit like Cinda Glenn, with long legs and short red hair. Her eyes were small but set brightly beneath high, arching brows. She was young, thirty years younger than the fifty-seven-year-old Harris, and she was pretty. After seeing the act he went backstage, sent flowers, and left presents, like an old-timer.

Bebe Allen was a California girl who knew nothing about the theater. She didn't know that Jed Harris had ever been involved with Broadway. He told her that he was a movie producer. "He made sure," Archie Carter remembered, "that Bebe learned nothing about his past."

On April 1, 1957, one month after they had met, Jed and Bebe were married, "as if you [he wrote to Gilda] had nothing to do with it."

Dramatically enough, the day after the wedding Jed ran into Gilda and Benny Davis in the casino of the Royal Nevada Hotel in Las Vegas. They all stopped and stared at one another. Then Benny pulled Gilda away. Jed had "Rags," the maître d', bring her a note. "I am in the foyer, Chasha," it read. "If you can, come out." She didn't.

Bebe moved into the Hollywood house and Harris began working on *Operation Mad Ball*. Its cast included Jack Lemmon, Mickey Rooney and, at Jed's instigation, the television comedian Ernie Kovacs. Bebe had a bit part in it too.

Naturally, there was trouble. Richard Quine, the director, finally had to ask Harris to keep off the set and to not speak with the actors at all. Harry Cohn was so disgusted that, as a dig, he gave the obstreperous Harris a tiny, windowless office. Nevertheless, Jed stayed on until the picture was finished. Then, according to Carter, "he sent Cohn a three-page letter telling him what a no-good prick he was."

Operation Mad Ball was a box-office success even though Columbia Pictures gave it minimal advertising support. Harris's share was ultimately worth $187,000. It was a score indeed, but now he was through in the movies too. Nobody would work with him: it simply wasn't worth the grief.

Upstairs in the Hollywood house, he lay in bed reading. Bebe was below in the living room, watching a television late show. Suddenly she appeared at the bedroom door. As she recounted the incident to Archie, she said, "Jed, I'm watching the oddest movie."

He looked up from his *Manchester Guardian* and peered over the reading glasses that were perched on the tip of his nose.

"I don't know what to make of it, or how to say this, but I'm so reminded—it's uncanny—" And then she simply blurted it out:

"Does *The Saxon Charm* have anything to do with you?"

He said nothing. He held her eyes in his as he might have when considering an actress for a walk-on. Finally, evenly and coolly, he replied, "What do *you* think?"

She stared. She didn't answer the question. She said nothing at all. She turned, went downstairs, and watched the rest of the movie.

"*The Saxon Charm* was never mentioned again," she told Carter.

Harris sold the house in Hollywood since there was no work for him and they moved back to New York. As long as it lasted, the money paid for an apartment on Sutton Place.

At the time, Jacques Traubee was a long way from Sutton Place. He was at the Royalton Hotel, and precariously at that.

The Royalton and the Algonquin are the New York theater's twin hotels. They face each other on West 44th Street, like alternatives. Show folk who are on top stay, dine, and are clever at the Algonquin. Those who are in trouble hole up in the Royalton.

Jacques Traubee was behind in his rent at the Royalton and was consequently delighted to see Harris stepping out of the Algonquin. After considerable backslapping, most of it on Traubee's part, he took Harris by the elbow and guided him up the street. "I'm broke, Jed," he said. "I'm behind in my rent. I think I'm going to get kicked out of the Royalton."

Harris was expressionless.

"Can you help me out?"

"What do you owe?"

"A few hundred."

He needed more than that and he'd given Harris thousands of dollars. Jed reached into his pocket and pulled out a packet of cash. He leafed off a couple of hundred-dollar bills. Traubee took the money and walked off muttering, "You son of a bitch."

Jed's turn would some soon enough. Living in the Sutton Place style was fast depleting the *Operation Mad Ball* money and Bebe was awarded a substantial part of the rest when she walked out the second and final time. Truly a child of Hollywood, she had scrawled her farewell in lipstick on the dressing table mirror like a Barbara Stanwyck movie, almost.

"Jed Harris. You are a fucking prick."

Harris's women were fast disappearing and, as a rule, not going on to better things. Bebe would be dead within ten years. Cinda Glenn was still down in Montego Bay, but Samuel Haas was older and ailing and spending most of his time in America. Not being married to him, Cinda had few rights. Louise Platt was luckier. Her second husband was Stanley Gould, a quiet, academic, dependable fellow, but her relationship with Abigail was marred by the child's connection to a marriage that Louise wanted to forget.

On New Year's Day of 1960, the forty-eight-year-old Margaret Sullavan was found dead behind the bolted door of a New Haven hotel room. She had been trying out a play called *Sweet Love Remembered*. Only two sleeping pills were missing from the bottle, but her death was presumed a suicide anyway.

Geraldine Morris was still available to Jed in her winter home in Cuernavaca, Mexico. He had a cash advance from Doubleday to write a memoir about *The Heiress*. Taking it, he accepted Gerrie's invitation to come down "for the whole winter, if you like." She was in bloom, beautiful and mature and knowing, yet still *hamishe*. "Let's face it," she said, "I went all the way back to New York's Jewish-girls-forever club."

Gerrie and Jed had the big house to themselves, and a staff of servants to cater to them. She felt that the conditions were perfect for his writing, but he wouldn't work. "Instead he was just impossible. He was an unhousebroken guest of wild proportions."

Seldom showing up for meals, Harris would sleep through the day and then get out of bed in the middle of the night, demanding not merely food but the services of the full staff. When he was available for dinner, he wasn't hungry. "My cook was brilliant," Gerrie Morris remembered, "but Jed had an affection for cheap food. It wasn't unusual for him to go out a half-hour before dinner and fill up on refried beans."

Nor did his bedroom performance offer any compensations for her. After his lifelong reputation as a sexual dynamo, Harris was temporarily impotent. It may have worried him, but he did not offer any explanation or analysis to

Gerrie other than a shrug. He never said that life was treating him badly, or unfairly, or all too fairly.

He did not get the *Heiress* memoir written until he got back to New York. It was mostly dictated to Shirley Berick and left for her to polish. The title, ultimately, was *Watchman, What of the Night?* and though the book was scantily reviewed because of a New York newspaper strike, the notoriously acid drama critic Claudia Cassidy did write about it in the *Chicago Tribune:*

He was small and ugly, or charming. He was the most conceited man on earth, or the most delightful. As a stage director he was an outrageous oaf or the gentlest and subtlest of persuaders. Actors loathed him or they adored him. He had no friends, or they never forgot him.

He sounded dead. As Arnold Weissberger, the dean of theatrical attorneys, had said of him, "When someone tremendously successful—especially in show business—becomes inactive and then disappears—naturally, you think he's dead."

Naturally, and because Jed Harris's life was now characterized by inactivity and disappearance, many people *were* beginning to think him dead. He had lived in Florida for a time, writing the book and failing to rekindle the romance with Gilda. He had roamed the country, making passing acquaintances as easily as ever. Michael Abbott hadn't seen him since *The Billy Rose Show* when the telephone rang. It wasn't four in the morning. It was seven, on a blizzarding New York day.

It was four in California.

"Dear boy?"

Abbott knew the voice at once.

"I am at the Beverly-Wilshire Hotel. I find myself in a bit of difficulty and I want you to do something for me. I'm just going over my checkbook and I find I've made an error and possibly a few checks that I wrote might be returned."

There had as yet been no greeting. It was as if Abbott were still working for Harris when in fact he was now an executive with Talent Associates, a television production firm, and it was a dozen years since they had last spoken.

"I want you to deposit five hundred dollars in my account at Bank Leumi on West 35th Street and Fifth Avenue." He used the Israeli bank, he told Abbott, as a statement of his pro-Jewish feelings. "I'll see you in New York in a week," he said before hanging up.

Abbott made the deposit "because Jed still had his magic" and a week later Harris indeed called for lunch. Over coffee, a check was dutifully handed over, made out to "Abbott Gold," which was Michael's real name. Jed enjoyed that.

Regardless of how it was made out, it bounced.

"How could you do that to me?" a hurt Abbott demanded on the telephone.

"What are you talking about, dear boy?"

"The check. The goddamned check bounced!"

"Don't bother me with things like that," Harris said, hanging up.

The next time Abbott saw Harris was on Madison Avenue, a year later. Jed was still in uniform, the fedora, the camel's hair coat, but the costume had lost its former crispness. Still, the famed saturnine head was tilted downward as usual.

Jed glared at the sidewalk, rejecting it.

Catching sight, Abbott turned "and I fled. I don't know why. I didn't want to fall into his clutches again. I didn't want him to come into my life again."

◈

"You always wanted to know what Jed Harris looked like," Edward Chodorov said to his wife Rosemary. "He's across the room with two men. Now don't stare at him because I don't want him over here. You can't start with Jed. You start with him and you get phone calls at four o'clock in the morning, and he starts taking over your life. So just look. He's the man sitting against the wall."

After Harris and his party left, the table captain approached.

"Mr. Chodorov, Jed Harris would like to know if he can join your table."

"Tell Mr. Harris I'm sorry but I'm talking business. I'm sorry. Tell him please forgive me."

The captain was back shortly.

"Mr. Harris insists on joining your table."

"Well you tell Mr. Harris that I am sorry but I insist that he shall *not* join my table," and Chodorov turned to his wife. "This isn't the end of it, you know. It's just the beginning."

The captain was back.

"If you will not allow Mr. Harris to join you at the table, will you join him at the bar?"

"I'm sorry, Rosemary," Chodorov said. "This is going to go on all night. I'd better get rid of him," and he got up and walked to the bar. Harris was sitting on a stool, swirling a snifter of cognac.

"Hi, Jed. What's cooking?"

"All I wanted to say was that when I looked across the room, I saw my

241

Eddie take out his glasses to read the menu. You used to be so young. It made me burst into tears."

Recalling the moment, Chodorov said, "That's how he did it. I said, 'God-damnit, come on over to our table, you bum.'"

When the three of them left the restaurant they stopped to watch a movie being filmed up the street. *The Sweet Smell of Success.* Invited onto the set, they were picking their way through the lights and wires when a pretty girl passed by. "Some starlet or extra," Chodorov recalled. Without saying a word or missing a beat Harris turned on his heel and followed her off and that was the last time Chodorov ever saw him.

◆

Martha Scott and Henry Fonda had organized a producing company called The Plumstead Theatre. They were presenting *Our Town* in a Broadway revival at the Anta Theatre. Although Henry Fonda seemed perfect as the Stage Manager, Thornton Wilder wasn't pleased with the way rehearsals were progressing otherwise.

"We've got to get back to what we had when Jed did the play," he told Miss Scott. "And that was without sweetness." The current director was underlining the play's sentiment, as usually happened with productions of the play. Perhaps that was inherent in *Our Town* no matter how often Wilder said, as he said now, "no nostalgia allowed."

Did he not know that Harris was still alive? That Jed was in fact standing in the theater lobby during dress rehearsal and determined to get in? The security guard was ill-equipped to cope with him. Jed demanded to see Martha Scott and Isabel Wilder. They were summoned and they came.

Jed looked old. He looked ill. He looked feverish to Miss Scott.

"Why?" he whispered with anguish. "Why didn't you ask me to direct this?"

She couldn't tell him why. She couldn't tell him that Henry Fonda had vetoed him under any circumstances. Having been married, however briefly, to Margaret Sullavan and having been her friend for a lifetime, Fonda couldn't forgive Harris's treatment of her. Her suicide had only made the actor angrier.

"He was one of a small group of people," Martha Scott said, "who felt that Jed had something to do with Margaret Sullavan's suicide."

She and Isabel Wilder talked to Harris for an hour, trying to calm him down. He finally left.

Now Traubee had to find *him* a room at the Royalton.

Jacques cautioned against despair. As he jovially knew, having scored and blown it since last seeing Jed, a reversal of fortunes could be as real and immediate as the Algonquin across the street. A certain theatrical arrogance could carry one's pride in the meantime.

And his financial circumstances notwithstanding, Harris could still observe the landscape of foolishness with zest. Upon the election of George Murphy to the Senate he quipped, "If they wanted a hoofer in Congress they should have elected Astaire."

But if shabby living conditions did not unduly depress him, like the hammiest tragedian he would demand royal *service*. He demanded it whether or not he paid his bills, "and," Traubee recalled, "if he did not get that service he would raise hell. That was a pretty funny thing for a deadbeat to do."

One of the Royalton's owners summoned Traubee to the office.

"You owe us about a thousand dollars," he said. "Not only are you not paying for your room but you've brought another fellow in here and he isn't paying his bills either. Give me your opinion, Mr. Traubee. Is this a way for us to run a hotel?"

Traubee tried to appear above it all.

"And how your friend *complains*. I don't want to lock you out—you're not the type of man to lock out. But you know as well as I that in the hotel business, if a guest doesn't pay his bills we just, well, *lock them out*. That's what is done.

"Now Mr. Traubee," the man continued in an urgent whisper, as if they were in a five-star hotel and a Duke was momentarily embarrassed. "Would you possibly be able to find yourself another place to live? Of course you can take all of your things. And when you have the money, why then you can pay your bill. And of course after that you would be most welcome to stay with us again.

"Oh, and one last item, if you don't mind. Would you also ask Mr. Harris to leave? *Please?*"

They moved from the Royalton to the Webster on 45th Street, a place that Traubee considered "just one step removed from a flophouse," but he took the descent in stride. Jacques Traubee would never lose a night's sleep in a fleabag.

While their belongings were being transferred by a boy they had hired off the street, Harris and Traubee walked through the Broadway area; beneath one marquee and another; past the successful shows of the day.

At last Jed took notice. He stopped in front of a theater and scanned its posters. The rave reviews. The ticket price scale posted in the box-office window. Then he turned to Traubee.

"I can get along without Broadway," he said, and Jacques stared him straight in the face.

Jed had certainly tried to get along without Broadway, although it had hardly seemed his option. He had alienated every professional associate, every potential source of work, every possible avenue of resurrection. It looked, rather, as if he was going to *have* to get along without Broadway.

Moreover, if he was going to get along without Broadway, it wasn't going to be as a Hollywood producer. He had alienated everyone out there too.

He had been announcing himself, lately, as a writer, but the fact had to be faced that Tom Reed had written *Night People*, not he. Archie Carter had written *Operation Mad Ball*, finally with Blake Edwards's help, not his.

The fact had to be faced that *Watchman, What of the Night?* had been off-handedly dictated to his secretary, Shirley Berick, and that she had cleaned it up and set it to sentences and paper. Not he. If he could get along without Broadway, it wasn't going to be as a writer.

Now, with all those strings run out, he had begun alienating the friends who had stood by him. He was checking them off and then checking them out. Some of his most loyal, or masochistic, women had finally had enough: Louise Platt, Cinda Glenn, Gilda Davis, Gerrie Morris, and, one way or another for certain, Margaret Sullavan. Then the last of the male friends had their fill: Fred Wakeman fled with *The Saxon Charm*. Archie Carter went back to his wife and family in Providence. Michael Abbott didn't want to see him and Ed Chodorov avoided him. Even Jacques Traubee, the last and best friend, was having moments of impatience.

"I can get along without Broadway," Jed had said to him, beneath the marquee and perilously close to vagrancy. "But can Broadway get along without me?"

DEATH MARCH

The tragic dimension is the waste—the waste of a life. Had he continued, had he not destroyed his relationships with people, he would have dominated the American theater as no one before or after. He started so young and with his talent he could have gone anywhere. As it is, his moment in the sun threw a shadow across the theater that endured for fifty years and no one escaped it.

That shadow was his legend.

—Archie Carter

CINDA GLENN came into a quarter of a million dollars in 1964 when the Samuel Haas estate settled her lawsuit out of court. It was one of the precedent-setting palimony cases.

Cinda was generous to her friends and an easy touch. In four years the money was gone, the last of it sunk into a Santa Barbara antique shop that she ran into the ground. At fifty-nine she was too old to perform and unqualified to do anything else. Her beauty was gone, as she had feared from the start. She returned to the little apartment on Madison Avenue, the haven she had always held on to, and she supported herself by continuing in the furniture business, in a manner of speaking: she sold everything in the apartment, piece by piece.

When the place was all but bare, her cat died. She did not, however, die

245

of losing her cat. On an early September morning in 1968, Cinda was found on the floor just outside of her apartment, dead of starvation.

Her only request was that *Variety* print her obituary, which it did.

◆

The last writer to come under the spell of the Harris charm was named Andrew Angus Dalrymple. He had sent his play, *More News in a Moment*, to Jean Dalrymple in the hope that "the similarity [of names] would encourage her to show me some favoritism."

Despite Jed's lifetime of deceptions and betrayals, once again Jeanie sent a good script his way, this time the young Canadian's comedy about bickering Irishmen in a Belfast betting parlor.

Whether or not a play is any good may be a matter of personal opinion, but its commercialism is a matter of consensus. To be successful on Broadway, a play has to satisfy large numbers of people; that is the box-office equation.

If there was ever a play in Jed Harris's pocket that seemed to have such a quality of mass appeal, it was Andrew Dalrymple's. Everyone who read it was enthusiastic about it. Since Harris plainly had neither the intention nor the nerve to dare for success again, all that remained to be tested was the limit of his endurance of failure.

Playing a part as if reading music, the playwright agreed to share royalties and credit with Harris. The familiar process of rewriting began, from Toronto to Palm Springs.

There was money for a while. Jeanie had raised the $175,000 needed to present the play. Jed announced *Great Day for the Race*, as it was now called, for the 1970 season. A cast was assembled, a rehearsal hall engaged. There was a first reading but the forebodings were dark. Harris may have committed the entire play to memory, but memory is not evidence of mental acuity. The truth was, his mind was *not* running smoothly. His comments at the reading were not meaningful, insightful, useful, or even coherent to at least some of those present.

That became irrelevant when "something terrible happened," as Andrew Dalrymple put it. "Thirty people were killed in one week in Belfast and the angels took flight. Backers of our comedy, people who'd pledged money, fell away in droves. The real life drama of Northern Ireland had caught up with us with a vengeance."

One might almost suspect Harris of having staged the Irish trouble himself.

With the investors gone, he could now pursue the *non*-production of *Great Day for the Race*, a pursuit for which he was better equipped.

Just why the name of Alice Carey came to him at that time is curious. It is difficult to trace the perambulations of any mind, and of Jed Harris's splendid but beleaguered mind especially. Was he trying to remember anyone Irish in his acquaintance for the sake of an Irish play? Surely he knew others besides the daughter of a woman who had cleaned his apartment almost twenty years earlier. Yet he telephoned Alice Carey, now an aspiring young actress. When she came to his small apartment on East 65th Street, he offered her a job as his production assistant.

It was in no way a euphemism for mistress. Jed would often be in bed when Alice arrived and he would invite her to sit on its edge while he rambled, but he made no sexual approaches until months later, and even those would be but gestures.

She was so awed by him, and had been since childhood, that she kept a journal beginning with her first day on the job.

He told me to call up some of the better book stores and get a book by Charles Lever. Then he asked me if I wanted to get married. I said, "Not particularly." "Your use of the word 'particularly,' makes me think there is a slight possibility of it," he said, and he mentioned George Moore, who, he said, started the Bloomsbury literary group in the nineteen hundreds. He said, "When confronted by a word like 'particularly,' Moore would say, 'Now what, *precisely*, do you mean by that?'"

When Jed got through with George Moore, touching on Leonard Woolf, he went on to an elaborate discussion of a production of *The Emperor Jones* which he once wanted to do at The Radio City Music Hall. He said how he wanted the lights and sound of the Music Hall to surround the audience and involve them claustrophobically.

After further ruminations on literature, theater, and politics, Harris brought up *Great Day for the Race*, which he praised to Alice as "the greatest Irish play since *Juno and the Paycock*. It's going to be my triumphant return to the stage."

At the end of that first day she was exhilarated. He had promised her that she could understudy the one female role in the play and in the bargain, she was to be paid $100 a week. It was not a large sum in 1970 but to Alice it was a munificent figure in light of the job's other ornaments.

Jean Dalrymple arranged for free office space at the New York City Center for Music and Drama, where she was a producer of revivals. The project must have appeared serious. Were they not assembling a new set of investors? But from the outset, Alice was aware of a reality gap. Jed stayed home in bed while she went to the office. It was she, a novice, who set up casting calls and auditions.

Then, Actors Equity asked him to put up the bond.

A producer is required to post an Equity bond to insure payment of two weeks' salaries for the actors should a play suddenly close. Harris was among an elite exempted from this requirement because of an eminence pre-dating the formation of Actors Equity. Now, the actors' association had decided that his financial position was too shaky for such courtesies.

"It was pathetic," Alice later said, "and worse, Jed didn't even know what an Equity bond *was*. When it was explained to him, he didn't want to put it up. And when Miss Dalrymple talked about doing readings for backers, he said he had never done that and never would. He said it was going to be like the old days, with just one backer. He wouldn't listen to anyone. There was nobody around with that kind of money to put up for a play and certainly not for a twenty-five-character play about the Irish trouble in Belfast *when there really was Irish trouble in Belfast*.

"Yes, it was pathetic."

Harris talked as if the production were going to open as scheduled, but "there is no visible money or means by which we will do it," Alice wrote in her journal. "And there is no talking to Jed at all. He was once *the* Jed Harris and now no one knows who he is."

As if to make certain that Alice knew who he was, he told and retold stories of his past.

I sometimes wonder whether Jed is senile, drunk or so immersed in reminiscences that he cannot quite grasp the present. He constantly repeats himself and even when I tell him that I've heard the story before, he delights in retelling it. What is interesting is that he tells it the same way each time, neither embellishing nor taking away.

Part of his past, too, were the old vaudeville sketches. "The only kind of comedy I truly love," he told Alice, "is low comedy. If you had only seen Willie Howard's sketch about the men lost and freezing in the Arctic; eating gefilte fish and chicken soup . . ."

Jed sits on the side of his bed and tells me the whole Willie Howard sketch. He begins to *look* like Willie Howard and I've never even *seen* him.

Alice started packing for Jed as soon as he answered the door. She knew why the landlord had come.

Harris did not seem embarrassed about being evicted for nonpayment of rent. Rather, he was regal in his contempt. "He acted as if it were the building's loss, his leaving," she remembered. "He sashayed out of there, manuscripts under his arm, pitying the landlord as someone too unfortunate to realize how important a person had been staying there."

When in need of a roof it is wise to make peace with one's family. Running into Jacques Traubee at an art gallery, Mildred Harris said she hadn't seen her brother in years. She told him that the ninety-year-old Mrs. Horowitz was seriously ill. When Traubee passed the news on, it gave Jed an excuse to renew connections.

He visited his mother in the nursing home. He moved in with his sister Sylvia. When the little place on Gracie Terrace almost burst from the squeeze, he went downtown to Mildred's apartment on University Place.

Mildred's daughter Nina was one child Jed did befriend into adulthood. He even went to her weddings. She had first married the writer Clifford Irving. "The ceremony was almost longer than the marriage," Mildred said. Nina's husband now was Mark Mersen, a television producer.

She had grown up to be a handsome woman and, by all accounts, a capable actress. Her last big role had been in a hit off-Broadway production of Jules Feiffer's *Little Murders*. It was a cartoon play. Absurdism was the theatrical fashion of the moment and, Nina recalled, "Jed was not devoted to it. He wasn't a hidebound realist but he did insist on organization and structure in a play. The fundamentals."

He also talked to her about suicide. "Not about committing it," she said, "but about *not* committing it. He thought the world would grant him the right to suicide if it comprehended the enormity of his disappointment. But," she shrugged, "he just wasn't the suicidal type."

Jed stayed at Mildred's apartment until the first telephone bill arrived. It was for more than five hundred dollars. He told his sister he couldn't possibly pay it and that made her so angry she called Nina and asked her to have Mark come and protect her when she threw Jed out.

Protection wasn't necessary. Whenever he was asked to leave, he left. Alice again packed for him. On the way out he took a couple of watercolors from the wall: they were of the sets for *Uncle Vanya*. Then the old man and the young woman trundled out of the building. It was eleven o'clock at night. He gave the cab driver Alice's home address. She had a studio apartment in the West Village. When she opened its door he went straight for the sofa bed.

"You can't stay here, Jed. We've got to put you in a hotel."

"The only hotel I'll take is the Algonquin. And," he added, "the only acceptable room is one with a good writing desk."

She checked him into the Royalton. That would last as long as his credit.

He stood in front of Scribner's book store on Fifth Avenue, across the street from the National Bank of North America. He handed Alice his personal check for twenty-five dollars. The account was long since overdrawn.

He told Alice that the bank manager would approve the check if she cashed it "because you're a young girl and you're cute."

Maybe he *was* Willie Howard.

The manager refused to cash any check signed by Jed Harris. Alice stood in the bank and wept. Jed now had two dollars.

He moved into a room in the Prince George Hotel on East 28th Street. He kept busy calling on acquaintances, ten dollars here, five there, and walking. It was on West 57th Street near Carnegie Hall that he noticed big Art Franklin farther down the block.

Art Franklin had grown up doing athletic pirouettes on Brooklyn streets. He'd dreamed of becoming a professional punchball player. A lack of punchball stadiums had led him instead to writing poetry, novels, plays, and even comedy material. The day he had met Jed Harris he jotted down in his diary, "A Hungarian without an accent is like a rattlesnake without a rattle." Thus suspicious, he began the friendship.

Now Jed's voice whistled down 57th Street. "Artie! Artie! Artie! It's so wonderful and strange and perfect to run into you like this!"

That was the way Franklin spoke, rather than Harris, but this is his recollection.

Jed was clutching a worn copy of *Great Day for the Race*.

"I was going to kill myself," he whispered as he came up to Franklin.

"Why? Why would you even talk about such a thing?"

"Because they just threw me out of the fucking Prince George Hotel."

"Oh? You got thrown out of the Prince George? On Twenty-eighth Street? In that case you're entitled to kill yourself."

"It piles up," Harris said. "I'm past seventy and this was the worst dump of all and there's no place left to go."

"But suicide? That's not for Jed Harris. Every schmuck in the neighborhood does that."

"Plus I'm starved."

"*Now* I understand. You're always crazy when you're hungry. Let's go over to P.J. Clarke's. We're just a few blocks away."

"In that case I won't kill myself."

They pushed through the door and into the popular East Side tavern. Mid-afternoon the place was quiet. As their drinks were set out, a voice called from the adjoining booth.

"Are you Mr. Jed Harris?"

"That's Danny Levezzo," Franklin said. "He owns the place."

"Fuck the Guinea."

"There you go again. He happens to be a lovely man and an old friend and for your information, asshole, he's a millionaire and very tight with the Vanderbilts. He's generous and he backs anything he believes in. You're lucking out and you don't even know it."

"So ask him to join us."

Levezzo, a muscular and handsome young man, expressed admiration when he was introduced. Years later, he too remembered the conversation.

"You have a son, Jones Harris, don't you?"

"He's my biological son and that's our entire connection and relationship," Jed said. "He hasn't done a goddamned thing his whole life."

"I'm sorry you feel that way," Levezzo said, "because he's a friend of mine."

Art kicked Jed under the table. "Is that right, Danny?"

"Yes, and I've always found him a gentleman. A nice young man. Matter of fact, he's about to marry a friend of mine's daughter."

Naturally, Harris said, "Who cares?"

"It's terrible that you feel that way about your own boy," Levezzo said. "But you did know that Jones is marrying Heidi Vanderbilt, didn't you?"

"A Vanderbilt!" Franklin exclaimed.

The restaurateur looked seriously at Jed. "Jones is marrying her in a couple of weeks. He would love your blessings. Why don't you meet his bride and come to the wedding?"

"You want Jed to see Jones and the girl?" Franklin said. "You *got* it."

"I hope you follow through on this," Levezzo said, rising and excusing himself.

"Art Franklin leaned across the table. "This guy can *help* you."

"I don't need help."

"Right. Two minutes ago you were jumping out the window of the Prince George Hotel. Don't you understand anything? We aren't talking about Jones. We're talking about this play," and he picked up the script. "You've got to let him read it," and with that, Franklin stood up in his seat.

"You need investors!"

"I don't need anyone's approval!" Jed shouted. "What the hell does this guy know about reading scripts?"

Franklin was already gone. "Five thousand dollars will get you a piece of this play," he said to Levezzo, "and it'll bail him out."

Several days later, Danny Levezzo called Franklin to say he liked the play but that even if he hadn't he would help Harris. He knew who Jed Harris was.

"Don't you fuck this up now," Art said to Jed as they walked to the restaurant to pick up the check. "Danny is a nice man and a smart man but he's got his pride so don't dump on him and don't blow the deal the way you've blown a million deals."

"Are you through?"

"No. Out of that five thousand dollars I want the three hundred you owe me."

"I'm giving you a thousand as your cut."

"I don't want a thousand. I just want the three hundred."

Franklin got the three hundred dollars when he helped Harris cash the Levezzo check. Then Jed went on a shopping spree at Bloomingdale's. He bought red silk pajamas and French shoes and a Palm Beach suit and then he spent the rest of the money on a trip to Miami Beach to see Gilda Davis.

"Don't you see?" he explained to Franklin before he left. "This five thousand is what I need to get the *whole* investment. I'll get the whole bundle from Benny Davis now."

◆

Jed never met Heidi Vanderbilt and Jones didn't invite either him or Ruth to the wedding.

◆

Jacques Traubee thought his life so far was but a prelude to a career in show business. That was the reason he'd wanted to meet Jed Harris in the first place. Now he could pursue that career because his real estate empire stood solid: in the Bronx, in Daytona Beach, and in Joplin, Missouri.

His first venture was taking an option on a play of Archie Carter's, *The Shrimp Boats Are Coming*. Jed promptly revised the script into the ground.

"What the hell do you know about plays?" Harris growled, when Jacques disapproved. "If I could get Claudette Colbert, I bet you'd do it then."

Traubee agreed, but Colbert never answered Jed's letter.

Now Jacques decided to produce *Great Day for the Race*. He knew that it could be mounted in London for a fraction of what it would cost on Broadway. Then he could bring it to New York. It was not an unusual idea. What was unusual was the friendship behind the business. Jacques believed that in the fate of *Great Day for the Race* lay the balance of Jed's life.

He flew to England in the hope of arranging a joint production with a London management. The first producer to read the script reacted with enthusiasm. This play just couldn't miss.

Moreover, the producer was London's most important, "Binky" Beaumont of H.M. Tennent, Ltd. Jacques Traubee's show business debut seemed at hand and what site more elegant than London?

He arrived for the appointment in a glow. He was certain that soon he too would be calling Mr. Hugh Beaumont "Binky."

The Tennent organization had offices atop the Globe Theatre in the West End of London. Traubee went up in the quivering little two-passenger elevator. The four-room suite was unpretentious, almost shabby, for a theatrical enterprise, especially one as powerful as Tennent. Traubee was ushered into Beaumont's oval office overlooking Shaftsbury Avenue. The elegant producer looked up from the desk, placed his cigarette in an ashtray, and rose. The dark suit was tailored close to his slim physique. He was so refined that his words seemed squeezed through a silver tube.

"How do you *do*, Mr. Traubee."

Jacques, continentalism itself, strode forth with a smile and an outstretched hand. He accepted the seat offered and sat basking in Beaumont's appreciation of *Great Day for the Race.*

"We are all enthusiastic, over here."

There was only one complication. Beaumont lighted a fresh cigarette and held it between the tips of his fingers.

"You must tell Mr. Harris that he will not be directing this production. We do not want him."

The producer explained, beginning with "Now look, Traubee," that Harris's inability to work with anyone else was well known. Beaumont himself had been involved with the 1946 London premiere of *Our Town.* It had been a disastrous experience. Harris was never at rehearsal and Isabel Wilder had demanded action. "Jed did not do his job," she later said, "he did not hold up his responsibility and Binky called him to order."

That amounted to Harris's being barred from rehearsals. On opening night he had been halfway back to America aboard an ocean liner. And that, Beaumont said, was only *one* reason why he would not hire Jed Harris to direct *Great Day for the Race.*

Traubee composed himself. Only then did he speak, and he spoke with a concentration that was dark and gathered.

"Listen, you son of a bitch," he began. "We're talking about one of the greatest directors in the history of the theater.

"I don't pretend to be a great expert. I'm just beginning as a producer although my business involves a kind of acting, I suppose. But I'll tell you this and I want you to remember it, Mr. Beaumont. I am not about to suggest to Jed Harris that he not direct this and I wouldn't have anything to do with a management that would suggest such a thing."

"Do calm down," Beaumont said, adding with theatrical bitchery, "You seem to be in love with him."

"Yes I am," Traubee replied. "I'm in love with him as a director, and as the man who made the American theater what it is. This man reached a tremendous peak when he did *Broadway* and *The Front Page*. He won a fucking Pulitzer Prize for *Our Town*."

"I know all about *Our Town*," Beaumont said. "We lost every penny on it over here."

"Do you know what he has gone through since then? This is a man who did it all when he was young and then something terrible happened to him. Whatever it was, he was never able to make a comeback from it. Everything was suddenly behind him.

"This is a man who just wasted the last thirty years of his life and possibly the last forty years of his life."

"There are many sad stories," Beaumont said wearily.

"Goddamnit!" Traubee exploded. "I'm not asking you to pity him. He worked on this script. All of these rewrites are *his* rewrites. I know what he did."

He paused to calm down.

"Sure," he continued, now quietly, "somebody else could direct it. The play would work. It's a terrific play. But we're not just talking about whether one play is a hit or not; whether it's going to make someone a couple of bucks. *This man's whole life is the theater and his life is on the line now.* Maybe he was stupid to give himself so entirely to the stage. Maybe I was smarter to give my life to real estate. But damnit, the excitement he created hooked me and a million other people on the theater. *Mr. Beaumont, this is Jed Harris we're talking about.*"

He stopped and swallowed hard. He stared at the suave Englishman.

Beaumont had listened. Then he considered. Finally, he capitulated. He changed his mind and agreed to co-produce *Great Day for the Race* in London. With Harris as its director. He asked only that two changes be made in the script.

"One deletion that is imperative," he said, opening the manuscript, "is this reference to our Royal Family." He found the page and read the line. "'Oh, that goddamned Royal Family is a bunch of Germans anyhow.'"

Traubee nodded. It wasn't an important line.

"Our only other quarrel," the producer said, "is with this BBC radio commentator. He is being obviously effeminate. It isn't a matter of prudishness or taste. We just think that such humor is a bit dated nowadays."

"That's all?" Traubee asked.

"I think that does it," Beaumont replied.

They shook hands and Jacques flew back to New York with the deal.

"No."

"What?"

"I won't make those changes."

"Stop being silly," Traubee said. "The British Royal Family isn't German. That goes back years. And fag jokes are old hat. These are trivial changes, Jed. The main thing is, we've got a production."

"I won't do it. Nobody makes conditions with me. Furthermore, I don't even feel like going over there and directing it."

And there was nothing Jack Traubee could do about it. That was the end of *Great Day for the Race.* Harris telephoned the author who never knew how close he'd come and yelled, "Cheer up, you dumb Canadian! I've been re-reading our comedy and it's as great as ever . . . It's an Irish *M*A*S*H!*"

But Andrew Angus Dalrymple settled for writing an article in the *New York Times* about his experiences with the play. It appeared on Sunday, September 10, 1972, and concluded

Jed, and all the other characters I've encountered these past years: . . . it's a privilege to have come so close.

◆

Whether terrified or charmed or both, almost everybody from the 1920s to the 1950s agreed that Jed Harris was *the* genius of the American theater, which in one way or another has been living in his distant, obscure shadow ever since.

It is 30 years that I myself have been dying to meet, not to mention interview, Jed Harris. But where was he, what was he doing?

"I've been everywhere. Florida, California, Maryland, Massachusetts. This year I've written two books, which I can't tell you about [a children's book, "The Rise of Elfi Katz," and a memoir, "Life Among the Goyim." Neither would be published.]

"Once I was talking with Hemingway down in Key West. He said, 'I don't care for show business and most of the people in it.' I said, 'Neither do I.' He said, 'Then why do you do it?' I said, 'It's something to do.'"

—Jerry Tallmer, *New York Post*, May 20, 1972

Harris had given the interview in the Algonquin bar but he was staying in a small and miserable room on the sixth floor of the Royalton. There he had joined the hotel's old-timers; men using the place as a retirement home; buying newspapers, picking up mail. Spending the days filling the days.

"Hello, Jed."

The man had picked up his mail too and now they were both in the elevator. Harris looked at him blankly.

"I'm Dan Petrie. The *Billy Rose Show.*"

Petrie was staying at the Royalton for nostalgia's sake. He was a successful movie director. Harris nodded brusquely, opened the British newspaper he had just received, and buried his nose in it.

His daily business included a visit to Charles Abramson on the eighth floor. The eighty-year-old Abramson had been a producer of musical comedies in the twenties. He was a natty fellow, his dyed hair plastered down, his mustache waxed. His pride was a collection of Italian silk ties and he considered himself unsurpassed in the tying of a Windsor knot.

The furniture in the room was his own and he was proud of that too. Unfortunately, some of the pieces were hidden by great piles of yellowed newspapers and curling scrapbooks.

Harris would tap on Abramson's door at eleven o'clock each morning. When Charlie's "Who's there?" went unanswered because Jed couldn't hear it, Abramson would open the door a few inches and peer over the chain. Harris would shout, "Goddamnit, what took you so long?!!" Then he would add in a whisper, "What are you doing? Let's have a cup of tea."

They would go downstairs and walk to a coffee shop. Over tea, Harris would abuse the waiter. Then, provoked by something Abramson said, he would call Charlie "a dirty kike." That would conclude the daily rite.

Harris spent his afternoons at the library, or browsing through bookstores, but as Abramson observed, "he never seemed broke to me." Jean Dalrymple was helping out. She could always come up with something. She sold one of the essays from "Life Among the Goyim" to the *New York Times* and the reminiscence about *Uncle Vanya* ran in the Sunday drama section. She put him in contact with book publishers, and while none of them found the rest of "Goyim" immediately publishable, a few thought his name still important enough to be worth a small advance. He accepted the advances, all of them.

The most profitable transaction was a movie windfall. Warren Beatty wanted to make a version of *Here Comes Mr. Jordan*. Buried among Harris's papers were the movie rights to the original play and its title, *Heaven Can Wait*. He had bought them years earlier and now they were worth $25,000 to Beatty.

Such things kept Harris going during these years when he was, as he put it, "wasting time waiting to die."

◆

Abigail was home in St. Louis with her husband and their two daughters when the telephone rang.

"Hello?"

No response.

"Hello?"

She tried to put the silent caller at ease. "Don't be afraid," she said. She tried comedy. "Hey, we lend money to *anyone*."

Still, silence. She was about to hang up when the whisper came through, a whisper she had seldom heard but would always recognize.

"Write to your father."

"Where?"

"Lee Leight. At Arnold Weissberger's office."

The theatrical attorney.

Then the telephone went dead.

◆

Pat Burroughs was freshly divorced and north of home the Christmas of 1976 when her paper hero materialized. The tall, pretty young woman with the long, straight brown hair and the North Carolina drawl had been stage-struck since childhood. She had acted, she had stage managed, she had painted scenery and kept track of props and fetched coffee at college and summer stock theaters. Now she was working on her doctorate in theater arts at Louisiana State University.

Pat Burroughs found the subject of her dissertation in New York City and despite the forty-year difference in their ages, he was not impotent with her. They went back to Louisiana, to a house in Mandeville across the lake from New Orleans. She worked on her thesis while he rewrote his memoirs.

Their life together was serene "but not for long," Pat recalled. The pictur-esque setting of Mandeville couldn't compensate for the town's sleepiness. They moved to a small apartment in the center of Charleston. From there they went to Sullivan's Isle, off the South Carolina coast. Then to Char-lottesville for a stretch and finally to Winston-Salem, North Carolina, where they lived with Pat's mother. They hadn't been in one place for more than four months.

The problem with "Life Among the Goyim," all the editors told Harris, was its theme. An audience for a Jed Harris book, they argued, would be interested not in his life as a Jew but in his theatrical reminiscences. The great years still had a few thousand dollars in them.

In reworking the memoir, Harris retained the few essays that dealt with his stage career and replaced the others with anecdotes about *Coquette*, *The Royal Family*, and *The Front Page*. But he found a private way to honor the theme of the original. He called the new book *A Dance on the High Wire*, a title drawn from a passage in "Life Among the Goyim."

"How utterly fascinating," she said. "I've often wondered what it's like to be Jewish."

257

"It's quite exhilarating," I said. "It's like dancing on the high wire in tight shoes."

Pat typed a fresh copy of the manuscript, packed a bag for him, and sent him off to sell the memoir in New York.

The chairman of Crown Publishers was a white haired, genial, and vigorous gentleman named Nathan Wartels. Jed decided to give him a crack at *A Dance on the High Wire* after spending the advance that another publisher had just given him on it. After all, Nat Wartels was an old friend.

A twenty-three-year-old Jake Horowitz had strolled down Central Park West with Nat Wartels after an evening of pinochle at Ray Malsin's apartment. "I have a great destiny," Horowitz had said, not specifying just what the great destiny would be. To Wartels, it had been a bitter optimism. "He seemed to feel as if the world owed him something. The world was going to pay for some unexpressed hurt it had done him."

Now that the world appeared to be making repayment for hurts that *Harris* had inflicted, a compassionate Wartels was trying to arrange a ten-thousand-dollar advance on the book. But, he warned, it couldn't possibly be paid in full until the manuscript was finished and accepted.

Harris erupted.

"Listen, you miserable kike. If you can't come up with that advance you can forget about the book altogether."

Wartels kept silent.

"Snot-nosed publisher," Harris muttered before starting to cough.

"I'll see what I can do," Wartels said. He advised Herbert Michaelman, his editor-in-chief, that they were going to publish an unsatisfactory book. "It has no narrative flow. It's just a collection of essays, not a memoir at all, but I want you to leave Jed alone. Don't worry about fact or fiction or consistency. Just make sure it isn't libelous."

Crown usually paid out its advances in fractions: one-third upon signing, one-third upon submission of an acceptable first half, and a final third upon a manuscript's satisfactory completion. Wartels gave Harris a full half of the advance, five thousand dollars. Michaelman didn't like it. He didn't like Harris, and he wasn't proud that such a book would be published during his tenure.

During the stay in New York, Harris stopped by at Arnold Weissberger's offices. He kept the attorney on retainer even though no retainer was paid and no legal work was done beyond pacifying the occasional publisher. Weissberger even went through the motions of billing Jed. "It was a matter of respect," he said. "We're talking about Jed Harris, after all."

When Harris stopped by at Weissberger's this time, it was not for legal counsel. He used the office as a mail drop. His correspondence was scanty. The only piece of mail that seemed to matter was the monthly Social Security check.

Its identity was concealed in an office envelope. Weissberger's secretary, Lee Leight, watched Jed casually slip it into the breast pocket of his out-of-style sports jacket. Like a man fresh from prison, or an alcoholic on line for a Christmas dinner, he was all buttoned up. His necktie was pulled close to the shirt collar. His belt was hooked one notch too tight. His jacket was closed and the trousers hitched high above the shoe tops. It was as if such grips could hold together whatever was left of the man and keep him from falling apart entirely.

Moments after leaving the office, Harris returned.

"What's this?" he asked the handsomely graying, well-groomed Miss Leight.

It was a bank check for one hundred dollars. It had been in the envelope along with the Social Security check. She examined it as if for the first time.

"It's from someone who said he was an admirer of yours," she said, handing it back. "A secret admirer. He insists on remaining anonymous. I'm sure that there were many people in the theater who respected and admired and liked you."

"Well tell him to shove it," Harris said. "I'm not taking money from anyone." And tossing the check on her desk, he turned and left.

The next day, he telephoned.

"I was just wondering, Lee. About that check you gave me yesterday. You haven't returned it, have you?"

She hadn't. He came by, took it, said nothing to her and left.

The three Harris sisters and Jean Dalrymple had decided to give him twenty-five dollars each, every month. The secret admirer story had been Jeanie's idea.

◆

"We're going to California," he announced to Pat Burroughs on his return. "I'm going to sell 'The Bitch Goddess.'"

It was February of 1979. The novel was not finished. There was little hope of selling it and no reason to try in California when all the publishers were in the East. But there was another purpose to this trip. That purpose became clear after his first visit—for treatment of emphysema—to the UCLA Medical Center.

"Hello, Meg?"

"I'm sorry. You must have the wrong number."

259

"Don't you know your own name? 'A room with a view—and you, / With no one to worry us . . .'"

The song ended with a cough.

"Jed, darling!"

Judith Anderson had retired from the stage to tend her flowers in San Ysidro on the outskirts of Santa Barbara. She had not seen Harris in many years.

"How do I get there from Los Angeles?"

She began giving driving directions, but the car was Pat's. It was bad enough that Jed was leaving her alone in the small and depressing Malibu apartment. She was hardly about to give him the car too, and be marooned there.

"No-no-no, I'll be coming by bus."

That was Miss Anderson's first hint that Jed would be arriving in less than first-class condition. Still, she pursued her usual day, gardening in the brilliant sunshine.

San Ysidro is one of the wealthiest communities in America. Judith Anderson's home was not its most splendid but the whitewashed eighteenth-century stone and timber house had a surpassing beauty. It was nestled in magnificent foliage. Flowers splashed through the garden. The interior was done in an elegant blue and white. Judith Anderson would never have to stay at the Royalton.

Harris hauled his suitcase from the taxi and lugged it through the gate, toward the front door. Judith was gardening. She rose, stretched and smiled, accepting his warm embrace. It made her intensely aware that "the only thing we had in common was the past and I had no interest in talking about it."

She showed him through the house. He asked where he could find a big table.

"Well there's one in the dining room of course."

"I'll have to see if it's right. This is going to be a wonderful place for me to work. I'm writing three books, you know."

"I was alarmed of course," she recalled. "It was quite mad, the whole idea." But then help came when the telephone rang with an invitation for dinner and a way to get them both out of the house.

"He delighted our hosts with his stories," she remembered. "As he began talking, I could just about see the young Jed all over again. Once, his conversation had sent words tumbling in merry cascades. I'd thought he was beautiful. So exotic. With his heavy eyelids and sensual mouth, the bulbous

Jewish nose. But now, after a while, it just seemed as if he wouldn't shut up.

"He was so *exotic*, and he had such long, elegant hands. But," she said, "as the evening wore on, it was all being played back in a grotesque man. The eyes were sunken, the lips curled and sneering, the nose outlandish.

"He'd become a monster."

To Judith's relief, when they got back Jed went directly to his room without making any sexual overtures. He did not appear again until five o'clock the following afternoon, when he padded into the living room, barefoot in his red silk pajamas, and announced to Judith and her maid that he was going to cook dinner.

He began drinking cognac. His breath reeked from the constant smoking and he was having trouble breathing. He cursed his way into the kitchen, opening drawers and slamming them shut. When Judith came in, he pushed her roughly.

"My only thought," she recalled, "was *knives!*"

Then he lost concentration and decided to dress. A short while later, Miss Anderson remembered, "he made an actor's entrance, wearing what he seemed to think was a California costume: an open neck shirt with an ascot. He hadn't shaved. He must have thought he looked the way he had when he was young."

He told Judith how wonderful it would be for the two of them to be living together.

"Here I'd be," he said, "sitting at the big table and writing my books. And you would be out there, planting and weeding in the garden."

"Forget it, darling," she said, and then he began to drink again. His speech was growing slurred, his manner even surlier. "In all the years I'd known him," she said, "he had never used foul language or become drunk. Now he raged. He raged with hatred for everyone. He hated his children, he hated me."

He lurched into the pantry and rummaged through the cabinets.

"Don't you have any goddamnned peanuts?"

He shuffled back into the living room, a fresh cognac in hand. He knocked a table over, and when he lifted his hand to strike Judith she fled to her bedroom, slamming the door and locking it.

He pounded. He bellowed. He made such a din that she turned the television set on to blot out the noise. Finally, "I think as much for his sake as mine," she recalled, "he gave up, went back to his room and fell asleep."

The next morning, all she saw was "a dirty, broken old drunk." She told him that he had to leave and he accepted that. "If he hadn't, I would have left myself. I was willing to be anywhere but there, in my own home. I couldn't deal anymore with the ugliness and heartbreak of Jed Harris in the gutter."

Just then, the telephone rang. It was the maid. Harris had already asked her to drive him to the bus station. "Please tell Mr. Harris," the maid said to Miss Anderson, "that I cannot drive him to the bus station. I'm *afraid* to."

"You'd better tell him yourself. I don't know anything about this arrangement," and she handed the telephone to Harris.

He listened to the maid. He waited and timed it. Then he spit into the mouthpiece, "You miserable little cunt. Who the hell are you to fuck up my day? You'd better get your disgusting body over here or I'm going to find you and wring your neck. Do you hear me?"

He hung up and turned to Anderson.

"He lifted his hooded eyelids," she remembered. "They were heavy now. 'She'll be here,' he whispered wearily to me."

Judith curtly replied, "You ought to pay her," and then she left the house.

Harris shuttled up and down the West Coast, alienating the few friends he had left at that end of the continent. Closing out all accounts. In San Francisco he cadged a few dollars from Jay Darwin, one of his old businessman benefactors. He'd dedicated *Watchman, What of the Night?* to Darwin. Then, back in Los Angeles, he borrowed fifty dollars from Donald Davis.

Nunnally Johnson was dead. His daughter Christie wanted nothing to do with her godfather. The gold chain around her backyard tree could not make up for her sense of him as a man who did evil among people. And Harris couldn't visit Dorris Johnson because the last time there he had put the touch on her brother Bob for ten dollars and some loose change.

Judith Anderson received a letter from him. The note said, "This is for your maid." A ten-dollar bill was included.

Jed's niece Nina lived in Los Angeles. She loved him. He never called.

By the summer of 1979, Pat Burroughs was crumbling from the pressures of his rages and demands, his appearances and absences, his violence and cruelty and his thirty-odd visits to the emergency room at the UCLA Medical Center.

He looked up from his newspaper. It was a small living room in the seedy garden apartment, there on a dirt road in Malibu. He had just read that Dick Cavett was in town to tape a special. With *A Dance on the High Wire* to be published in the fall, Jed told Pat, an interview on Cavett's nationally syndicated program would make wonderful publicity.

Robin Breed, who produced *The Dick Cavett Show*, had never heard of Jed Harris but she gave the message to Cavett anyhow. A theater buff, he was thrilled but shocked. He thought the legend had long since been dead.

They all went to lunch, Cavett, Breed, Harris, and Pat Burroughs, and "Jed sort of auditioned," Miss Breed recalled. "He told anecdotes for nearly four hours. It was exhausting, especially because he sent out vibrations that put me a little on edge."

The Dick Cavett Show was usually videotaped in New York but Cavett had such a feeling of having found a long-lost legend that he asked Miss Breed to find studio space in Los Angeles. A director was engaged and a crew hastily assembled.

It was a half-hour program. Some guests were given two segments. Cavett had not yet decided how many to devote to Harris and so Miss Breed told the director to just keep going; the decision on length would be made later.

At the Metromedia studio in Hollywood, Pat Burroughs walked up behind a cameraman and looked over his shoulder as the taping began.

"She was Jed's memory bank," Miss Breed recalled. "His fund of anecdotes was awesome and he could pull names and dates out of nowhere, but the sequence was shaky. She would remind him of who came before and after—things like that."

Well-known people become accustomed to stares and because of that they seem to develop swelled heads, not just metaphorically. Actually bigger heads. They are our Martians, giant famous faces supported by prosthetic bodies. Jed seemed to always have had this celebrity's physique, but now his head overwhelmed the failing body. Even his separate features had become outsized, ears and nose and chin pulled from the face like globs of clay. Only the eyes were small, squeezed out like beans from beneath the burdensome lids.

His brow was broad and when he spoke his eyebrows rose and fell beneath furrows. There were great vertical creases too, through the cheeks and between the eyebrows. Had he once really been likened to a Spanish don? Now there was a film of morticianly suntan brushed by the makeup man across the once ivory flesh.

The big television cameras glided noiselessly along the buffed vinyl of the studio floor. The echoing room was dark except for the one end that was the focus of all its energies.

"When I was rehearsing on a stage with a play," Harris was telling Cavett on camera, "it was the only time that I was happy."

He sipped water through the bent hospital straw. "An affectation," Miss Breed said. "Just a prop."

He responded alertly to Cavett, except when the question was loaded in some way. Then he didn't seem to hear. He would raise an eyebrow and say "oh?" or "pardon?" in what seemed a stalling maneuver rather than an evasion. For invariably, a sly response would follow.

He kept lighting cigarettes, Salems, and coughing.

"Very few people know anything about the theater," he said hoarsely. "In my work I am endlessly patient, but very often with people I have a low tolerance. Well, most people in the theater are idiots; fools of one kind or another. You try to be tolerant but they just wear you out. I used to be very hard on actors. I just disliked them. I dreaded to have to talk to them."

It was past the one-hour mark. The engineer kept reloading videotape. Jed had a sandwich during a break, and a cup of coffee. He coughed intermittently and seemed to have trouble clearing his throat, but he lighted continuous cigarettes. With each of them he spread his fingers across his face, as always.

"The theater is a rather mindless place," he resumed. "You have to have a knack, a feeling for it, to make a delightful entertainment."

He talked about *A Doll's House* and how Ruth Gordon's talent overcame a certain lack of beauty.

The technicians stopped in their tracks. They listened and stared, and couldn't take their eyes off him.

He talked about *Our Town* and of course the last scene in *The Green Bay Tree*.

"Why are some people afraid of you?"

Harris smiled and drew in on the cigarette.

"I don't know," he said. "They're probably justified," and he went hoarsely on to another subject.

"Do you see your son Jones?"

"As rarely as possible. I don't particularly like him. I don't like my children better than anybody else's. [Having the child] is something [Ruth Gordon] did willfully. It was part of being an actress, having an illegitimate child by a famous director. It had nothing to do with me."

As if satisfied with the telegenics of that exchange, Cavett smiled.

"Well, it's good news to hear you're active again. Directing again."

"I don't know. We'll see, we'll see. As you get older and you know death is imminent—around the corner, could happen anytime—you get no fear of it. You just accept it. As natural. And . . . it's a rather pleasant time in that way."

The show finished, they all went to eat at the Brown Derby. Harris fell asleep at the table. "The air had gone right out of him," Robin Breed said. "But at least we had nearly three hours of him on tape."

The air was going out of Pat Burroughs too. The medical and emotional strain had become unendurable. She told Jed that she was going back to Winston-Salem whether he came along or not. He said he would. He wasn't feeling well. They loaded their sorry belongings into the trunk and back seat of the Thunderbird.

Pat drove. Jed really couldn't have. His cough had gotten worse. He was having a terrible time breathing. He was gasping for breath. By the time they reached Texas he was too ill to continue even as a passenger. Pat arranged for him to be admitted to a New York hospital and brought him to the San Antonio airport. His flight delayed, he urged her to go on ahead. Then he telephoned Jacques Traubee in Daytona Beach.

"When are you coming to New York?"

"Tomorrow, Jed. No, not tomorrow. The next day. Why?"

"I'll come down there and fly to New York with you. I want to fly to New York with you."

"There's no sense in that. I'll *see* you in New York."

The following day, Harris showed up at Traubee's Castaways Hotel in Daytona Beach.

"What are you doing here?"

"I thought we were going to New York," Harris stammered. "I guess I forgot."

Now, wearing a wool robe over a sweater, he wandered through Traubee's apartment on Central Park South in New York. Jacques was in bed, reading.

"You know a lot of sporting people," Jed wheezed. "Is there anyone you could call, they could advance me twenty or twenty-five thousand dollars on this new book of mine? It's going to make a barrel of money. I'll assign all the rights and in the meantime I'd be able to get myself a house in the country and hire a young man to do light duties and take dictation."

"I'll look around," Traubee said with terrible sadness. "I don't know anyone offhand."

Harris paused at the bedside. "Maybe I'll fix myself some breakfast."

"Jed. It's eleven o'clock at night."

"I'm sorry. I'm taking this very strong medicine. If I don't take it I'm in great pain. I don't know which is worse, the pain or the disorientation."

Only days later, when Traubee was back in his penthouse apartment atop the Castaways Hotel, Jed checked into the New York University Medical Center on First Avenue and 30th Street with pneumonia and congestive heart failure.

They put him into the Intensive Care Unit, "but he was not in danger," according to one of the senior nurses. "He was alert and basically oriented."

The fluid in his lungs was relieved by diuretics. He was given digitalis tablets to strengthen his heart. When his lungs were clear and his condition became stabilized he was taken out of Intensive Care and put into a private room.

His demands for service were persistent, his treatment of the staff outrageous. "To tell the truth," the senior nurse said, "we were in more pain than he was." One young nurse who made the mistake of coming into his room to make him comfortable was plumping up the pillow when he whispered, "Your boyfriend sucks cunt."

She fled in tears and refused to return. After that, nobody wanted to go into his room.

At the first sign that his stabilization would continue, they checked him right out. "He was the first patient in my memory," the senior nurse said, "who was ever thrown out of a hospital."

He returned to Winston-Salem, to Pat Burroughs and her mother, and there he recuperated until the galley proofs of *A Dance on the High Wire* were ready. Then he wrote to Nat Wartels for help in finding an apartment. "Maybe somebody went to Europe, or something like that. Because I can't pay those hotel bills in New York."

But it was always to be the Royalton.

Each morning he would take the subway downtown to the Crown offices and spend the day carping about real and imagined mistakes in the proofs. Herbert Michaelmore would steel himself when he heard the author rasping, wheezing, and swearing down the corridor to complain about a book that never should have been published in the first place.

"I'm not feeling too great today," Jed muttered to Nat Wartels, one afternoon. "I'm a little tired. Under the weather. Do you mind if I sit down?"

"We've got a rest room for employees who don't feel well. Why don't you go in there and lie down on the sofa?"

"I'd rather sit here," Harris said, plopping down on a small fiberglass chair in Wartels's cluttered office. He let his eyelids fall shut. His face was pale and there was a film of white froth on the edge of his lips. Wartels walked to the outer office and told his secretary to call a doctor, but instead Harris went to Jean Dalrymple's.

"Jed! Jed!"

He had fallen asleep sitting at the dining room table, talking to her while she cooked. Now Jean was standing there in a fright. He sat up, blinked, shivered, and was awake.

"Is there anything the matter with you?"

"Nothing at all," he said. "I'm perfectly all right. The only trouble is that

I haven't had any sleep in three weeks. The medicine they give me either keeps me awake or puts me to sleep."

"I can't stay in here and watch you if I'm supposed to prepare dinner. Why don't you sit in one of those big armchairs while I'm cooking? Otherwise you're going to nod off again and fall off your chair."

"I'm okay."

Moments later, while working in the kitchen, Jean heard a crash and rushed in to find him on the floor. He wasn't hurt, only shaken.

◆

Jed and Mildred went to the 57th Street offices of the Public Broadcasting System to see the first two half-hours of the Cavett interview. No date had yet been set for a broadcast, but it seemed as though there would be two segments and probably more.

Robin Breed wasn't there. Harris had been annoying her. After cashing the five-hundred-dollar check he had received for the interviews, he had told her that it must have been lost in the mail and demanded another. Then he asked her to live with him.

Several remarks had been edited out of the interviews. Harris had called one playwright "a fag" and another "a Commie." These deletions were presumably made for fear of libel. Jed had asked for a deletion too. He wanted his remarks about Jones to be dropped. It was the first time he had ever shown any consideration for his son's feelings.

The request was ignored.

◆

He must have spent a terrible night. The symptoms of a man with his condition—congestive heart failure with complications—include breathing difficulty, mental disorientation, fever and chills. It is likely that, in that sorry little room of his in the Royalton, he was trying to raise his head high enough to fall asleep: stuffing sweaters and coats beneath his pillow so that the congestion would flow down from his throat and he could breathe. It was then, probably, that the heart stabs began.

Unable to reach either Mildred or Sylvia, he called his sister Florie and tearfully told her that he would die if he didn't get to the hospital and he hadn't the taxi fare. According to the story he told the other sisters, Florie didn't believe him. All his life he had called one or another of the sisters to threaten them with his death. Now Florie had more serious problems. Her son was desperately ill.

Harris took the elevator downstairs, pushed through the hotel's front door and out into 44th Street and the rainy night. He carried no umbrella and his old raincoat absorbed more water than it repelled as he stumbled east in the general direction of the hospital. But he was too ill and too weak to walk.

He stepped off the sidewalk and into the street, waving toward the headlights of the oncoming cars. At last, a truck stopped for him. He hauled himself into its cab. That was how he got to the hospital, or so he told his sister Mildred.

The floor staff was not delighted to see him again. He made his first demand even before getting into the hospital pajamas. He pulled out a handful of creased newspaper clippings that he'd brought along. They were about *Broadway, The Front Page, Our Town, The Heiress.* Photographs. An old *Time* magazine cover.

"Put them up," he gasped between coughing fits. "Post them so they'll know who I am."

The nurse's aide got the thumb tacks.

"Not on the wall, you ass! I want them on the fucking door!"

"It was as if there was a monster in there," the senior nurse recalled.

But when Mildred and Jean came to visit, he was a model patient. He opened his eyes, smiled brightly, and spread his palms in mimicry of a vaudevillian.

Sylvia visited, and a defensive Florie, still insisting that she hadn't refused to help him get to the hospital. Abigail moved in with Mildred for the duration and was at the hospital every day; Jones less often.

As Harris's condition deteriorated, his howling escalated. The staff argued three times a day about who would bring him his meals. There was always the likelihood that the tray would be hurled, and even a weakened Harris could hit a departing nurse with a cup of coffee at ten feet.

"Everything in his system was collapsing," the senior nurse remembered, "and then, suddenly, he 'crapped out' with a cardiac and respiratory arrest."

The nurses came running, the aides, orderlies, interns, the floor resident. They leaped on his bed and pounded his chest while the electrocardiograph machine was rolled into the room. The crowd on the bed opened up to let a doctor in and he injected adrenaline directly into Harris's heart.

"We put tubes in every orifice of his body," the senior nurse said, "starting with the endotracheal tube in his throat so that the respirator could breathe for him. I think he was on every kind of machine and tube that we had, with catheters threaded into his veins and arteries to monitor every aspect of his heart's condition."

Naturally, the floor staff delighted in his silencing and when he gestured for pencil and paper the nurses tittered among themselves, giggly about the prospect of Mr. Harris committing his obscenities to paper.

He snatched the writing materials from the young woman who brought them, and he scribbled. They watched through the glass wall of his room. He thrust out the sheet of paper. The aide looked at it and looked again. She brought it outside.

His demand for a half-dozen newspapers was written upside down and backwards. It was a vaudeville hallucination. Harry Kahane, "Professor Backwards," had been a popular act in the twenties, writing upside down and backwards.

When his kidneys shut down he was put on a dialysis machine and then given intravenous injections to maintain his blood pressure and heart rate. "That was a continuous drip," the senior nurse explained. "It stops, he stops."

He drifted toward a semicoma while on the respirator. "We couldn't get a definite reading on his level of consciousness, it kept changing. That was why we had to put him 'on all fours.'"

"On all fours" is hospital argot for being strapped down at the arms and legs. This is done so that the patient cannot rip out the tubes. The body is inclined to repel these invaders unless, of course, the body is in a coma.

The respirator made him uncomfortable too. The machine forces air into the lungs with a bellows. Then sucks the air out. It breathes for the patient. Again, the body may resent this usurpation of its functions. Some patients will resist the machine even when they are conscious, despite knowing that they need the respirator to breathe.

"They need it to live," the senior nurse said, "and still they fight the machine." But Harris didn't fight the machine. He fought the sedatives. He stayed awake.

"One by one," the nurse said, "his organ systems shut down, and one by one they were artificially maintained. We put him on one of the 'launching pads.' That's what we call the two cubicles we use for hopeless patients."

When Harris's liver went, the itching began. Restrained, he could not scratch. The jaundice turned him yellow while the itches had him writhing on the bed and twisting against the straps.

"It was the torture of the damned," the nurse said.

Finally he slipped into the coma. Its mercy was deceptive, for the struggle was now only joined in silence, the interior drama betrayed by the blisters that popped up along his body, excess fluids puffing his face, the skin breaking down.

Pat Burroughs learned of the siege from Jones, calling him when she was unable to reach Jed. She would not leave the hospital from the day she arrived, standing guard at Harris's room door and firmly directing visitors. Mildred, Sylvia, Florie, and Jean Dalrymple would have to receive permission from Pat if they wished to visit Jed. Argument was futile. Jones sided with Pat.

Curtains were drawn around the bed, for the staff's sake. "He was in the worst possible condition you could be in," the senior nurse said, "and still be alive. Every morning we would come in and ask, 'Jesus, is he still here?'"

Then he died, on November 15, 1979.

"If you're going to do what I do," the nurse said, "you can't be superstitious or religious. But if there's anything to the idea of being punished in the way you die for the way you lived your life, I'll tell you this: the only other patient we ever had who suffered the way Mr. Harris did was Giuseppe Gambino. You know. The Mafia don?"

◆

Michael Abbott was at a small dinner party when a young woman turned to him at the table and said, "I'm glad you came after all."

"I don't understand."

"I heard so many wonderful stories about your days with Jed Harris and how important that friendship was and now, for you to have to come to a dinner party on the day he died . . ."

The blood drained from Abbott's face.

"What do you mean?"

"You know . . . the *Times*. It was in today's *Times*."

Abbott felt a momentary paralysis. Pushing himself from the table, he rose and walked unsteadily to the bathroom.

"I wept in there," he remembered. "I was hysterical. I sobbed uncontrollably. I didn't know why."

He washed his face and returned to the dinner table to smile and chat and stay until a decent hour.

"I got out of there as fast as I could without being rude. I never did fully understand the powerful grip that Jed had gotten on me."

◆

Harris was cremated. The funeral service was held at Frank E. Campbell's on upper Madison Avenue. A small group didn't quite fill the first few pews in the chapel. Among those who came were Mildred, Sylvia, Florie; Jed's daughter Abigail and his niece Nina, of the honey hair and the *pachkes* in the park. Lillian Gish, Marc Connelly, Edward Chodorov, José Ferrer, Michael Abbott, Jacques Traubee, Jean Dalrymple.

Jones's marriage had ended in divorce. He arrived at the funeral home with Pat Burroughs. He was carrying the urn containing his father's ashes. The couple turned up later, at the reception in Jean Dalrymple's apartment. Michael Abbott was showing everyone an inscribed gold wristwatch that Jed had given him as a twenty-third birthday present.

"He never gave *me* a watch," Jones said.

"I'm sorry," an embarrassed Abbott replied.

"Don't even talk to me," Jones snapped. "I've always hated you."

"Oh?"

"When I was a kid and you were working for my father, he'd always tell me what a brilliant stage manager you were. Then he'd look at me and say, 'Jones, you're a nothing and you'll always be a nothing.'"

He was still holding the urn of ashes. He carried it around for days.

◆

In its January, 1931 issue, *Theatre Arts Monthly* had published

A SKETCH OF JED HARRIS

By John Anderson

Only recently have we come to notice the *regisseur* in our theatre—perhaps because there have been so few to notice—and to understand that what he does to a play is the final act of creation in the drama; more important, in its medium, than the work of an orchestra conductor.

The fact that he makes his stage vivid, or fast, or brooding or what not, is invariably hailed as an event in itself. That is the business of any competent craftsman, and the fact that Jed Harris is a good craftsman is the least of it.

Brooks Atkinson has said that his work is centrifugal, which describes its true energy perhaps better than any other word. It encompasses the energy and intuition and thoughtful preparation with which he approaches any production, whether he hires a director or directs himself. In either case it is ultimately a dramatic thing of its own.

It encompasses his feeling for living dialogue, his conscious manipulation of his players across the stage, and the injection of subtleties which apparently mean nothing, but which take on, in his general scheme, the strength and body of larger design. I mean by that the contrivance of Lillian Gish's entrance in *Uncle Vanya*, where she merely fluttered across the stage, without speaking to anyone, and vanished. Perhaps not everyone in the audience caught the quiet moment of that capricious movement, but in itself it told the whole story of Tchekov's play, as a sort of thematic announcement of human symphony.

I mean, too, that marvelous pause in *Coquette* where he held the stage empty until an old, fat negro mammy could lumber up the stairs, but as she heaved her bulk up, to a vague humming of her own, her solemn movement changed the accent of that play from comedy to tragedy. It was an inflection which let the play tip toe from one mood to the other simply through the slowing influence of her walk, a transition superbly contrived and profoundly effective.

It is a method which made the balcony in the duplex apartment in *The Royal Family* the sort of balcony that actors would unconsciously think of for *Romeo and Juliet* because it emanated from an intellectual appraisal of the material and the honesty of craftsmanship to state that material in its own unflinching terms.

What he says, how he looks and how he behaves are negligible to the essential fact of his undeniable artistry, as negligible as Toulouse-Lautrec's deformity when you look at his pictures, or Michaelangelo's broken nose in the presence of the Medici chapel.

If Jed Harris was a Michaelangelo of directors, or even a Toulouse-Lautrec, the world will never know it. We may believe descriptions of performances by Burbage, Kean, Bernhardt, the Barrymores, or Duse but we can never experience them. These are performing arts. Only the medium endures.

We may even have reason to doubt that Jed Harris would seem to us the great director the *Theatre Arts* essay describes. The occasional records of other past performances on scratchy discs or film suggest that there are fashions in performing art. Opera singers of the past seem grandiose to us, ballet choreography florid, and actors histrionic. Most likely, Harris's directing genius would seem old-fashioned to us as well. But he was a genius of the stage according to the standards and values by which he worked; a genius of his time. Even his bitterest enemies conceded that.

We know, too, that he provoked those enemies. It seems reasonable to conclude from all the facts and reports and memories that the independence of spirit, the originality of judgment and the arrogance of decision that sent this meteor streaking to theatrical success were the very qualities, when perverted by frustration and neurosis, that undid him.

An admirer such as Mr. Anderson in *Theatre Arts Monthly* might be expected to minimize his personal qualities as "negligible to the fact of his essential artistry," and that might make sense in a strictly artistic appreciation. However, Jed Harris's creative impulse was a factor of his psychology; it was a compulsive and powerful impulse. It may well be that his major creation was himself. Certainly he was an actor and his life a performance. The connection between the complex nature of the man—personality, emotional makeup, intellect and artistic drive—and the nature of his work is the web of his tragedy.

On April 5, 1981, Jed Harris was inducted into The Theater Hall of Fame. It is no more than a list carved into a marble wall in a corner of the lobby of the Gershwin Theatre in Manhattan. But it is the only hall of fame that Broadway has.

The charter members, installed as a group in 1972, included the first friends that Harris alienated, George Abbott and George S. Kaufman. Also in that original group was Moss Hart, who had survived Harris's painful schemes to become one of Broadway's most celebrated writer-directors.

Elected to this hall of fame in the intervening years had been every Broadway eminent that panels of experts could think of, including many of the cast of characters in Harris's life: Judith Anderson, Harold Clurman, Laurence Olivier, Lillian Gish, Katharine Hepburn, Maxwell Anderson, S. N. Behrman, Marc Connelly, Thornton Wilder, Helen Hayes, Ina Claire, Walter Huston, Noël Coward, Henry Fonda, Ruth Gordon, Osgood Perkins, José Ferrer, Margaret Sullavan, even Willie Howard. Everyone but Jed Harris.

They had been elected, recognized and honored because they had not only performed well but performed *properly*. They had made no enemies and, most to the point, they had finished on top.

Harris did not meet these requirements. His success had been very great but it had not been lifelong. He had predicted before it all began that he'd burn out young. Instead, arrogance, egoism, cruelty, and Machiavellianism had kept his talent from being spent and that was his greatest tragedy.

Those in the Hall of Fame had exercised and nurtured their abilities. Jed Harris had not. That is why the Wonder Boy, the late Meteor, was being admitted to this select group as an afterthought.

Jones Harris accepted the scroll on behalf of his father. It was presented by Joseph Papp, the head of the New York Shakespeare Festival. A fiercely independent, maverick producer, Papp was an appropriate choice.

His remarks to the black-tie audience were drawn from ancient reports. "Sheer terror," "genius," "the myth." Polite applause followed the final references to this man of the past, this vaguely familiar name from the Barrymore era or some such. He had all but invented Broadway yet had chosen to stand apart and alone, whatever his reasons, whatever the consequences. Jed Harris's should have been the first name carved into the marble wall that stood for a Broadway Hall of Fame. Had he been offered the honor, he would doubtless have rejected it.

The author is grateful to the following for permission to reprint excerpts from previously copyrighted material:

From *People in a Diary*, by S. N. Behrman. Copyright © 1972 by S. N. Behrman, by permission of Little, Brown and Company.

From *A Dance on the High Wire* by Jed Harris. Copyright © 1980 by Jed Harris. Used by permission of Crown Publishers, Inc.

From "Miss Pinchot's Two Notes Clue to Death by Gas," by George Kivel and Grace Robinson published in the *Daily News* on January 25, 1938. Copyright 1938, New York News, Inc. Reprinted by permission.

From the *New York Post*, May 15, 1938 and May 20, 1972. Reprintd by permission of the *New York Post*. © 1972, New York Post Corporation.

From the *New York Herald Tribune*, 1937. © I.H.T. Corporation. Reprinted by permission.

From *Present Indicative*. © Noel Coward, 1937. Reprinted by kind permission of the Estate of Noel Coward.

From *Theatre Arts Monthly*, January 1931. Reprinted by permission of *Theatre Arts*.

From Chappell Music Company, copyright © 1928 by Chappell & Co., Ltd. Copyright Renewed, Published in the U.S.A. by Chappell & Co., Inc. International Copyright Secured. All Rights Reserved. Used by permission.

From the Dick Cavett Show, including excerpts on pages 73, 74, and 263, 264. Copyright 1979 by Daphne Productions, Inc. Used by permission.

INDEX

275

278

280

DISCARD